CASS SERIES: STUDIES IN AIR POWER
(Series Editor: Sebastian Cox)

AIRWAR

D0782095

CASS SERIES: STUDIES IN AIR POWER

(Series Editor: Sebastian Cox)

ISSN 1368-5597

AIRWAR:
THEORY AND PRACTICE

PHILLIP S. MEILINGER

FRANK CASS
LONDON • PORTLAND, OR

First published in 2003 in Great Britain by
FRANK CASS PUBLISHERS.
Crown House, 47 Chase Side
London, N14 5BP

and in the United States of America by
FRANK CASS PUBLISHERS
c/o ISBS, 5824 N.E. Hassalo Street
Portland, Oregon, 97213-3644

Website: www.frankcass.com

Copyright © 2003 P. Meilinger

British Library Cataloguing in Publication Data:

Meilinger, Phillip S.
  Airwar: theory and practice. – (Cass series. Studies in air power; 14)
  1. Air warfare – History 2. Air warfare – Philosophy
  I.Title
  358.4'14'09

ISBN 0-7146-5310-1 (cloth)
ISBN 0-7146-8266-7 (paper)
ISSN 1368-5597

Library of Congress Cataloging-in-Publication Data:

Meilinger, Phillip S., 1948–
Aiwar: theory and practice/Phillip S. Meilinger.
    p. cm. – (Cass series – Studies in air power, ISSN 1368–5597; 14)
  Includes bibliographical references and index.
  ISBN 0-7146-5310-1 (cloth) – ISBN 0-7146-8266-7 (pbk.)
  1. Air warfare – History. I. title. II. Series

  UG630 M357 2003
  358.4–dc21

2002033932

Typeset in 10/11.5pt Imprint by FiSH Books, London
Printed in Great Britain by MPG Books Ltd, Victoria Square, Bodmin, Cornwall

Contents

To Wart, Ernie and Beccajon

Series Editor's Preface

The Cass Studies in Air Power Series has always sought to take a broad perspective on air power and to include studies encompassing economic, biographical and human aspects of the subject, as well as straightforward historical studies. This is the first book in the series to address the more theoretical and doctrinal aspects of air power, and, though it is firmly grounded in history, it would be true to say that it is aimed more at the airman than the historian.

In the realm of military theory, airmen have always tended to be less prolific than their army or naval counterparts. In part, this may stem from an innate suspicion of those who preach elegant theories but do not have the necessary skills to carry them out. Pilots tend, quite naturally, to have the greatest respect for those of their fellow airmen who display the greatest skill in the air, rather than those who display formidable intellectual powers on the ground. In almost every air force in the world it is the pilots who reign supreme, to the extent that, certainly in the Royal Air Force, navigators and other aircrew specialists have often felt themselves to be second-class citizens. Theorising is now institutionalised in manuals on doctrine and has thus become the province of the doctrine writers, and here, too, many front-line aviators remain indifferent or antagonistic to the product. This suspicion of theorising has a corollary, which is an underestimation of the value of history as a tool for the modern airman. Whereas an infantryman or paratrooper can see very clearly the close parallels between his activity and that of his forebears on the Somme or at Bastogne, many airmen do not feel such an immediate affinity with their ancestors flying over Berlin or the Yalu River.

In this volume, Colonel Meilinger quotes General Michael Dugan's exasperation with airmen's own ignorance of the wider aspects of their trade when compared with soldiers and sailors, and his words will strike a chord with anyone who has had to lecture on air power history to a class of young air force officers. Yet, whether they realise it or not, every military airman flying today does so in accordance with a doctrine of some sort, and since doctrine is in large part the formalisation of ideas based on previous practice, they are indeed dependent on the experience of their forebears. It cannot be otherwise when air forces, as large multi-billion dollar businesses, spend, comparatively speaking, so little of their time actually engaged in their core activity of fighting. History is vicarious experience, and the author brings that experience to the page and sets out its relevance to today in very clear terms.

Phillip Meilinger has for many years been one of those rare individuals, an airman who both studies history and uses it as an informed tool to enable him to analyse current air power problems and future solutions. In this series of essays, written over a number of years, he uses history not only to inform but also to challenge. In doing so, he follows in the tradition of fellow countrymen and military theorists from A. T. Mahan to Colonel John Warden. Military doctrine and ideas are themselves subject to constant challenge, and in the following pages the author assaults a few modern shibboleths, whether it be an unthinking and slavish adherence to 'jointness', or a perceived gap in airmen's thinking on the use of air power in non-nuclear strategic operations. Many, both airmen and historians, will find much with which they do not agree in these pages, but whether we agree with the analysis or not it is impossible to read these essays without being forced to reanalyse and often reassess our own position.

If there is a connecting theme to many of these essays, it is their attempt to lift the eyes of airmen, firstly from the head-up display, and then further up again from the battlemap, and to show them not only air power's intellectual roots but also its wider and enduring principles and impact. Military pilots are enjoined that it is not healthy to keep their 'heads in the cockpit' when flying, but instead to remain aware of what is happening beyond their instruments. In this work, Phillip Meilinger is aiming to achieve a similar result with their intellectual as opposed to their physical horizons.

Sebastian Cox

Introduction

Air power is the ability to project power or influence through the medium of the air and space to achieve strategic, operational or tactical objectives. Note that space is included in this definition. Although at some point space may become a separate entity and medium of war, that has not yet occurred, and it is unlikely to do so for at least another decade. Even then, the integral connection between air and space operations will be so close and symbiotic as to be seamless.

Air power includes far more than air vehicles: it encompasses the personnel, organization and infrastructure that are essential for the vehicles to function. On a broader scale, it includes not just military forces but also the aviation industry, including airline companies, aircraft/engine manufacturers and all their personnel. On yet another plane air power includes ideas on how it should be employed. Without these ideas, or doctrine, the effective employment of air power is impossible. In 1991, Iraq had a large collection of airplanes, but it did not have air power.

For nearly a century there has been a fundamental difference of opinion as to whether or not the airplane has altered the strategies of war or merely its tactics. If the former, air power can be seen as a revolutionary leap in the conduct of war; but if the latter is true, then air power is simply another weapon that joins the arsenal along with the rifle, the tank, the submarine and the radio. I believe that air power has brought about a revolution in war, because it has altered virtually all aspects of how it is fought, by whom, against whom, and with what weapons. Flowing from these factors have been changes in training, organization, administration, command and control, and doctrine. War has been fundamentally transformed by the advent of the airplane.

Much of this transformation can be explained by listing air power's most basic characteristics. Before the Wright Brothers ever flew, the likes of Jules Verne and H.G. Wells had already identified the unique strengths and weaknesses of the airplane. Its inherent strengths were as follows:

- *ubiquity* – the ability to operate in the third dimension above the earth, unconstrained by the limitations of terrain;
- *speed* – aircraft operated far more quickly than surface forces; even in World War I aircraft traveled an order of magnitude faster than their surface counterparts;
- *range* – the air weapon could travel great distances in one leap to strike at an enemy far beyond the front lines;

- *potency* – while striking deeply in an enemy country, aircraft could deliver significant ordnance; in World War I, German bombers took off from their bases on the Continent, flew to the industrial heartland of Britain, and dropped two tons of bombs each;
- *flexibility* – the combination of the above factors that allowed aircraft to perform a variety of missions, over a wide area, in a very short period of time.

On the other hand, there were inherent limitations of air power, and these too were recognized early on in the airplane's development:

- *technology and capital dependent* – not every country has the industrial, scientific or financial resources to build modern aircraft;
- *transitory* – aircraft cannot live in their medium as can surface forces; aircraft must land to refuel and rearm. Even the great bombing missions of World War II lasted but a few hours;
- *weather and the night* – the natural phenomena of rain, wind, clouds and the darkness of night itself present formidable barriers to flight;
- *cannot hold ground* – for surface advocates this is the most damning limitation; only troops can occupy and therefore control events on the ground.

It is crucial that all military officers, and especially airmen, recognize these inherent strengths and weaknesses, so that they can better and more effectively employ the air weapon. On the other hand, I would also argue that as time has passed over the first century of flight, the strengths of air power have grown stronger, while the weaknesses of air power have grown weaker. Aircraft can now fly farther, longer and higher, while also delivering greater ordnance far more precisely than ever before. The fact that a modern air force requires great technological sophistication as well as great resources means that only a few countries can match the USA in this area. At the same time, however, aircraft are not as transitory; air refueling allows aircraft to stay aloft for intercontinental round-trip missions, unmanned air vehicles can now stay airborne for days at a time, and satellites remain in orbit around the earth for years. The weather and the dark are not the formidable obstacles they once were due to the development of radar, infrared imaging and the space-based global positioning system. As for air power's inability to hold ground, it has become one of the more unusual paradoxes of modern warfare that this weakness is now seen as one of air power's great strengths. The use of ground troops has become too dangerous and too costly, while the world often sees their use as 'provocative'. Hence, we stopped short of Basra in the 1991 Gulf War in order not to offend our Arab allies, and at the outset of the Kosovo crisis in 1999, the US President and NATO declared that ground troops would not be sent. Over the past decade, the USA and Europe have wanted to use military power to project influence, but have been unwilling to do so if it entailed high risk or the probability of casualties. Air power is the preferred weapon in such circumstances.

My operational career as a US Air Force pilot and staff officer has intertwined with my intellectual career as a historian, educator and defense analyst. It has been my intention to use my historical training and methodology to shed light on current and future problems. It is my belief that both views are crucial to a military officer or, for that matter, any national security decision-maker. In my own life, I have unquestionably benefited from having a foot in both worlds.

The collection of essays that follows is a mixture of historical enquiries regarding both events and ideas, combined with attempts to look forward to see future trends in war. As a consequence, I see parallels in history with contemporary events. Thus, for example, the interservice rivalries of the 1920s and 1940s are not so different from those of the 1990s. Although the topics covered here span the history of flight, there are certainly gaps in the story. I make no claim that this is a history of air power. Rather, it is a collection of my thoughts on various important aspects of air power history and theory, strategy and tactics, and operations and organization, from both an American and an international perspective.

As this book goes to press, the USA and some of its allies are engaged in a 'War on Terrorism' as a result of the attacks on 11 September 2001. Predictions at a time like this are always risky, but even at this early stage there seem to be interesting insights into this most unusual war.

The 'clash of civilizations' hypothesized by Samuel Huntington is partially coming true, although some would call it a clash of 'cultures'. The biggest surprise to Americans has been the depth of hatred felt towards them by the terrorists and their supporters. We have difficulty understanding why this war has occurred and how we should respond. It is therefore useful to recall the old saw from the Vietnam War era: 'we must win the hearts and minds of the people'. By that it was meant that the grievances of the Viet Cong were largely political, economic and social, not military. In order to combat effectively the Viet Cong, we had to respond with political, economic and social policies. Similarly, Islamic peoples have grievances against the USA, partly because we support Israel, partly because we continue to punish an Islamic country, Iraq, and partly because we maintain a significant military presence in the Gulf Region. It is no use arguing the rationality or validity of those views – they exist, and we must deal with that reality. If we are to enlist Islamic support for the war on terrorism, we have to address these social, economic and cultural concerns.

In this vein, it is apparent that the Clausewitzian paradigm of war is in need of revision. To terrorists, war is not a continuation of policy, politics or political intercourse: it is an end in itself. It is deeply rooted in culture and, in this case, religion as well. It is not based on a 'rational actor' model so familiar to those in the West. Our unshakeable attraction to Clausewitz means that we will continue to be shocked and surprised by adversaries who simply do not think like we do and who do not see war as fundamentally political. Until we break from this fatally flawed paradigm, we will be unable to anticipate problems in many areas of the world.

One of the biggest challenges facing us in this war is that of intelligence. Knowing your enemy has always been basic to waging war effectively, but this principle is more important when fighting terrorists and other non-state actors. Their infrastructures and military forces will be small, transitory and dispersed. They will deliberately hide among the civilian population, daring us to strike, and it will be extremely difficult to locate precisely these terrorists and then track them 24 hours a day. Yet, we must have that type of accurate information in order to combat them and bring them to justice. Recall the USA's difficulty in locating Manuel Noriega in Panama (he finally walked up to the Vatican representative's house and surrendered), Hussein Aideed in Somalia (US Delta forces on the ground raided the wrong house, and we never did catch him), and Saddam Hussein all through the Gulf War. At the time of writing, we have not yet located Osama bin Laden, although we have been looking for him for nearly a decade.

Once we locate the people or their base camps, weapons stockpiles, etc., we have to hit them. There are really only two ways to do so. We either fly there or we walk there. Ideally, the countries where terrorist cells are located will arrest the terrorists within their borders, but we cannot count on such good fortune. For the USA, air power is the obvious option, as it has been for the past decade. The technology to track and identify targets, and then pass that information to orbiting strike aircraft in near-real time, is constantly being improved. The time needed to complete this 'sensor to shooter' cycle continues to decrease. The goal is to put ordnance within 15 feet of a target within minutes, at low risk to ourselves and with little collateral damage. Such accuracy is routine, and the technology is now available that reduces the time factor to single-digit minutes. The problem in Afghanistan has been the inability of commanders to make decisions quickly enough to hit time-sensitive targets.

Decision-making has been held at Central Command headquarters in Tampa, Florida. On numerous occasions, targets were located and identified, but because approval to strike them resided out of the theater, the 'sensor to shooter' cycle slowed to a crawl. Too often, by the time commanders finally made a decision 15,000 miles away, fleeting mobile targets had disappeared. This is a human, not a technological problem.

Unfortunately, patience is not an American virtue, so there are always some who argue that we should send in masses of ground troops, quickly. There is a need for a ground presence, but it will almost certainly not entail large numbers of conventional US forces. The Northern Alliance, a defeated group of ragtag irregulars, was given new purpose, new hope and new options as a result of US and British air strikes in Afghanistan. After several weeks of steady pounding from the air, the Taliban collapsed when the Alliance began a ground offensive. The rapidity of that collapse caught most by surprise. It was common to compare US air strikes and capabilities with the unhappy Soviet experience of the 1980s. The day Kabul fell, there were those still arguing that only a massive infusion of US ground troops, supported by tanks and heavy artillery, could dislodge the Taliban before winter. That, seemingly, was the lesson taught by the Soviet experience. In truth, there is no comparison between the two conflicts, as the Taliban learned to their dismay.

This relationship between air power and a significant ground force – where regular US troops are not present in significant numbers – is a unique aspect of this war. Sharing intelligence, coordinating combat actions, ensuring re-supply, and maintaining close communications between US air forces and opposing the Taliban are a challenge. How well this relationship has worked and what needs to be improved should be studied closely. It is likely such ad hoc coalition efforts will be encountered more frequently in the future.

Another interesting feature of this war that warrants scrutiny is the close cooperation between air power and special operations forces (SOF). These highly trained elite units are being used to pinpoint targets for air strikes or in some cases neutralize those targets themselves, in the event of air strikes being inappropriate. Our degree of reliance on SOF, in the absence of US ground forces, is unprecedented. (I would add here that the SOF, so useful in Afghanistan, includes the elite British commandos.) In a sense, SOF are unique types of air-delivered precision munitions. We may be seeing a new concept of war employing air power, SOF, the CIA and other government agencies working together closely to achieve political goals.

Airlifting and air dropping supplies into a combat zone, while also conducting air strikes against enemy forces, is nothing new. What is new, however, is that in Afghanistan humanitarian air drops to civilian refugees were being conducted almost at the same time and to the same locations as were combat strike sorties against the Taliban. This led to unusual and sometimes tragic errors: cluster bomblets are painted bright yellow, but so are emergency food packages. Several casualties occurred to unsuspecting Afghanis attempting to retrieve what they thought were food supplies. Changing the colors of either the munitions or the food packages will help solve this particular problem, but the unique requirements of waging war and humanitarian airlift, simultaneously, raises new challenges that need to be worked out. At the same time, it also has become apparent that the delivery of food and medical supplies has a large political component to it. There are several competing factions in Afghanistan: if we do not supply all of them equally, are we taking sides in a postwar political power struggle?

Access to bases near a crisis area is a serious issue. Projecting military power relies on forward bases for its effectiveness. It is possible but not efficient to fly strike missions from bases over a thousand miles distant. In Afghanistan, long-range bombers dropped most of the ordnance, while carrier-based fighters also played a major role. Land-based fighters, on the other hand, were of only marginal use due to the distances involved. Access to close-in bases can be denied either by enemy action or, as in this case, by political circumstances. Neighboring countries were unwilling to allow aircraft on strike missions to use their airfields. An obvious solution to this access problem is diplomacy – negotiating basing agreements – but this is unreliable. More long-range bombers are also a possibility, but there are many missions that require the tactical flexibility of fighter-bombers. We need to give our fighters greater range. The limit of 500–700 miles without refueling now possessed by most of these aircraft is simply not adequate.

The USA must be wary of letting its rhetoric outstrip its abilities. President George Bush has declared a global war on terrorism, but such a broad attack must raise eyebrows. There are dozens of terrorist organizations located worldwide, most of which had nothing to do with the attacks on 11 September. More importantly, one person's terrorist is another's freedom fighter. Although there is little doubt that al-Qaeda is composed of terrorists, there is substantial disagreement over designating as terrorists such organizations as the Hamas, the Irish Republican Army or the Chechnyan rebels. Labels have political implications. Similarly, the USA will gain some strange bedfellows while tracking down the main perpetrators of the September attacks. In the recent past, for example, the USA has branded Iran and Syria as backers of terrorist activities. Similarly, the regimes in Pakistan, Uzbekistan and Tajikistan have seldom been accused of being budding democracies. Yet, the support of all these countries is needed to track down the worldwide network of bin Laden and al-Qaeda. It seems clear, therefore, that we will have to cut deals with some unsavory individuals in order to neutralize even more unsavory ones. In general, however, the danger for the USA is in establishing an unachievable goal – the destruction of terrorism worldwide. Although such a sweeping call to arms has domestic political benefits, it also sets a bar that may be too high for the military to achieve. Eradicating al-Qaeda and its Taliban supporters in Afghanistan is a major undertaking. Attempting to eliminate terrorists everywhere, while also punishing the regimes that support them, may be impossible. The Bush administration could be setting itself up for overall failure, even if it proves successful in specific operations.

There are too many people that I have met and worked with over the years and who have shaped my thoughts on these subjects to possibly remember them all, but I would especially thank Dave MacIsaac, Al Hurley, Denys Volan, Jon Reynolds, John Shy, Tony Mason, Dick Hallion, Mike Terry, Duane Reed, Mike Wolfert, John Warden, Dan Kuehl, Al Gropman, Alan Stephens, Ian MacFarling, Vincent Orange, Denny Drew, Dave Mets, Karl Mueller, Dik Daso, Pete Faber, Hal Winton, Bob Pape, Doc Pentland, Buster McCrabb, Mark Conversino, Mark Clodfelter, Bill Holley, Rob Owen, Andy Lambert, Phil Sabin, Seb Cox, Christina Goulter, Pete Gray, Bill Arkin, Dave Deptula, Chris Bowie, Tom Ehrhard, Jack English, Chuck Gagnon, all my students at the School of Advanced Airpower Studies and the Naval War College, and of course, Barbara. In many ways, these essays are the product of the long and stimulating relationships I have had with all of them. I thank them.

1

Giulio Douhet and the Origins of Air-Power Theory

When becoming dean at the School of Advanced Air Power Studies at Maxwell AFB, Alabama, I moved to include a course in the curriculum that focused on the evolution of air-power theory. In my view, most textbooks used for courses on military theory tended to ignore air power. The two major compendia of essays on the subject, the two versions of Makers of Modern Strategy, *each contained but a single chapter on the subject of air power theory. I thought this strange and regrettable. In truth, I soon discovered that very little of a rigorous and analytical nature had been written about air-power theory or its theorists. This was true even of the first and perhaps most important of the early theorists, Giulio Douhet. I therefore decided to research and write such a study myself. Although Douhet's influence on his contemporaries has been oft debated, he remains today one of the most quoted, and misunderstood, of air-power theorists. Echoes of his basic arguments are still heard today.*

General Giulio Douhet of Italy was among the first to think deeply and write cogently about air power and its role in war. Many of his ideas and predictions were wrong, but echoes of his basic concepts are still heard more than 60 years after his death. Indeed, the victory of the Coalition in the 1991 Gulf War is an example of what Douhet predicted air power could accomplish. Specifically, his formula for victory – gaining command of the air, neutralizing an enemy's strategic 'vital centers', and maintaining the defensive on the ground while taking the offensive in the air – underpinned Coalition strategy. Certainly, not all wars have followed or will follow this model, but Douhet's theories of air-power employment have become more accurate as time has passed and the air weapon has become more capable. This chapter will re-examine the theories of this first great air theorist, analyze them based on their own internal logic, and reassess them.

Giulio Douhet was born in Caserta, near Naples, on 30 May 1869. His father came from a long line of soldiers, while his mother was from a family of teachers and journalists. He performed well in school, graduating first in his class at the Genoa Military Academy. Giulio was then commissioned into the artillery in 1888 at the age of 19. Soon after, he attended the Polytechnic Institute in Turin and continued his studies in science and engineering.

His performance continued to be excellent, and his graduate thesis, 'The Calculation of Rotating Field Engines', became a standard text at the school. Douhet's professional ability was also evident, and as a captain in 1900 he was assigned to the General Staff. While there, he read closely all reports regarding the Russo-Japanese war, which broke out in 1903, and early on predicted that Japan would emerge victorious. Few Westerners agreed with him at the time. Also while on the General Staff he continued his technological bent and wrote several papers advocating mechanization of the Italian army. In 1901, he published a series of lectures titled 'Mechanization From the Point of View of the Military', and three years later wrote a pamphlet on the subject, 'Heavy and Military Mechanization'. Significantly, although Douhet saw a role for heavy trucks to move men and supplies in a theater of operations, he did not predict the development of armored vehicles for use on the battlefield. In addition, he viewed mechanization solely in terms of Italy's peculiar geographic, economic and political limitations. Technology would compensate for Italy's inherent weaknesses in manpower and natural resources. This theme would later repeat itself in his writings on air power.[1]

In 1905, Italy built its first dirigible and Douhet immediately recognized its possibilities, becoming a keen observer of what he believed was a revolution in military technology. He followed aeronautical events closely, and when Italy's first airplane flew in 1908, Douhet commented: 'soon it will be able to rise thousands of feet and to cover a distance of thousands of miles'.[2] Two years later – only seven years after Kitty Hawk – Douhet predicted: 'the skies are about to become a battlefield as important as the land or the sea...only by gaining the command of the air shall we be able to derive the fullest benefit from the advantage which can only be fully exploited when the enemy is compelled to be earth bound'.[3] However, the superiority of the airplane over the dirigible was not yet obvious to everyone. Douhet's superior, Colonel Maurizio Moris of the Aviation Inspectorate, was a staunch supporter of the airship. He and Douhet had several clashes over the issue, most of which Douhet lost. In fact, as late as 1914 Italy was still spending 75 per cent of its aviation budget on dirigibles.[4]

At the same time, Douhet realized the aircraft could become a dominant weapon only if freed from the fetters of ground commanders who did not understand this new invention. He therefore advocated the creation of a separate air arm, commanded by airmen.[5] During this period he became close friends with Gianni Caproni, a bright young aircraft engineer who held similar views on the future of aircraft. The two men teamed up to extol the virtues of air power in the years ahead.

In 1911, Italy went to war against Turkey for control of Libya, a war that saw aircraft used for the first time. Amazingly, aircraft were used not only for reconnaissance but also for artillery spotting, transportation of supplies and personnel, and even bombing of enemy troops, supplies and facilities – both in the day and at night. In short, most of the traditional roles of air-power employment were identified and attempted during the very first year they saw combat.[6] The following year, Douhet, now a major, was tasked with writing a report on the meaning of the Libyan War for the future employment of aircraft. Perhaps because his superiors and colleagues were less enthusiastic about air power than he was, Douhet's comments were muted. Most of his report dealt with the organization, training and equipping of the Italian air arm. He did note, however, that although some thought the primary role of aircraft was reconnaissance, 'others' believed that aircraft should be used for 'high-altitude bombing'. As for who would control air power, Douhet suggested that aviation units be assigned to each army corps, but slyly he added: 'this would not prevent, where necessary, grouping such flights with the Army Group, or for that matter, the formation of independent air units'. Also of interest, he called on Italian industry to embrace the new invention and to develop its potential for both commerce and the national security. The relationship between the civilian aircraft industry and the strength of a country's military defense was an important subject, and one to which he would later return. Finally, when discussing the types of aircraft the air force should have, Douhet suggested that a 'general purpose type of aircraft' be developed that could fulfill the roles of reconnaissance, air combat and bombardment.[7] Significantly, this aircraft should be capable of carrying a heavy load of bombs. Overall, this report left interesting clues to where Douhet's ideas on air power would soon lead.

That same year, Douhet was given command of the Italian aviation battalion at Turin and wrote 'Rules for the Use of Airplanes in War', one of the first such manuals in any air force. Of note, his superiors made him delete all passages referring to the airplane as a 'weapon'; to them it was merely a 'device' to support the surface forces.[8] Douhet's incessant preaching on such matters irked his superiors, and he soon became known as a 'radical'. Moreover, in early 1914 he ordered, without authorization, the construction of several Caproni bombers. In truth, Douhet had tried to go through proper channels, but his superior, Colonel Moris – who was still enamored with the dirigible – dragged his feet. Characteristically, Douhet became impatient and took matters into his own hands. Such presumption, coupled with a personality variously described as dogmatic, assertive, persistent, impatient, tactless and supremely self-confident, earned him exile to the infantry.[9] Unfortunately, Douhet's methods for advancing the cause of air power tended to work at cross purposes to his goals.

Douhet was serving as a division chief of staff at Edolo when Europe blundered into World War I. He was unable to resist a prophecy. In August, barely a month after the beginning of the conflict, he wrote an article titled 'Who Will Win?', in which he stated that modern war had become total war. Moreover, because of the industrial revolution, weapons could be produced in such mass quantities, the quick wars of annihilation predicted by many were a thing of the past. Douhet warned instead that the new war now begun would be long and costly. Nonetheless, he concluded that in the long run the difficulties of fighting on multiple fronts would spell defeat for the Central Powers. Although Italy had at that point declined to enter the war on the side of the *Entente*, Douhet called for a military buildup, especially in air power, in the event neutrality could not be maintained. Even in his peripatetic position in Lombardy, now-Colonel Douhet peppered his superiors with ideas on air power. In December 1914 he wrote that an air force must be built whose purpose was 'to gain command of the air' so as to render the enemy 'harmless'. He continued: 'to gain command of the air is to be able to attack with impunity any point of the enemy's body'.[10] In another essay he suggested that 500 bombers be built to strike 'the most vital, most vulnerable and least protected points of the enemy's territory'.[11] He maintained that such an armada could drop 125 tons of bombs daily.

After Italy plunged into the war in 1915, Douhet was so shocked by his army's incompetence and unpreparedness that he frequently wrote his superiors suggesting organizational reform and increased use of the airplane. The diary he kept at the time was filled with angry, sarcastic and frustrated remarks regarding his superiors and their war strategy. Rejecting the offensively oriented ground strategy of the General Staff, he commented ruefully, 'to cast men against concrete is to use them as a useless hammer'. In another entry he noted there were reports that Italian soldiers at the front did not even have rifles. Perhaps, he offered, 'if an enemy attacks they could always beg a mule to kick him'.[12] In yet another memo to his superiors the colonel advocated that a bomber force drop 100 tons of explosives on Constantinople each day until the Turkish government agreed to open the Dardanelles to Allied shipping.[13] Typically, he even wrote the Italian Commander-in-Chief, General Luigi Cadorna, about his concerns and was twice reprimanded for his intemperate remarks.

Beginning in 1916, Colonel Douhet started corresponding with several government officials, including Leonida Bissolati, a Cabinet Minister known to be an air power advocate. His letters to the Minister were especially candid, even for Douhet. In one letter he roundly criticized the Italian conduct of the war and then noted: 'we find ourselves without a reserve, in a crisis of munitions, with all our forces engaged in an offensive already halted, with the rear threatened by old and new enemies, exposed to being attacked at any moment and overcome decisively in the shortest moment'.[14] A copy of Douhet's scathing missive reached General Cadorna, who labeled it 'calumnious'. As a result, in September 1916 Douhet was arrested and court-martialed for 'issuing false news...divulging information differing from the official communiqués...diminishing the prestige and the faith in the country and of disturbing the public tranquillity'.[15] He did not deny writing the letter to Bissolati, but insisted he was motivated strictly out of love for country and a desire to see Italy win the war. But his reputation as an agitator had preceded him and the verdict of the court was 'guilty'. Douhet was sentenced to a year in jail at the fortress of Fenestrelle; he began his incarceration on 15 October. One can only speculate on whether Douhet was actually relieved to have finally brought matters to a head. In a mood that echoes of resignation mingled with frustration, he confided in his diary: 'they [the government] can no longer say that they were not warned'.[16]

Colonel Douhet continued to write about air power from his cell, not only finishing a novel on air warfare but suggesting in a letter to the War Minister that a great Inter-Allied Air Fleet be created. He envisioned a fleet of 20,000 airplanes, mostly provided by the United States, whose role would be to gain command of the air and carry out a decisive air attack on the enemy.[17]

Meanwhile, the fortunes of the Italian army continued to plummet, culminating in the disaster of Caporetto in October 1917 when the Italians lost 300,000 men. Released from prison that same month, Douhet returned to duty, and, because calamity breeds change, he soon became Central Director of Aviation at the General Air Commissariat, where he worked to strengthen Italy's air arm. He also continued his close relationship with Caproni, and it is likely the two had a role in determining the force structure and philosophy of the new US Air Service.

Shortly after entering the war in April 1917, the United States sent a mission to Europe headed by Colonel Raynal Bolling to decide which aircraft were most suitable for construction in the United States. A member of the Bolling team, Major Edgar Gorrell, had several talks with Caproni, who persuaded him to purchase the rights for several hundred of his heavy bombers for construction in the United States. Soon after, Gorrell wrote Caproni requesting information on German industrial targets for use in planning Allied bombing missions. It is probable Douhet helped Caproni compile this information, since at that same time he was also collecting intelligence on the location of German factories. Although the Caproni bomber contract was not fulfilled, the relationship established between these men planted the seeds for US air power.[18]

At the same time, Caproni provided Gorrell with a copy of a polemic written by an Italian journalist and friend of Douhet, Nino Salvaneschi, titled, 'Let Us Kill the War, Let Us Aim at the Heart of the Enemy!' This propaganda pamphlet accused Germany of endless atrocities, thereby justifying any and all actions taken to defeat it. Although Germany had attempted to bomb Britain into submission by Zeppelin attacks, the airship was unable to achieve decisive results. The Allies now had, however, large aircraft (not coincidentally, Capronis) capable of carrying tons of bombs. These aircraft, termed 'battleplanes' by Salvaneschi, meant that: 'The sky is the new field of combat and death which has unbarred her blue doors to the combatants'. The purpose of these battleplanes was 'to kill the war', and this was done not by destroying the enemy army, but by destroying its 'manufactories of arms'. This would, in turn, leave the enemy with insufficient strength to carry on the war.[19] Gorrell was impressed with Salvaneschi's piece and distributed copies of it within the American Air Service. Over the months that followed, Gorrell wrote a memo on the desirability and feasibility of strategic bombing that was remarkably farsighted. Perhaps not surprisingly, there were strong similarities between Gorrell's memo, Salvaneschi's piece and the ideas then being expounded by Douhet.[20]

In June 1918 Douhet retired from the army, disgusted with the inefficiency and conservatism of his superiors, and returned to writing. Soon after the Armistice he became upset with the government for not dealing adequately with veterans of the war. He therefore started a newspaper, *Duty*, that dealt largely with domestic, economic and political issues. In this position he learned that the government had launched an official investigation into the battle of Caporetto. The report concluded that defeat was a result of organizational and leadership deficiencies, many of which had been noted by Douhet. The retired colonel therefore petitioned to have his court martial re-examined. This was done, and when it was realized his criticisms and predictions had been accurate, the judges decided Douhet had indeed primarily been interested in the safety of his country and not in personal gain. The verdict was overturned in November 1920, and he was promoted to general.[21]

Douhet did not return to active duty, but instead continued his literary efforts. In 1921 he completed his most famous work, *The Command of the Air*, and to show how completely his reputation had been restored, the book was published under War Department auspices. During this same period Douhet became a supporter of the Fascist party and Benito Mussolini, even participating in the 'March on Rome' in October 1922. When Mussolini assumed power soon after, he endorsed Douhet's ideas and appointed him Commissioner of Aviation. Douhet was unhappy as a bureaucrat, however, and hoped instead to be appointed as chief of the air force. Such an offer was not forthcoming, so after only a few months the general retired a second time to devote himself to writing. This he did for the next eight years, publishing dozens of essays and articles on air power, as well as several novels and plays. Unfortunately, few of his many works have been translated into English. Indeed, fully one-half of the first edition of *Command of the Air*, which is a lengthy appendix discussing the principles of flight and technical details of aircraft and sea plane construction, has never been translated and remains largely forgotten.[22]

Giulio Douhet died of a heart attack on 15 February 1930, while tending his garden at Ceschina, near Rome.

Douhet was profoundly affected by the trench warfare of World War I. Like most of his generation, he was appalled by the carnage and feared such a catastrophe would recur. He believed that wars were no longer fought between armies but between whole peoples. All the resources of a country – human, material and psychological – would be focused toward the war effort. Whereas Napoleon sometimes gained victory with a single battle, now a series of battles and a series of armies were needed. The *nation* would have to be exhausted before it would admit defeat. This was becoming increasingly difficult in an age of industrialization when the implements of war could be produced in a seemingly inexhaustible supply.

What made the attritional war of 1914–18 more horrifying was advancing technology – specifically the machine gun – which gave an overwhelming advantage to the defender. Defense behind prepared positions had always possessed inherent advantages, so an attacker required a preponderance of force to ensure success – usually a three-to-one superiority was considered necessary. The World War proved to Douhet that new technology required a greater superiority for an attack to succeed; and 'succeed' was a misnomer if it meant the slaughter of thousands. He was convinced that technology had granted the defense a permanent ascendancy in land warfare. Paradoxically, however, he argued that although technology had caused the trench stalemate, it would be technology – in the form of the airplane – that would end it. Only aircraft could overcome the fundamental problem of a prolonged war of attrition caused by mass armies equipped with modern weapons.

Douhet argued that air power was revolutionary because it operated in the third dimension and was unhampered by geography. Indeed, it was not the weapon that was revolutionary but the medium of the air itself that granted flexibility and initiative. Aircraft could fly over surface forces, which then became of secondary importance. If ground no longer needed to be controlled, then the forces used to control it diminished in significance. Contrary to conditions on the surface, he continued, the aerial offense was stronger than the aerial defense because the vastness of the sky made it virtually impossible to defend against the airplane. In Douhet's formulation, the speed of aircraft relative to ground forces plus its ubiquity – the ability to be in so many places in a short period of time – equaled offensive power. Writing before radar, he argued that a defender could not know the exact time and location of an attack, and this gave an enormous advantage to the offense, virtually assuring tactical surprise. On the other hand, defense would require a huge air fleet because each point protected would need an air contingent at least the size of the attacking enemy. This was precisely the opposite of the situation on the ground, because it meant successful air *defense* required the preponderance of force. This led Douhet to term the airplane 'the offensive weapon par excellence'.

Just as the possibility of aerial interception was discounted, so too ground-based air defenses were dismissed. Antiaircraft guns were deemed wasteful because they seldom hit anything. Douhet sarcastically conceded that ground fire might down some aircraft, much like muskets shot in the air might occasionally hit a swallow, but it was not a serious deterrent to air attack. He added that those who believed artillery was an effective counter to the airplane 'had confused aircraft with snails'. Douhet stated flatly: 'I am against air defense because it detracts means from the Air Force...I am against it because I am absolutely convinced that...it cannot achieve its aim'.[23] Thus, in Douhet's eyes, the best defense, indeed the only defense, was a good offense. This is also why he eschewed an air reserve. All aircraft were committed; holding forces in reserve exemplified the outdated and defensive thinking of surface commanders. The speed and range of aircraft created their own reserve, because they were able to react quickly and engage in different locations long before surface forces could move there.

These beliefs regarding the nature of modern war and the inherent characteristics of the airplane led Douhet to a theory of war based on the dominance of air power. His most fundamental precept[24] was that an air force must achieve command of the air – what today we would call air supremacy.[25] Without it, land and sea operations, and even air operations, were doomed. Moreover, a country that lost control of its airspace was forced to endure whatever air attacks an enemy chose to carry out. Command of the air meant victory.

Because it was virtually impossible to predict the specific time and place of an air attack, Douhet saw little chance of an air battle occurring. He reasoned that a stronger air force would be foolish to seek out its weaker enemy in the air, but should instead carry out the more lucrative task of bombing the enemy's airfields and aircraft industry – 'destroying the eggs in their nest'. The weaker force also had no incentive to seek an air engagement that was likely to lead to its destruction. The only hope for the weaker side was to strike even more violently at an enemy's homeland. Douhet thus envisioned a rather peculiar scenario in which opposing air forces studiously ignored each other while flying past to destroy the other's airfields and factories – something akin to 'mutual assured destruction' without nuclear weapons. He realized, however, that achieving aerial dominance was not an end in itself but rather enabled air power to conduct its primary task of reducing an enemy's will and capability to wage war.

The objective of war had always been to impose one's will on the enemy by breaking their will to resist. This, in fact, was what happened to Germany, Austria and Russia in the Great War – their armies were still largely intact in the fall of 1918, but the will of these nations to continue the fight had dissolved. In Douhet's view, air power could break a people's will by destroying or neutralizing a country's 'vital centers', those elements of society, government, military and industrial structure essential to the functioning of the state. Because of their value – as well as their immobility and vulnerability – these centers were protected by fortresses and armies. It was therefore necessary to defeat these armies and reduce these fortresses to expose the soft, inner core. Once disarmed, a country would then usually surrender rather than suffer the humiliation of an enemy occupation. Over time, many began to equate destruction of the army with the object of war, rather than merely as a means to an end. The Great War demonstrated that such a goal could have catastrophic consequences. Douhet reminded his readers that the true objective in war was the enemy's will, and only aircraft could strike it directly, overflying and ignoring the surface conflict below. In short, aircraft could obviate the bloody first step of destroying the enemy army, which now became superfluous.

Douhet was perhaps the first to realize that the key to air power was targeting, because although aircraft could strike virtually anything, they should not attempt to strike everything. It was necessary to identify those objectives most important and to hit them most forcefully. Choosing the proper targets was not an easy task and would require great insight; it was in this area that air commanders would prove their ability. The choice of targets would depend on a number of circumstances, including economic, military, political and psychological factors, and would therefore be variable;

but Douhet identified five basic target systems as the vital centers of a modern country: industry, transportation infrastructure, communication nodes, government buildings and the will of the people.[26]

To Douhet this last category was the most important, because the total wars of the new industrialized age were no longer a contest between armed foes: all people were combatants, women and men alike, and their collective will must be broken. Douhet stated bluntly that this could be done most effectively by urban bombing. This would terrorize the population, but that is precisely why it would have such great effect: 'normal life could not be carried on in this constant nightmare of imminent death and destruction'.[27] In 'The War of 19__', which described a fictional war between Germany and a French–Belgian alliance, Douhet had German bombers striking cities immediately after the outbreak of war to make a 'moral impression' on the population.[28]

Significantly, Douhet implied such terror bombing might not be necessary because gaining command of the air would be so psychologically devastating, the destruction of the vital centers would be unnecessary. The side that had lost control of its own airspace would realize what was in store for it and surrender rather than face devastation. Thus, war would become so horrible it would be humanizing. This paradox generated in Douhet a strange ambivalence about the righteousness of air power that he never fully resolved. Also of interest, his emphasis on the importance of gaining command of the air implies its achievement was comparable to clashes between opposing armies, when a decisive battle meant victory in the war: 'once a nation has been conquered in the air it may be subjected to such moral torture that it would be obliged to cry "Enough" *before* the war could be decided upon the surface'.[29] In other words, he came close to identifying the enemy air force as the key vital center. In a sense, therefore, Douhet was also stressing the need for a decisive counterforce battle, just as were the land war theorists he so decried.

Douhet did not advocate that aircraft attack or assist surface forces. The strength of air power lay in its use as a strategic weapon, not a tactical one. He did concede, however, that the air campaign might take six days or six months, 'depending on the intensity of the offensive and the staunchness of the people's hearts'. This meant that although command of the air and the subsequent devastation of a country's vital centers would probably produce victory, it might still be necessary for air power to defeat the enemy's ground forces if surrender was not immediately forthcoming. And if all else failed, ground troops would occupy enemy territory. To Douhet, this last option would seldom be necessary, and even the need for the defeat of the surface forces was unlikely.[30]

Because Douhet viewed air attacks on a country's vital centers as of primary importance, he saw little use for 'auxiliary aviation' (pursuit or attack aircraft). His ideas on this subject grew more radical over time. In the first edition of *Command of the Air* (1921), he recognized the utility of auxiliary aviation; however, in the second edition of 1927, Douhet went much further. Stating that he had been deliberately mild in his earlier edition so as not to cause too much consternation, it was now necessary to be completely honest. He therefore maintained that, in truth, auxiliary aviation was 'worthless, superfluous and harmful'. Auxiliary aviation was merely a collection of airplanes; it was not air power. He was convinced that an army or navy without control of the air above it was an army or navy about to be destroyed. Command of the air was therefore essential and was the key strategic objective. Once achieved, and if tactical operations were still in progress on the surface, aircraft could be of assistance. But diverting assets to surface support while the strategic air battle was still raging was folly. If command of the air was lost, the war was lost, regardless of the situation on the surface.

Remember that Douhet was formulating a theory of war applicable to Italy: a country of modest resources, powerful neighbors and mountainous northern borders.[31] He believed it relatively easy to defend the mountain passes – as indeed Austria had done against Italy in the Great War. Certainly, auxiliary aviation would be useful in that defense, but to what end? Victory on the surface was prohibitively expensive if not impossible. For Italy, it was wiser to hold on the ground while attacking in the air. Douhet admitted, however, that a country with great resources – like the United States – could afford to build both a strategic and an auxiliary air force.[32]

To implement his ideas, Douhet called for an Independent Air Force (IAF). Air power divorced from army and navy control was essential because it 'could not depend, like Cinderella, on the generosity of older sisters', but must see to its own needs. Even the most conservative soldier and sailor recognized how essential aircraft had become to their operations. Although denying Air power could be a decisive factor in war, they realized victory was unlikely without it. To Douhet, this realization was dangerous if it meant surface commanders would demand air power, under their control, to support tactical operations. In this circumstance the aviation defense budget would be fatally split between independent and auxiliary air power, a situation that would help no one.

The IAF would be composed largely of 'bombardment units' and 'combat units'. The former were long-range, heavy-load-carrying aircraft of moderate speed. Although Douhet considered it unlikely that enemy aircraft could intercept a bomber force, such an eventuality was possible, so he called for 'combat units' or escort aircraft that would carry machine guns to ward off enemy interceptors. Of note, because he did not anticipate an air battle would actually occur, he claimed that he did not believe such defensive armaments would really be required, but would be included as a comfort to aircrew morale. The only other aircraft type Douhet thought necessary was a fast, long-range reconnaissance plane to fly over enemy territory photographing potential targets. Reconnaissance was necessary for effective targeting, because it was desirable not only to pinpoint objectives but also to determine the effectiveness of air attacks on those objectives. In the revised edition of *Command of the Air*, Douhet combined the functions of bombardment and escort into one aircraft, the battleplane. He envisioned battleplanes flying en masse towards an enemy's vital centers, carrying both bombs and defensive machine-guns.[33]

Significantly, unlike many other writers of the period who tended to glorify air warfare, especially the role of the fighter pilot, Douhet took a decidedly non-romantic view. There are no passages in his writings that speak of the exhilaration of flight, the conquest of nature by man and his machine or the near-mystical experiences of those who have become unfettered by the tyranny of geography. He did not compare the pilot to a modern knight who was bold, chivalrous and dashing, but portrayed the aviator simply as a determined and stoic professional who unremarkably went about his deadly business. And this business was indeed a deadly one.

Because most attacks would be on area targets, Douhet did not believe bombing accuracy was especially important: if targets were so small as to require high accuracy, then they were probably not worthwhile targets. These area attacks would be made using a mixture of high explosive, incendiary and gas or biological (aero-chemical) bombs. The explosives were used to produce rubble; the incendiaries to start fires in the rubble; and the aero-chemical bombs to prevent firefighters from extinguishing the blaze. Although in *Command of the Air* Douhet states merely that these bombs should be used 'in the proper proportion', in 'The War of 19__' German battleplanes carry bombloads in the ratio of one explosive, to three incendiary, to six aero-chemical bombs. Douhet thus recognized that a combination of different types of weapons can produce a greater result than any single weapon. Of note, during World War II, Allied bombers often carried a mix of both high explosive and incendiary bombs so as to achieve the results suggested by Douhet.

The general also maintained it was essential that air attacks be carried out en masse. In the air, as on the surface, piecemeal attacks were counterproductive. His emphasis on mass in the air – remember his call for 20,000 aircraft in 1917 – was every bit as pronounced as that of the surface generals of the Great War. He considered it equally important that these mass strikes be carried out rapidly. The speed and range of aircraft provided the flexibility to strike several targets simultaneously. This simultaneity would cause paralysis and collapse: air strikes would occur so rapidly and massively over a wide area, the collective will of a country would simply disintegrate. In today's parlance, Douhet was referring to 'parallel operations' – the ability to operate against several different target sets, at both the strategic and tactical levels, simultaneously. It would take several decades before the accuracy and effectiveness of aircraft and their weapons would allow such parallel operations, but the principle Douhet outlined in 1921 was certainly a viable one.

Douhet also stressed that because defense against air attack was impossible, there had to be an air fleet-in-being to attack immediately and relentlessly on the outbreak of hostilities. Unlike with surface forces that could have weeks or even months to prepare, there would be no time to mobilize air power in future wars. A country not ready for war would lose command of the air and, with it, the war itself. Indeed, an unstated conclusion of this position is that air power would be particularly effective at 'first strike' or in a preventive war. If mobilization was not a factor in air warfare, and if air defense was impossible, then obviously the country that struck first would enjoy an enormous, almost insurmountable, advantage. Assuming Douhet's formulation, therefore, in times of crisis there would be a tendency to use the air weapon precipitously. Thus, even more so than in the era before the Great War, when mobilization by a country was tantamount to a declaration of war, the inexorable, almost inevitable, nature of air attack might mean that the slightest twitch in times of crisis could lead to catastrophe. The air weapon, by its nature, was a device with a hair trigger.

Douhet believed that the strength of a country's air force was integrally related to the condition of its civil aviation industry. In a greater sense than with either land or sea power, he viewed military air power as dependent on the civil sector. Douhet saw a strong and symbiotic relationship between an air force, the aviation industry, the government and a country's commercial vitality. He argued that the government must subsidize and support civil aviation in three general ways. First, it should establish air routes consisting of airports, emergency landing fields, radio and signal beacons, and weather stations. Second, it must fund research and development – aircraft and their special high-performance engines were too expensive for industry to assume the financial burden for their development. Douhet also believed civil airliners should be capable of performing military missions. He envisioned airliners with the same specifications as battleplanes, and thus able to augment the air force in war.[34]

There is some validity in this idea. Although it has not been possible to achieve complete commonality, the technological relationship between civil and military aircraft has always been close because scientific advances often benefit both sectors. During the 1930s, it was commercial designs like the Boeing 247, Lockheed 'Vega' and Douglas DC-3 that led to military aircraft development. Even today it is no coincidence that Boeing and Lockheed airliners closely resemble US Air Force tankers and cargo aircraft. Even so, the increasing complexity demanded of military aircraft is making this decades-old technological marriage tenuous. Finally, Douhet expected civil aviation to establish an 'airmindedness' among the population. Not only must a pool of pilots and aircraft mechanics be trained for use in war, but events like air shows and demonstration flights would educate people to the importance of aviation and the economic, social and military benefits it could bestow. The people must think of themselves as an air-power nation.

In evaluating the writings of Douhet, it must be noted that there were really three theorists with that name writing about air power over a 20-year period. The first was a relatively young man, fascinated by machines and gadgets, who witnessed heavier-than-air flight in 1908 and began dreaming about its possibilities. Over the next four years, he sketched out an outline of the importance of aircraft and how they would be used in war. By the time Italy had entered World War I, Douhet had already decided upon the basic thrust of this theory: war had become total and stagnated, and air power would provide the antidote. It would do this by taking the offensive at the outset of war and by bombing the vital centers of the enemy country. World War I merely provided more detail and specificity to his theories. The stalemate and horror of land warfare was even worse than he – or most anyone else – had imagined. The few and fairly weak attempts at strategic bombing had seemed to provide disproportionately large results. Douhet therefore expanded upon his earlier ideas, threw in a few examples from the war, and produced the first edition of *Command of the Air* in 1921.

The response to his work was fairly muted. Perhaps because of the inevitable revulsion to war experienced by most of Europe in the wake of the Armistice, or perhaps because of the turmoil in the rise of Mussolini and the fascist state, Douhet's book caused little stir initially. During the six years after the publication of his book, the 'second theorist' continued to think and write, out of the public eye, and in the process his radicalism grew. The result was the second edition of *Command of the Air*, which, as we have seen, was more extreme than the first. The role of the army and navy in Douhet's revised work was reduced, with a corresponding increase in the importance of strategic air power. As a consequence, the utility of auxiliary aviation was deemed nil. Finally, Douhet placed even greater faith in the ability of the bomber to penetrate enemy airspace and destroy its targets. Escorts were unnecessary. Unlike the first edition, the 1927 version of *Command of the Air* had a noisy reception.

The third Douhet was the man who spent the last three years of his life reacting to the firestorm created by his revised work. Because of his reputation and personality, as well as the primitive state of aviation even into the mid-1920s, it had been easy to ignore Douhet. Clearly his superiors, even those involved with aviation or sympathetic to it, had not taken him too seriously. As a consequence, his writings up to 1927 had generated little debate within his profession. After that date, however, such was not the case. Mussolini clearly approved of air power, new airmen like Italo Balbo were becoming national heroes and gaining international reputations, and the aircraft themselves were becoming increasingly capable. The ideas of Douhet were thus becoming a threat to the proponents of land and sea power, whom he was constantly attacking. For the first time, Douhet was forced to engage in an intelligent, albeit heated, debate with his military peers. He was not used to having to defend himself from incessant and virulent attack. Nonetheless, given the gusto with which he responded to his critics between 1927 and 1930, largely through the pages of *Rivista Aeronautica*, he certainly seemed to enjoy the controversy. What effect did this long overdue dialogue have on his theories? The impact was mixed. On the one hand it forced him to clearly define terms like 'command of the air', and this clarification enhanced his theory.[35] On the other hand, however, it drove him to dig in his heels even more adamantly regarding the dominance of air power over surface warfare.

The increased radicalization of Douhet's ideas, spurred by the heated debate in the professional military journals, culminated in his last work, 'The War of 19__'. This fictional account was written in the last months of his life but not published until soon after his death. In many ways, this piece combined and magnified Douhet's most extreme positions. The entire war lasts less than two days, and dozens of major cities lay in ashes. The battleplanes of the victorious Germans suffer enormous losses, but succeeding waves continue and are unstoppable. The morale of the civilian population quickly collapses and the political leadership sues for peace, while the land forces of the belligerents have barely even begun their mobilization and assembly. The war of the future is therefore rapid, violent, relatively bloodless (compared to the Great War) and dominated completely by air power. It was this vision – almost hopeful and utopian in some respects – that was to dominate air-power theory for the next decade. It is therefore imperative at this point to examine more closely Douhet's assumptions and conclusions, many of which were, quite simply, wrong.

Douhet initiated a fundamental debate, never resolved, over whether air power is unique and revolutionary, or whether it is just another arrow in a soldier's or sailor's quiver and thus evolutionary. Debate hinges on the alleged decisiveness of air power.

Can air power be decisive in war? Perhaps it depends on the definition of that term. Some use it to imply that air power can (or cannot) win wars independently of other arms, but it is unlikely any service can win a war alone in the modern age, so that definition is not useful; moreover, few airmen would ever make such a claim. Others define decisiveness in terms of destruction of an enemy force or the occupation of territory. Douhet argued these were not the objects of war and were often irrelevant. Trafalgar did not end the Napoleonic wars, and although Hannibal occupied most of Italy for a decade and destroyed several Roman armies, he still lost the war.

A more useful meaning of the term is to identify the force predominant in achieving the desired goal. If that goal includes the quarantine of a belligerent, as in the Cuban Missile Crisis of 1962, then sea power will dominate. If, on the other hand, the goal is to topple a dictator and restore democracy, as in Panama, then ground forces will dominate. But there are other instances, as in the Gulf War, when air power is dominant. Using this meaning, Douhet believed passionately that air power could be decisive in war and thus revolutionary. He did, however, stumble in several key respects.

One of Douhet's more glaring errors was his overestimation of the psychological effects of bombing. He believed people would panic in the face of a determined air attack. To a great extent, however, Douhet can be excused for this mistake since he had little empirical evidence to draw upon, and what existed was quite supportive. For example, in 1925 military theorist Basil H. Liddell Hart commented on the psychological effect of German bombing attacks on Britain in World War I:

Witnesses of the earlier air attacks before our defence was organized, will not be disposed to underestimate the panic and disturbance that would result from a concentrated blow dealt by a superior air fleet. Who that saw it will ever forget the nightly sight of the population of a great industrial and shipping town, such as Hull, streaming out into the fields on the first sound of the alarm signals? Women, children, babies in arms, spending night after night huddled in sodden fields, shivering under a bitter winter sky.[36]

Douhet had read of such panic during the war and had noted it in his diaries. Clearly, these reports had made a deep impression on him. In truth, there were many such descriptions in the literature of the time, and even former British Prime Minister Stanley Baldwin proclaimed glumly in 1932 that 'the bomber would always get through'.[37] Such warnings were clearly believed: during the Munich crisis of 1938, fully one-third of the population of Paris was evacuated from the city so as to avoid a possible German air assault.[38] The problem with such apocalyptic predictions was that they failed to address whether morale was even a relevant issue in a tightly organized police state – as were Germany and Japan during World War II. In addition, the dire predictions of Douhet and others erred by underestimating the resilience of human beings in the face of adversity. Civilian morale did not break in World War II with anywhere near the rapidity or finality predicted by Douhet: cities were not inhabited by mere rabble who would collapse at the first application of pressure.[39] It may be, as one observer noted, that Douhet's theories assumed wars occurring between the democratic countries of Europe.[40] In democracies the government is responsive to the wishes of the population. However, this is not generally the case in a dictatorship where the leaders may ignore the desires of the people, and indeed, the state police may prevent the people from making their wishes known. In such a circumstance the morale of the population, even if affected by aerial bombardment, may be irrelevant to the despot. Similarly, a country in the throes of civil war may not be responsive to *any* government, or a government may have little control over its population. In such situations the moral effect of bombing would be negligible or at least would not operate using the mechanism envisioned by Douhet.

The physical effects of aerial bombs were similarly exaggerated, but in this case Douhet should have known better. He postulated absurdly uniform and effective bombing – no duds, no misses, no overlap, no difference in the composition and construction of targets struck. In fact, he seemed to assume all wars occurred in clear weather and all pilots and bombardiers – and their equipment – performed flawlessly. For example, he stated that a 100 kg bomb (220 lb) would destroy anything within a 50 meter diameter, meaning that a target 500 meters in diameter would require ten tons of explosives. Because aircraft of the day could carry two tons, it would take five aircraft to effect this destruction. Magnanimously, Douhet doubled that number and claimed ten aircraft would 'destroy entirely everything that exists upon an area of 500 meters diameter'.[41] Such calculations were simplistic in the extreme. For example, a circle that size has an area of approximately 0.19 square kilometers. London was about 1,000 times as large at that time (about 75 square miles or 196 square kilometers). Thus, even using Douhet's hopelessly optimistic figures for bomb effectiveness, it would still have taken 10,000 tons of high explosives to level London, or a force of 5,000 aircraft. Even so, had such an air fleet been available, the results expected by Douhet would not necessarily have been forthcoming. One historian has noted that in the first six months of the Germans' Operation Barbarossa in 1941, the Soviet Union lost 40 per cent of its population, 63 per cent of its coal, 58 per cent of its steel, 68 per cent of its pig iron, 60 per cent of its aluminum, 38 per cent of its grain, 95 per cent of its ball bearings and 99 per cent of its rolled, non-ferrous metals.[42] Those are staggering statistics, and had they been attained by a strategic bombing force they would have been the envy of any air commander. But of course the Soviet Union not only did not collapse, it went on to defeat Germany. Modern nations have a toughness and resilience undreamed of by Douhet.

Douhet also proposed that aero-chemical bombs be employed with the high explosives, which he believed would be especially effective against urban targets. General Nicholas N. Golovine noted, however, that based on wartime experience 25 grams of poison gas were needed to 'put out of action' one square meter. Again using London as an example, 5,750 tons of poison material would have been required 'for an effective gassing'.[43] Added to the tonnage of high explosives noted above, including an appropriate number of escort aircraft, and also assuming some attrition of the striking force, an attack on London of the destructive magnitude envisioned by Douhet would have required nearly 20,000 aircraft. Yet, 'The War of 19__' lasts only 36 hours because more than two dozen of the major cities in France and Belgium have been reduced to ashes – and this by only 1,500 aircraft using bombs of a mere 50 kg, a size so small as to be virtually useless. Although repeatedly claiming his methods were scientific and mathematically precise, it is nonetheless true that for a trained engineer, Douhet's mathematical and technical gaffes, as well as his sophomoric attempts to estimate bomb damage 'scientifically', are baffling. Where is the empirical evidence supporting his assertions regarding the effectiveness of high explosives against reinforced structures? He had none. It gives little comfort to realize he was not alone in these errors.[44] Unfortunately, this attempt to imbue air power with a false 'scientism' has never been fully overcome. It would seem to be a peculiar penchant for air-power theorists to devise technological solutions to what are often very human problems.

To make matters worse, Douhet then stated breezily that in order to achieve optimal bomb dispersion, crews should be trained to 'scatter their bombs' in a 'uniform fashion'.[45] Nothing more clearly exposes a key flaw in Douhet's theories: he was out of touch with the details; he showed no understanding of the tactics needed to implement those concepts. Apparently, Douhet was not an aviator and, as a consequence, was frequently guilty of serious missteps such as his bizarre comment (see above) that pilots should be trained to scatter their bombs uniformly, even in the heat of combat.[46] Moreover, Douhet had an irritating tendency to exaggerate his prophetic powers. In *The Command of the Air* he quotes at length from a piece he published in 1910 in which he predicts the coming dominance of the airplane. However, other pieces he wrote during that same period were far more conservative. As noted above, his official report on the Libyan War was strongly muted, dealing mostly with organizational and technical matters. In addition, in 1910 he published an article titled 'The Possibilities of Aerial Navigation' that was similarly unremarkable. Douhet sang the praises of the airplane, but stopped far short of calling for an independent air arm or even emphasizing the role of strategic bombing in future wars. Instead, he stressed the reconnaissance and tactical aspects of aircraft and their importance in battle and coastal defense.[47] It is thus an interesting insight into Douhet's personality that he felt the need to backdate his air-power theories to well before World War I. Being an early air theorist was not enough; he had to be the first.

Douhet was also guilty of virtually ignoring the air battle required to attain command of the air. Because the airplane's inherent attributes of speed and range granted it tactical surprise, he believed command of the air could be achieved without a fight. (In 'The War of 19__', the air battle lasts a mere three hours.) There has always been a tension in war between the strategies of annihilation and attrition. Land warfare had definitely reached a stage in World War I where the latter predominated. Air power has promised annihilation but generally provided attrition. The counterforce battle Douhet stated would be eliminated by air power was still necessary in World War II, but the trenches were moved to 20,000 feet. Nearly 80,000 Royal Air Force crew members and a like number of Americans were lost in the air battle over Germany. Indeed, that battle revealed it was wiser to meet the Luftwaffe in the air than it was to attack the German aircraft and engine factories. In effect, Allied bombers became the bait that brought the Luftwaffe's planes, and pilots, into the air where they could be destroyed. One reason Douhet discounted the air battle was that few had occurred on a major scale in the Italo-Austrian front during the war.

It is also possible Douhet ignored the air battle because to admit its likelihood would contradict one of his main tenets, that air power eliminated the counterforce battle. Toward the end of his life it appears he began to modify these views. In 'The War of 19__', the German battleplanes suffer horrendous losses – 100 per cent of the attacking force is shot down by enemy pursuit in the initial waves – but succeeding waves press on and ultimately achieve victory.[48] In other words, Douhet conceded defense was possible, at least tactically. It would have been useful if he had explored more fully the distinction between tactical and strategic air superiority, and how they could be achieved.

Douhet's premise that the weaker air force must assume an ever more violent offense because defense is futile was refuted by the Battle of Britain: radar stripped away the airplane's surprise. It is well to remember, however, that this 1940 battle has been the only clear-cut defensive air victory in history.[49] Today, electronic warfare – the jamming of communications and radars – and especially stealth technology have tilted the balance back in favor of the aircraft as an offensive weapon for those who have invested in such technology. The Gulf War presented a situation predicted by Douhet: attacking aircraft (F-117 stealth bombers) arrived over targets unannounced, destroyed those targets, and then departed, with impunity, all because they had achieved tactical surprise.

The Italian theorist also erred in foreseeing only total war, perhaps because his view was colored by a conflict that seemingly had no rational objectives. The political scientist Bernard Brodie accused him of failing to understand that war must follow policy, but this misses the mark.[50] Rather, Douhet expected that as in the Great War, future wars would be similarly inane. More of a cynic than a realist, he was profoundly skeptical of human nature and rejected arguments that war could be carefully guided or finely tuned to reflect political will: 'War...is a kind of irrepressible convulsion, during which it seems to lose or suspend every human sense; and it [humanity] appears to be invaded by a devastating and destructive fury'.[51] Fortunately, he was not completely correct; World War II was not as devoid of clear objectives as the Great War. Moreover, limited wars, like those in Korea and Vietnam, became the norm in the second half of the twentieth century, and in many of these wars – as against the Viet Cong for example – air power, as he envisioned it, is largely inappropriate.

Douhet denigrated limitations imposed by law and morality, and continued to advocate aero-chemical attacks on cities even after Italy had ratified the Geneva Protocol of 1925 which prohibited their use. This, too, showed Douhet's pessimistic view of human nature. He was certain total war would rationalize any type of activity and stated:

> He is a fool if not a patricide who would acquiesce in his country's defeat rather than go against those formal agreements which do not limit the right to kill and destroy, but simply the ways of killing and destroying. The limitations applied to the so-called inhuman and atrocious means of war are nothing but international demagogic hypocrisies.[52]

Given the World War hecatomb it is not surprising Douhet was so pessimistic. But as horrendous as the destruction in World War II was, no belligerent resorted to gas warfare, although most possessed the means to do so.[53] Moreover, since 1945 there have been several conventions held regarding the law of war, and a variety of rulings have been proposed. Most of these limitations are contained in the 1977 Geneva Protocols, and although these were rejected by the United States, it still follows their basic thrust.[54] This was shown in Desert Storm when Coalition airmen went to great lengths to restrict the types of targets struck and weapons employed so as to minimize civilian casualties and collateral damage. Now that precision bombing has become more routine, it is likely such scrupulous targeting will become standard practice.

Another example of Douhet's shortsightedness was his failure to forecast advances in surface technology. Although stating 'everything in this world undergoes improvement', he foresaw no evolution in surface weapons and claimed ground war had reached perpetual equilibrium. Thus, he ignored the development of tanks and armored doctrine, which played a major role in restoring mobility to the battlefield. Tanks, which were used by most of the major belligerents during the war and which underwent significant improvement in the decades that followed, are not even mentioned in *Command of the Air*. Significantly, however, the French army in 'The War of 19__' does possess a strong tank contingent; but France loses the war before they can ever be put to use. Obviously, Douhet is making a point. The surface stalemate of the Great War was certainly very real and had an enormous psychological impact on those who fought in it, but one must ask what happened to the Giulio Douhet who wrote so presciently concerning the potential of ground force mechanization in his early career. A skeptic might ask if this was because such ideas would have undermined his theories regarding the primacy of air power.[55] Also of note, Douhet took pains to single out small-caliber machine-guns as contributing to the trench stalemate of World War I. He did not mention the enormous and continually growing use of large-caliber artillery, which also played a major role in the stalemate. Since Douhet was an artillery officer, this omission is curious. One possible explanation is that Douhet was reluctant to call attention to a weapon whose explosive impact bore at least some resemblance to that of an aerial bomb. He did not want anyone to think of air power as flying artillery.

Douhet also missed the mark on air defense. There is a counter to air attack; yet, he insisted antiaircraft fire and interceptors were ineffective and would remain so. Moreover, Douhet denied to defensive air power the same flexibility, speed and ability to mass that he granted the offense. Even before radar this is not understandable. By as early as 1917, the British had established a sophisticated system of air defense consisting of multiple 'spotting stations' connected by telephone to a central headquarters in London. This headquarters was tied by telephone to the various airfields housing the interceptor squadrons. These airfields, in turn, maintained contact with their aircraft while airborne via wireless. The system was relatively effective and Douhet must have known this.[56] In one of his more memorable and maladroit comments, Douhet mused: 'Nothing man can do on the surface of the earth can interfere with a plane in flight, moving freely in the third dimension'.[57] Once again one searches for the lieutenant who began his career as an artillery officer. He must have known that German gunners shot down 1,588 Allied aircraft during the war, and that because of improvements in fusing, the number of rounds fired to achieve a hit fell by one-half between 1915 and 1918.[58] Continued improvements in air defenses should have been expected, yet he ignored them.

It is important to note that Douhet's argument regarding the inherently offensive nature of the airplane was predicated on the belief that only aircraft could stop other aircraft. Given the vastness of the sky, there was some merit to this position, though not as much as Douhet claimed. There is even less merit, however, if it is admitted that antiaircraft guns can also be effective against air attack. In such an instance, the numerical advantage gained by an attacker achieving tactical surprise and avoiding airborne interception evaporates quickly. Theoretically, if antiaircraft guns are extremely effective, interceptor aircraft are not even necessary for a successful defense. Moreover, Douhet seemed to assume that in order for a defense to be effective it must stop all of an attacker's aircraft. World War II proved this was far from the case. Even in those instances when the defense – using both interceptors and antiaircraft guns – was able to shoot down 'only' 20 per cent of an attacking bomber force, the effect on the attacker was near catastrophic. As the US strikes on Schweinfurt in the fall of 1943 showed, such loss rates were unacceptable, but were well within the capabilities of a defender to achieve. In truth, although Douhet – like many of his contemporaries – vilified the generals of the Great War for foolishly falling into a 'cult of the offensive', the Italian air theorist followed much the same path. In this sense at least Douhet was philosophically at one with the surface generals he so roundly criticized.

Somewhat surprisingly, Douhet did not adequately address the issue of objectives, even though he recognized their importance and saw targeting as the most important task of the air commander. In the exasperated words of Bernard Brodie: 'How could one who had so little idea of what it is necessary to hit be quite so sure of the tremendous results which would inevitably follow from the hitting?'[59] Although general target sets are mentioned, there is nowhere a systematic examination of what it would take to dismember a country's industrial system. This may partly be a result of his belief that the will of the people was of such overwhelming importance as a target that it was unnecessary to elaborate on the other vital centers. In addition, disassembling these centers was not nearly as simple as Douhet suggested. For one thing, aircraft cannot operate at will anytime or any place. Rather, there are many limits that may be imposed on air power: political restraints and goals, range, national boundaries, darkness, weather, the electromagnetic spectrum, even the duration of the war itself can significantly affect target selection. Yet, Douhet believed that because aircraft operated in the third dimension, they had no limits, and all targets could be quickly and effectively attacked. This interpretation is too facile. Targets are not destroyed simply because they are attacked, and merely identifying targets to be struck is no substitute for a coherent air strategy.

What is most surprising, Douhet is not alone in this shallow thinking. None of the classic air power thinkers – Mitchell, Trenchard, Slessor, de Seversky, *et al*. – ever went beyond the most fundamental stages of attempting to identify the key vital centers of a country. Moreover, the question of which specific target sets within those vital centers – precisely which industries, transportation nodes and command and control facilities were most important – and in what order of priority they should be struck, is simply not discussed. The theorists at the Air Corps Tactical School at

Maxwell Field in the 1930s made some initial enquiries in this area and quickly concluded that just as targeting is the key to air power, so too is intelligence the key to targeting. Unfortunately, although military intelligence organizations had existed in some form for centuries, the type of information they gathered was generally that needed at the tactical level: how many troops does the enemy have, where are they located, what are the capabilities of their weapons, where are their supply depots, etc. Airwar now required fundamentally different types of intelligence regarding a country's industrial and economic structure and potential. Because intelligence agencies that could provide this type of information did not yet exist, Douhet and others were left with vague and simplistic platitudes. It was a serious oversight that the vital connection between targeting and intelligence was not identified and seriously addressed. Of interest, it took Desert Storm to furnish the third pillar of this trio: the key to intelligence in modern war is the ability to assess the results of an air campaign on a complex system. Given the interdependent and linked nature of modern societies, neutralizing a certain target does not necessarily mean a strategic gain is achieved or that it was the one intended. In addition, the *pace* of airwar has now become so rapid that near real-time intelligence has become essential. Moreover, precision weapons demand precision intelligence: if one can now strike a specific office in a large military headquarters, then one needs to know the correct office.

Another example of Douhet's exaggeration is his attitude towards the army and navy. Although Douhet paid lip service to the other arms, he saw little use for them, and his tendency to move from the dominance of air power to its omnipotence grew. Because he did not expect surface forces to be decisive, he gave little thought to their future. In the defense department he envisioned the surface forces would have degenerated into impotence – merely serving to guard Italy's mountain passes and harbors. Douhet's thinking therefore became dangerously one-dimensional.

Finally, he failed to see the importance of history, of looking to the past to illuminate the present. In this regard he was in the same position as the nuclear theorists following World War II. There was little empirical evidence upon which to base a model of how nuclear weapons would be used in war, so their theories became intellectual exercises that relied on the force of logic. Similarly, what little evidence did exist from World War I, Douhet chose to ignore: 'the experience of the past is of no value at all. On the contrary, it has a negative value since it tends to mislead us'.[60] He took this position not because he believed history was useless, but because it provided the wrong lessons for air power. Paradoxically, however, at the same time he was denigrating the lessons of the Great War, he was building a theory of air power based on that war repeating itself. The result was a curious mixture of past and future, with no apparent anchor in either dimension.

World War II was seen as a test of Douhet's theories, and most found them wanting. Detractors noted he was proven wrong on many counts: the land war did not stagnate; there was a prolonged and deadly air battle necessary to gain command of the air; civilian morale did not collapse; aero-chemical bombs were not employed; and auxiliary aviation (tactical air power) proved enormously valuable. Defenders of Douhet see a different picture: command of the air did in fact mean the difference between victory and defeat; the German and Japanese war economies were devastated; and although not destroyed, civilian morale was severely damaged by bombardment. Moreover, advocates maintain Douhet's theories were never given a fair test because the basic tenet of his war-fighting philosophy – hold on the ground while attacking in the air – was never carried out. This resulted in a diversion of effort that detracted from the potency of the air offensive. The arguments of these advocates are not credible. Millions of tons of bombs were dropped over a period of six years, a scale far in excess of anything imagined by Douhet, and the results did not fulfill his prophecies. (It should be remembered, however, that Douhet's theories presumed the use of gas bombs. It is impossible to say whether or not their use would have made a significant difference in the results of the air campaigns waged by Germany, Japan, Britain and the United States.

A seemingly more reasonable approach was to maintain that atomic weapons vindicated Douhet; after all, an invasion of Japan proper was unnecessary, and the only battle of the home islands was the one conducted by the American B-29s. Atomic weapons seemed to grant new relevance to Douhet because a handful of bombs could now devastate a country as he had predicted.[61] Such arguments may be even less credible than the claims Douhet was not given a fair test in World War II. If the only circumstance that makes Douhet relevant is nuclear holocaust, then he is totally irrelevant.

Given the limited wars of the postwar era, especially Vietnam, it increasingly seemed that Douhet's ideas on air power were best confined to the dustbin of history. This has now changed, because the thawing of the Cold War and the collapse of the Warsaw Pact, coupled with the decreased presence of forward-deployed US troops, has put a premium on the ability to project power over great distances. This requirement is a natural characteristic of air power, and the efficacy of the air weapon was never demonstrated more clearly than in the Gulf War. For decades, airmen described air power using terms like furious, relentless, overwhelming, etc., but to a great extent these were just words because the technology did not exist to make them true. The airwar in the Gulf finally lived up to the prophecies of the previous seven decades.

One of Douhet's ideas that has become increasingly relevant is his call for a single department of defense. Douhet advocated such an organization as early as 1908 when he wrote a stinging essay titled 'The Knot of Our Military Question', which criticized the lack of cooperation between the Italian army and navy. He suggested a single ministry of defense headed by a civilian. At the same time, he called for a military chief of staff to coordinate the combat operations of the services.[62] His proposal was ignored, but it was an idea he would return to later. In *Command of the Air* he enlarged his defense ministry to include an air force, but the services were still united under a single civilian head, and military operations coordinated by a chief of staff. Douhet's rationale was not based on economic efficiency but on military necessity. War could not be subdivided by medium – air, land and sea – it was a whole, and only those understanding the use of military forces in all three mediums could understand war: 'There are experts of land, sea and air warfare. But as yet there are no experts of warfare. And warfare is a single entity, having a single purpose'.[63] He therefore proposed a national war college to educate soldiers, sailors and airmen in the overall conduct of war.

Douhet was also perceptive in noting the tension between separateness and joint action between the services. It was not inconsistent that he called for a unified defense department on one hand and an air force which dominated that defense department on the other. Service cooperation did not mean equality. It would be dangerous to merely divide the defense budget into three equal parts if the roles played by those parts were not equal. Hard choices had to be made, and to Douhet the logic was inescapable. Since land and sea forces could not survive in the face of air attack, it was folly to pretend those arms were the decisive forces in war and should be supported by air. The opposite was true. air power was now the key arm, and armies and navies must support it.

Although Douhet was the first and most noted of the early air-power theorists, the extent of his influence is debatable. Largely because he wrote in a language that was not common currency among military thinkers – a circumstance exacerbated by the fact that he deliberately confined his writing to the professional journals of his own country – Douhet initially was not well known outside his native land. The British, for example, may have heard of his ideas, but the first article to appear in the official journal of the Royal Air Force did not appear until 1933.[64] *Command of the Air* was never required reading at the RAF Staff College between the wars, and one historian states flatly that Douhet had no influence in Britain prior to World War II.[65] The situation in France was somewhat different. French airmen were followers of aviation developments in Italy, and in 1933 the magazine *Les Ailes* published a partial translation of *Command of the Air*. French air leaders, specifically Generals Tulasne and Armengaud, were receptive to his ideas.[66] In 1935, Colonel P. Vauthier wrote an analysis of Douhet's theories titled *La Doctrine de Guerre du General Douhet*, which further elucidated the Italian's theories and disseminated them to a wider audience. In fact, it is likely that the accounts of Douhet that began appearing in British and American periodicals about this time were based on the French works and not the original Italian. German military leaders were even more receptive to new ideas than were the French. Because of their failure in the Great War, German military leaders made a point of closely monitoring foreign developments. Although *Command of the Air* was not published in German until 1935, it appears Hitler was initially taken with Douhet's ideas: he appreciated the terroristic aspects of his air bombardment theory, and this was evident at the time of the Munich crisis in 1938. The Luftwaffe as a whole, however, was not similarly influenced, and the official doctrine with which it entered the war focused on army cooperation.[67]

Douhet had his earliest and greatest influence in America, but even then it was not great. In 1922, the Italian air attaché wrote about *Command of the Air* in *Aviation* magazine, and Billy Mitchell later admitted that he had met with Douhet during a trip to Europe the same year. About that same time, and perhaps even as a result of that meeting, a translation of excerpts from *Command of the Air* made its way into Air Service files, and in 1923 a longer translation circulated at Air Service headquarters. One historian claims Mitchell heavily 'borrowed from' this translation, and it, in turn, formed the basis of early Air Service Tactical School texts that dealt with strategic bombardment.[68] This is questionable, but by the mid-1930s articles discussing Douhet began to appear in US military publications, and a translation of the second edition was circulated around the Air Corps in 1933.[69]

In sum, it is apparent that European and US airmen were aware of Douhet's writings in the decade prior to World War II. Given that many people in many places were attempting to come to grips with the new air weapon, it is virtually impossible to draw clear lines of influence between them. That many of the ideas percolating throughout the various air forces were quite similar to those expounded by the Italian air general does not mean those ideas were based on Douhet. What is clear, however, is that by the end of World War II and as a result of the strategic bombing campaigns that were conducted throughout, the theories of Douhet were commonplace. This notoriety became even greater in the decade that followed, given the emergence of nuclear weapons delivered by air power. Although equating Douhet solely with the destruction of cities and their populations is simplistic and incomplete, his name has nonetheless become synonymous with a particular version of air warfare.

Giulio Douhet has generated intense and partisan debate over the past seven decades. Undoubtedly he had many things wrong, but he also had many things right. World War II and Desert Storm proved the accuracy of his fundamental premise – command of the air is crucial to success in a conventional war. Despite Douhet's many theoretical deficiencies, the scope and audacity of his work indicate a man of great intellect. Considering it took over two thousand years of warfare on land and sea to produce Jomini, Clausewitz and Mahan, we should not be overly critical of the airman who began writing a theory of airwar scarcely one decade after the invention of the airplane.

NOTES

This essay originally appeared as a chapter in *The Paths of Heaven: The Evolution of Airpower Theory* (Maxwell AFB: Air University Press, 1997), which was written by the faculty and students of the School of Advanced Airpower Studies. An earlier version of this essay had appeared as 'Giulio Douhet and Modern War', *Comparative Strategy*, Fall 1993.

1. Frank J. Cappelluti, 'The Life and Thought of Giulio Douhet', PhD Dissertation, Rutgers, 1967, 3–7, 10.
2. Giulio Douhet, *Command of the Air,* trans. Sheila Fischer (Rome: Rivista Aeronautica, 1958), from the Introduction by Gen. Celso Ranieri, ix. The Italian Air Force considers this the official translation of Douhet's major works; I have therefore used it where possible. Unfortunately, this version does not contain complete translations of 'Probable Aspects of Future War' or 'The War of 19__'. These works are contained in the Ferrari translation of 1942 cited in note 28 below.
3. Douhet, *Command of the Air*, trans. Fischer, 22.
4. Cappelluti, 'Life and Thought of Giulio Douhet', 66.
5. Ranieri, 'Introduction', x.
6. Renalto D'Orlando, trans., *The Origin of Air Warfare*, 2nd edn (Rome: Historical Office of the Italian Air Force, 1961), *passim*; D. J. Fitzsimmons, 'The Origins of Air Warfare', *Air Pictorial*, December 1972, 482–5.
7. D'Orlando, *The Origin of Air Warfare*, 214–16.
8. Douhet, 'Summing Up', trans. Fischer, 123.
9. Cappelluti, 'Life and Thought of Giulio Douhet', 69; K. Booth, 'History or Logic as Approaches to Strategy', *Royal United Services Institute (RUSI) Journal* 117 (September 1972), 35; Claudio Segrè, 'Douhet In Italy: Prophet Without Honor?' *Aerospace Historian* 26 (June 1979), 71.
10. Cappelluti, 'Life and Thought of Giulio Douhet', 70, 84.
11. Ranieri, 'Introduction', x.
12. Cappelluti, 'Life and Thought of Giulio Douhet', 90. These diaries were published in 1920 and 1922.
13. Ibid., 109.
14. Ibid., 127.
15. Ibid., 133; Thomas Mahoney, 'Doctrine of Ruthlessness', *Popular Aviation*, April 1940, 36; John Whittam, *The Politics of the Italian Army, 1861–1918* (London: Croom, Helm, 1977), 201.
16. Cappelluti, 'Life and Thought of Giulio Douhet', 129.
17. Ranieri, 'Introduction', xi; Cappelluti, 'Life and Thought of Giulio Douhet', 138. In late October 1918, a few weeks before the Armistice, the Allies did indeed form an Inter-Allied Air Force, commanded by Gen. Hugh Trenchard of the Royal Air Force; its mission was to take the war to Germany via strategic bombing of its vital centers.
18. Caproni's diary, December 1917. Translated portions of this diary plus the correspondence between Douhet and Caproni and between Caproni and Gorrell are located in the Air Force Archives at Maxwell AFB, Alabama, file 168.661. See also J. L. Atkinson, 'Italian Influence on the Origins of the American Concept of Strategic Bombardment', *The Air Power Historian* 5 (July 1957): 141–9; William G. Key, 'Some Papers of Count Caproni de Taliedo: Controversy in the Making?' *Pegasus*, January 1956 Supplement, 1–20. Both these sources argue that Caproni was the mouthpiece of Douhet.
19. Nino Salvaneschi, 'Let Us Kill the War, Let Us Aim at the Heart of the Enemy!' Milan, 1917, copy located in the Air Force Archives, file 168.661-129, 24, 47, 62.
20. For the contents of the Gorrell memo, see Maurer Maurer (ed.), *The US Air Service in World War I*, 4 vols (Washington: GPO, 1978), II: 141–51.
21. Cappelluti, 'Life and Thought of Giulio Douhet', 155–58.
22. Translations of Douhet's works have been sporadic at best. Key items that have not been translated into English include the 93-page appendix to the first edition of *Command of the Air* noted above, his war diary, 'The Army of the Air' (an

essay written in 1927), and his novels on air warfare. In addition, 'Recapitulation', which is a collection of Douhet's letters to the editor of *Rivista Aeronautica* written between 1927 and 1930 and published in the Dino Ferrari translation of 1942, includes only Douhet's responses – not the critical letters from Italian airmen, soldiers and sailors that he was responding to.

23. Douhet, 'Summing Up', trans. Fischer, 144. Douhet distinguished between air defense and protection from air attack: one cannot stop the rain, but he can carry an umbrella to avoid being soaked. Nonetheless, he believed civil defense actions such as underground shelters and evacuation plans were of little use. The people must expect to be bombed and endure its horror. From 'Danger From the Air', trans. Fischer, 198.

24. I use the term 'precept' rather than 'principle' because Douhet rejected the latter term. In his view, common sense should prevail in war. Unfortunately, when a concept was elevated to the status of a 'principle', it too often became a dogmatic assertion divorced from common sense.

25. The current US Department of Defense definition for air superiority reads: 'That degree of dominance in the airbattle of one force over another which permits the conduct of operations by the former and its related land, sea and air forces at a given time and place without prohibitive interference by the opposing force'. Air supremacy is defined as 'That degree of air superiority wherein the opposing air force is incapable of effective interference'. Douhet's concept of command of the air is closer to our notion of air supremacy.

26. Douhet, *Command of the Air*, trans. Fischer, 47–8. In a memo written in 1916, Douhet was a bit more specific, listing the following as potential targets: 'railroad junctions, arsenals, ports, warehouses, factories, industrial centers, banks, ministries, etc'. Cappelluti, 'Life and Thought of Giulio Douhet', 107.

27. Douhet, *Command of the Air*, trans. Fischer, 48.

28. Douhet, 'The War of 19__' in *Command of the Air*, trans. Dino Ferrari (New York: Coward-McCann, 1942), 367–8. This translation was reprinted by the Office of Air Force History in 1983. Although a brief introduction has been added, the pagination of the essays themselves remains the same as in the original.

29. Douhet, 'Summing Up', trans. Fischer, 171. Emphasis in the original.

30. Douhet, *Command of the Air*, trans. Fischer, 83–4.

31. There is little indication Douhet attempted to spread his ideas outside Italy. Virtually all of his works were written for Italian magazines and journals. Although he probably attempted to influence the Bolling Commission during World War I, this was so the United States could serve as a useful ally and partner.

32. Douhet's reference to the United States is significant and exemplified today by the US Army's helicopter fleet, one of the largest air forces in the world with more than 5,000 aircraft, whose sole mission is to support ground operations. Douhet would not have dreamed of diverting so many resources to such a mission.

33. During World War II some B-17s were modified to carry extra armor and machine guns. These aircraft, YB-40s, were mixed in with the bomber formations striking Germany. It was soon discovered, however, that these modified battle escorts were too heavy to keep up with the bomber stream after the bomb release point, so the experiment was discontinued. By contrast, the small size of the air-to-air missiles carried by today's F-15E – the modern equivalent of the battleplane – allow a defensive capability that does not diminish the plane's offensive punch.

34. Perhaps the most effective use of civil aviation in the Gulf War was as cargo aircraft – a use not envisioned by Douhet. The activation of the Civil Reserve Air Fleet brought over 300 commercial airliners under military control, and these aircraft moved over 400,000 personnel and 95,000 tons of cargo to the Middle East. This was 64 per cent of the passengers and 27 per cent of all cargo moved by air.

35. Douhet, 'Recapitulation', trans. Ferrari, 220.

36. Basil H. Liddell Hart, *Paris, Or the Future of War* (New York: Dutton, 1925), 39. In 1937, Air Chief Marshal Hugh Dowding, commander of RAF Fighter Command, stated that bombing attacks on London would cause such panic, defeat could occur 'in a fortnight or less'. ACM Sir Hugh Dowding, 'Employment of the Fighter Command in Home Defence', lecture to the RAF Staff College, reprinted in *Naval War College Review* 45 (Spring 1992): 36.

37. Eugene M. Emme (ed.), *The Impact of Air Power* (Princeton, NJ: Van Nostrand, 1959), 51–2. See also 'War in the Air and Disarmament', *The American Review of Reviews*, March 1925, 308–10, and H. de Watteville, 'Armies of the Air', *The Nineteenth Century and After*, October 1934, 353–68. For an overview of popular literature on this subject, see I. F. Clarke, *Voices Prophesying War, 1763–1984* (London: Oxford University Press, 1966).

38. George H. Quester, *Deterrence Before Hiroshima*, rev. edn (New Brunswick, NJ: Transaction, 1986), 98.

39. The best studies on the morale effects are The US Strategic Bombing Survey, Report no. 64b, 'The Effects of Strategic Bombing on German Morale', 1947; Fred C. Iklé, *The Social Impact of Bomb Destruction* (Norman, OK: University of Oklahoma Press, 1958); and Irving L. Janis, *Air War and Emotional Stress* (New York: McGraw-Hill, 1951).

40. 'What Lessons from Air Warfare?' *US Air Services*, Apr 1938, 7–8. This editorial argues that the civil war in Spain was simply not a condition anticipated by Douhet.

41. Douhet, *Command of the Air*, trans. Fischer, 17.

42. Barry H. Steiner, *Bernard Brodie and the Foundations of American Nuclear Strategy* (Lawrence: University Press of Kansas, 1991), 94.

43. Lt. Gen. N. N. Golovine, 'Air Strategy', *Royal Air Force Quarterly* 7 (April 1936), 169–72. Golovine was a Russian expatriate who had served in World War I. Douhet gave no estimates on the amount of incendiary bombs needed to burn a target. They had not been used extensively during the war, so there was little experience on which to base calculations. Gen. Billy Mitchell, in his 1922 manual 'Notes on the Multi-Motored Bombardment Group' (p. 81), estimated that only 30 tons of gas were required to render an area of one square mile 'uninhabitable'. That's about one-third the amount suggested by Golovine.

44. For example, one US Navy officer stated in 1923: 'There is scarcely a city in America which could not be destroyed, together with every living person therein, within, say, three days of the declaration of war'. 'Airplanes, and General Slaughter, in the Next War', *Literary Digest*, November 17, 1923, 61. Amusingly, the first page of this article has a picture of the hapless Barling Bomber with the caption: 'A few of these could wipe out a city'. Likewise, in 1920 the chief of the aircraft armament division in the US Army declared that a 100 lb bomb would destroy a small railroad station or warehouse, and a 1,000 lb bomb would completely demolish a large factory. William A. Borden, 'Air Bombing of Industrial Plants', *Army Ordnance*, November–December 1920, 122.

45. Douhet, 'Summing Up', trans. Fischer, 185.

46. Lee Kennett, *A History of Strategic Bombing* (New York: Scribner's, 1982), 55.

Kennett states Douhet's name does not appear on the lists of licensed Italian pilots through 1918. It should be noted, however, that when Douhet took command of the Aviation Battalion in 1913 he was already 43 years of age – too old to take on the arduous task of learning to fly the dangerous and flimsy aircraft of the day. Douhet did, however, work closely with Caproni in developing an aircraft stabilization device and an aerial camera, as well as designing a special bomb that was flight-tested in 1912. So although he may not have been a pilot, Douhet understood many of the technical problems of flight. Cappelluti, 'Life and Thought of Giulio Douhet', 59; Caproni diary, March 1913.

47. Giulio Douhet, 'Le Possibilite dell' aereonavigazione', *Rivista delle Comunicazioni*, August 1910, 758–71. I am indebted to Captain Marcello Ceccarelli of the Italian Navy for translating this article.

48. Besides making it clear in 'The War of 19__' that one should not be in the first wave, Douhet also tantalizes his readers by referring to 180 'explorer' aircraft in the German air force. These were high-speed pursuit planes whose mission 'had not been exactly determined'. They encounter French pursuits during the war, but play no significant role. Why were they even mentioned? From Douhet, 'The War of 19__', trans. Ferrari, 342, 383.

49. Douhet would no doubt have maintained the Germans bungled the operation by shifting to urban attacks before they had achieved command of the air – a violation of his most cardinal precept.

50. Bernard Brodie, *Strategy in the Missile Age* (Princeton, NJ: Princeton University Press, 1959), 37.

51. Cappelluti, 'Life and Thought of Giulio Douhet', 80.

52. Douhet, 'Probable Aspects of Future War', trans. Ferrari, 181.

53. Although poison gas was not used in World War II, the Italians did employ it against Ethiopian civilians in 1935. In a sense, therefore, Douhet was correct in maintaining that humanitarian impulses would have little braking effect on a country; it would seem that fear of retaliation prevented the use of gas in World War II.

54. W. Hays Parks, 'Air War and the Law of War', *The Air Force Law Review* 32 (1990), 1–226.

55. An exception to his technological myopia is Douhet's enthusiasm for submarines, which he saw as dominating surface fleets as aircraft dominate armies. Indeed, there are some similarities between aircraft and submarines – including their stealth characteristics.

56. Maj. Gen. E. B. Ashmore, *Air Defence* (London: Longman's, Green, 1929), 93–4. Ashmore was the chief of the London Air Defence Area during the war.

57. Douhet, *Command of the Air*, trans. Ferrari, 9.

58. Kenneth P. Werrell, *Archie, Flak, AAA and SAM: A Short Operational History of Ground-Based Air Defense* (Maxwell AFB: Air University Press, 1988), 1–2; Edward B. Westermann, 'Fighting for the Heavens from the Ground: German Ground-Based Air Defenses in the Great War, 1914–1918', *Journal of Military History* 65 (April 2001), 667. Golovine states the improvements in antiaircraft defenses in World War I were even more dramatic: in 1916 it took 11,000 shells to bring down a plane; in late 1918 it required only 1,500. Golovine, 'Air Strategy', 170.

59. Bernard Brodie, 'The Heritage of Douhet', *Air University Quarterly Review* 6 (Summer 1963), 122.

60. Douhet, 'Summing Up', trans. Fischer, 132.

61. This is the thesis of Brodie, Cappelluti, Louis A. Sigaud, *Air Power and Unification: Douhet's Principles of Warfare and Their Application to the United*

States (Harrisburg, PA: Military Service Publications, 1949); Lt. Col. Joseph L. Dickman, 'Douhet and the Future', *Air University Quarterly Review* 2 (Summer 1948), 3–15, and Cy Caldwell, 'The Return of General Douhet', *Aero Digest*, July 1949: 36–7, 90–2.

62. Cappelluti, 'Life and Thought of Giulio Douhet', 18–22.
63. Douhet, 'Summing Up', trans. Fischer, 187.
64. Anon. [Brig. Gen. Tulasne], 'The Air Doctrine of General Douhet', *Royal Air Force Quarterly*, 4 (April 1933), 164–7.
65. Robin Higham, *The Military Intellectuals in Britain, 1918–1939* (New Brunswick, NJ: Rutgers University Press, 1966), 257–9. On the other hand, one historian has seen strong similarities between Douhet and the early writings of J. F. C. Fuller; he therefore speculates Douhet may have had a significant, though indirect, influence on the RAF. Brereton Greenhous, 'A Speculation on Giulio Douhet and the English Connection', in *La Figura E L'Opera Di Giulio Douhet* (Italy: Società di Storia Patria, 1988), 41–51.
66. Watteville, 'Armies of the Air', 360–3.
67. Horst Boog, 'Douhet and German Politics: Air Doctrine and Air Operations, 1933–1945', in *La Figura E L'Opera Di Giulio Douhet* (Italy: Società di Storia Patria, 1988), 81-107.
68. Raymond R. Flugel, 'United States Air Power Doctrine: A Study of the Influence of William Mitchell and Giulio Douhet at the Air Corps Tactical School, 1921–1935', PhD Dissertation, Oklahoma, 1966. Flugel compared the text of *Command of the Air* with some of Mitchell's writings and with those in the Tactical School texts. The words and phrases used are quite similar. However, Flugel erred mightily: instead of using the recently discovered 1923 translation, which presumably Mitchell would have used, he employed the Ferrari translation of 1942. Because the two versions have significant differences, Flugel's charges of plagiarism remain unproven.
69. This was the translation done by Dorothy Benedict with the assistance of Captain George Kenney. It is based on the French translation in *Les Ailes* of 1933, and can be found in the US Air Force Archives, file 168.6005-18. For other writings about Douhet at the time see: Col. Charles DeF Chandler, 'Air Warfare Doctrine of General Douhet', *US Air Services*, May 1933, 10–13; 'Air Warfare Trends', US Air Services, August 1933, 8–9; L. E. O. Charlton, *War From the Air: Past, Present, Future* (London: Thomas Nelson, 1935); and 'Air Warfare', *Royal Air Force Quarterly* 7 (April 1936), 152–68.

2

Trenchard and 'Morale Bombing': The Evolution of Royal Air Force Doctrine before World War II

In continuing my investigation into the roots of air-power theory during its golden age before World War II, my research inevitably turned me toward Hugh Trenchard. He was known as 'Boom' by contemporaries not only because of his explosive voice, but also because of his willingness to act quickly and forcefully. He has long been termed The Father of the Royal Air Force (RAF) and for good reason. It is unlikely the RAF would have survived as a separate service had Trenchard not been its chief in the decade from 1919 to 1929.

Despite his strong leadership, which was unquestioned within the RAF, Trenchard wrote and spoke very little regarding his thoughts on the proper employment of air power. Yet, it was widely assumed that because he spoke of air power as a psychological weapon that could break the will of the civilian populace, Trenchard was thereby advocating the deliberate bombing of that populace. This was not the case, nor was it true within his service as a whole. Unfortunately, the confusion arising from the connection of Trenchard to morale bombing and thus to the urban area bombing of World War II has remained for decades.

Like their counterparts in the United States, British air leaders believed in the efficacy of strategic air power almost from the inception of the airplane. Perhaps this was because both countries traditionally were sea powers. Naval war is in many respects economic war; although battles occur, the primary objective is generally to apply pressure on a country's commerce and economy, thus causing such hardship that a country elects to make a change in policy. To an extent, air power flows from the same basic premise. Early airmen argued, however, that the new medium could apply such pressure more comprehensively and quickly. This offered important possibilities, because the catastrophic experience of the Great War suggested that traditional methods of warfare no longer served a useful purpose. If war was to be at all viable it had to be fought in a more rational fashion and not require the destruction of an entire generation. British airmen returned to the basics.

The object of war was to force an enemy to bend to your will, and this was accomplished by breaking either his will or his capability to fight. Armies generally concentrated on the latter by seeking battle. Hugh Trenchard, the commander of the RAF from 1919 to 1929, came to focus instead on the 'will' part of that postulate. Trenchard's ideas were to shape RAF thinking throughout the interwar period, and his influence on the RAF cannot be overestimated. The near-genius he brought to the task, despite his notoriously poor communicative skills, was crucial. Trenchard believed that the airplane, employed in mass, was an inherently strategic weapon that was unmatched in its ability to shatter the will of an enemy. Yet the British tradition of economic warfare could not be erased. The combination of these two distinct premises resulted in a unique blend, an air-power theory that advocated attacks on enemy industry designed to break the morale of the factory workers and, by extension, the population as a whole. Trenchard's instinctive beliefs on this subject found form in the official doctrine manuals of the RAF. It was, in turn, taught and institutionalized at the RAF Staff College where most of those who would lead their service in World War II were educated. This doctrine centered on the presumed ability of strategic bombing to destroy the morale of an enemy nation. Unfortunately, the meaning of the term 'morale bombing' was never completely clear, even to airmen, and this has caused enormous confusion ever since.

There is a tendency to read the history of RAF Bomber Command in World War II backwards from the fire bombing of Dresden in 1945 to the ideas of Hugh Trenchard in 1919. Because Air Chief Marshal Arthur Harris, the Air Officer Commanding-in-Chief of Bomber Command, carried out a ruthless and single-minded strategy of urban area bombing, and because he was a protégé of Trenchard, many historians have seen a direct linkage between Trenchard and Harris's conduct during the war.[1] This connection seems plausible because the common term tying them together was 'morale bombing'. In reality, the similarity is apparent rather than real. The two men meant quite different things. My purpose in this chapter is to trace the evolution of strategic doctrine in the RAF between the wars, paying special attention to the concept of morale bombing, how it originated with Trenchard in World War I, and how it evolved over the next two decades. First, however, it is necessary to clarify some other terms.

Although the terms doctrine, strategy and policy are sometimes used interchangeably, they actually have different meanings. Doctrine, in essence, is a set of fundamental beliefs regarding the best way to fight wars and conduct campaigns. Doctrine is based on both theory and practice, and it tends to be relatively unconstrained by factors such as politics or economics that are crucial in war but which are not generally determined by military leaders. Ideally, practice should play the most important role in the formulation of doctrine. The histories of previous wars and campaigns serve as the empirical database upon which doctrinal theories are founded. In the interwar period, however, those charged with formulating air doctrine were operating in an evidential vacuum. The experiences of air power were limited and the lessons obscure. Indeed, air power was not the decisive factor in the Great War, so air theorists who saw their weapon as revolutionary deliberately discounted the experiences of the war: it taught the wrong lessons. As the American Billy Mitchell put it: 'In the development of air power, one has to look ahead and not backward and figure out what is going to happen, not too much what has happened'.[2]

The RAF had more experience with air power in war than most countries, not only in World War I but also in operations between the wars. However, the lessons of the war tended to emphasize the importance of tactical air operations – reconnaissance, artillery spotting, ground support and air cover over the battlefield – and these were not things an independent air force wanted to stress. If the purpose of the air arm was to support ground operations, then why was it a separate service? Although the imperial air control duties of the RAF in the decades between the wars were useful and important, they did not necessarily translate into the sizable budget, force structure or importance that would make the RAF the equal of the other services.

As a consequence of this studied disregard for the main pillar of doctrinal formulation – actual experience – air thinkers were forced to rely on the other key input, theory. Air doctrine therefore became increasingly theoretical during the 1920s and 1930s, speculating on the effect of future technologies, employed by future aircrews, trained with future equipment, who would drop various types of future bombs on people and structures. It was *assumed* this bombing would provide definable results – although at the time these were speculative and untested. In truth, these exercises in logic were articulate, cogent and seemingly rationale – but at base they were still theoretical.

Strategy is the use, in peace or in war, of a variety of military, political, economic, cultural or psychological levers in order to attain national objectives. It tends, hopefully, to be realistic rather than theoretical, and is devised only after a careful calculus of strengths and weaknesses and the objectives sought. In that sense, it should not be idealistic; it should not seek a goal that the country is too poor or too militarily weak (either physically or psychologically) to achieve. A country's political leaders determine goals and devise a national strategy to achieve them. Military leaders, in turn, use that guidance to devise a military strategy focused on achieving military objectives that will lead to the accomplishment of the national objectives. Often, political reality will modify doctrine and produce a strategy that a military force is less than fully prepared to carry out.

Policy is somewhat different in that it entails a measure of detail and bureaucracy that induces limitations or modifications based on existing laws, regulations, or other economic, political or cultural factors. Even more so than in strategy, policy considerations put limits on the more 'pure' form of war espoused by doctrine. It is the nature of bureaucracies that policies sometimes work at cross purposes to strategy or doctrine.[3]

To illustrate: RAF *doctrine* formulated between the wars emphasized, as we shall see, daylight precision bombing of strategic industrial targets which would undermine the will of an enemy populace to carry on the war. When World War II broke out, however, British leaders knew the RAF was too weak to carry out such a doctrine; therefore, the *strategy* devised was to use the RAF in a defensive mode in France to complement the British Army, and Bomber Command was relegated largely to psychological operations – leaflet dropping – against Germany proper. At the same time, it was a *policy* of the government in 1940 to continue manufacturing the Fairey Battle, even though the light bomber was obsolete and manifestly unsuitable for carrying out either the approved doctrine or strategy. Instead, a policy decision was made that to ensure the viability of Fairey as an aircraft manufacturer, to keep the skilled workforce employed and practiced, and to have new aircraft – any aircraft – rolling off an assembly line for national morale purposes, policy would temporarily outweigh the dictates of strategy and doctrine. Battles were produced well into 1940, by which time they were barely suitable even as training aircraft.[4]

Air strategy and policy between the wars and during World War II, as determined by the British government, have been adequately examined. Works by Montgomery Hyde, Malcolm Smith, Barry Powers and Neville Jones have covered these subjects intelligently and rigorously.[5] However, the doctrine devised and evolved by the RAF between the world wars is a surprisingly overlooked subject. It is necessary to examine the operational concepts and doctrine that were so hesitatingly and painstakingly being formulated by the aviators and leaders – the practitioners – of the RAF.

Britain, like all belligerents, entered World War I with a small number of rudimentary aircraft and with little or no doctrine on how to employ them effectively. Over the course of the next few years, the RAF, which became a separate service in 1918, grew to be one of the largest and most effective air arms in the world. Although playing a peripheral role throughout the conflict, air power's potential captivated the imagination of the public, politicians and military thinkers. This fascination for air power was especially apparent regarding a single aspect of its many roles and purposes, that of strategic bombing. The actual experiences of the bomber forces, scanty though they were, were to be a source of debate for the next two decades.

The first strategic air campaign in history was waged by Germany. Beginning in early 1915 rigid airships, Zeppelins, began making the long night-time journey from their sheds on the North Sea to drop bombs on military and industrial targets in Britain. At first, these attacks were conducted with impunity, but fighter planes, artillery and searchlights were soon cobbled together into a makeshift air defense system. This defense was reasonably effective: the last great Zeppelin attack of the war was 19 October 1917, when five out of eleven airships went down. The Germans thereafter concentrated on large, multi-engine aircraft, Gothas and later Giants, which were faster and more maneuverable than the airships and thus were considerably more difficult to intercept and shoot down.

The fear bordering on panic these bombing strikes caused among the

British population and its government – for the next two decades – is difficult to exaggerate. Because Britain had remained sheltered behind its moat for centuries, this fear was worse than it would have been for a country that had no such tradition of invulnerability. The psychological effect of losing this shield was enormous. As a consequence, the government appointed a well-known general, the South African Jan Smuts, to study the problem. He was assisted in this task by the commanding general of the Royal Flying Corps (RFC), Lt. Gen. David Henderson. Smuts turned in two reports, the first being a fairly straightforward plan for a well-organized and capable defensive network centered on London. The other effort was more theoretical. In it, Smuts called for a separate air force that combined the units of the fleet (the Royal Naval Air Service) and the army (the Royal Flying Corps) into a single command. In words cited by airmen ever since, Smuts then went on to prophesy: 'the day may not be far off when aerial operations with their devastation of enemy lands and destruction of industrial and populous centers on a vast scale may become the principal operations of war, to which the older forms of military and naval operations may become secondary and subordinate'.[6]

Although there had been talk since the beginning of the war of combining the army and navy air arms into a single unit in the interests of efficiency and standardization, it was the catalyst of the German air attacks and the resultant recommendations of the Smuts report that were the deciding factors. The RAF was established on 1 April 1918, and its mission was to prevent further German air incursions and to strike Germany in retaliation. The new position of Air Minister was given to Lord Rothermere, and Henderson was appointed his deputy. The position of Chief of the Air Staff (CAS) was extended to Maj. Gen. Hugh Trenchard, who had been Henderson's subordinate as commanding general of the RFC units in France. The new arrangement proved unsatisfactory. Lord Rothermere by all accounts was a difficult and erratic personality who understood little about air power. Neither Henderson nor Trenchard could work with him effectively – though it should be noted no one ever accused Trenchard of being easy to get along with. As a result of immediate and acrid strife, all three men resigned within a fortnight in April 1918. Rothermere and Henderson then disappeared from the military aviation scene. The new Air Minister was Sir William Weir, and the new CAS was Maj. Gen. Frederick Sykes. After a somewhat unseemly display of petulance Trenchard was returned to France in May, only this time as commander of the newly created Independent Force, the formation of which was pushed by Sykes.[7] It contained a contingent of bomber squadrons, pulled from other units in France, whose purpose was to carry the war to Germany. In one sense this was a demotion for Trenchard – he now commanded barely 10 per cent of the British air units in France – but in another sense it was significant because it forced him to concentrate on the mission of strategic bombing. This concentration was to have long-term consequences.

Early in the war, Trenchard's thoughts on air power had begun to coalesce into the form they would take so forcefully in the interwar years. In a memo of September 1916, he wrote that the aeroplane was an inherently offensive weapon:

> Owing to the unlimited space in the air, the difficulty one machine has in seeing another, the accidents of wind and cloud, it is impossible for aeroplanes, however skilful and vigilant their pilots, however powerful their engines, however mobile their machines, and however numerous their formations, to prevent hostile aircraft from crossing the line if they have the initiative and determination to do so.[8]

This concept would be a recurring theme among air theorists up to the present, but Trenchard's emphasis contained a single-mindedness that bordered on stubbornness. Because the aeroplane was an offensive weapon it had to be 'guided by a policy of relentless and incessant offensiveness': the deeper British planes flew into German territory the better, almost without regard for the losses incurred or physical damage caused. He believed that the *act* of the offensive was essential because it granted the attackers a 'moral superiority'. This attitude – the aerial equivalent of the French Plan XVII – helps explain not only why Field Marshal Douglas Haig thought so highly of Trenchard, but why he acquired a reputation among some as a stubborn and uncaring commander who squandered the lives of his men in a vicious battle of attrition every bit as deadly as that on the surface.[9]

The question of precisely how aircraft should be used offensively behind German lines was crucial. Trenchard argued that because he lacked sufficient pursuit aircraft to perform escort duty, it was necessary to attack enemy airfields to keep the Germans out of the sky and thus ensure air superiority for the Allies – a prerequisite for the successful conduct of military operations.[10] Beyond that, he insisted that air operations be conducted in conjunction with the ground effort. The situation for the British Army throughout the war was precarious, and Trenchard realized it was the mission of the air arm to protect the fragile forces of Haig. Consequently, he envisioned an air campaign focusing on what today we would term 'interdiction' targets: railroad marshaling yards, bridges, supply depots and road networks that were primarily involved in providing men and material to the front. As he phrased it:

> I desire to emphasize that operations conducted by bombing squadrons cannot be isolated from other work in the air, and are inseparable from the operations of the Army as a whole . . . If an offensive is being undertaken on the ground, the work of bombing machines should be timed and co-ordinated so as to produce the maximum effect on the enemy'.[11]

In addition, Trenchard foresaw possibilities for strategic bombing of overarching value and singled out several industries as particularly important: iron and coal mines, steel mills, chemical and explosives factories, armament industries, aero-engine manufacturers, submarine and shipbuilding works, gun foundries and engine repair shops. Significantly, one reason for selecting many of these targets was their large size and easy identification; blast furnaces, for example, had 100-foot towers and their fiery ovens could be seen for many miles at night.[12] The problems of navigation and target identification hinted at here were to continue for the next several decades.

In his official report after the war, Trenchard reiterated his previous stance that the aerial needs of the British Army in France had had first priority, but after this was assured, the bombing of Germany became 'a necessity'. Its objective was to achieve 'the breakdown of the German army in Germany, its government, and the crippling of its sources of supply'. Recognizing that he had insufficient forces to collapse German industry, he nonetheless attempted to hit as many different factories as possible, as often as possible, so that no one felt secure anywhere within range of his bombers. The object of bombing factories was to adversely affect the morale of the people. Using a subjective and unprovable statistic, which earned him much (largely deserved) ridicule, Trenchard stated that the psychological effects of bombing outweighed the material at a ratio of twenty to one.[13] Every mission conducted by the Independent Force during the war was flown against military targets.[14] Thus, it is important to understand that Trenchard was not advocating the bombing of German population centers with the intention of causing a popular revolt (the concept put forward by his contemporary in Italy, Giulio Douhet). Rather, Trenchard was implying that the act of bombardment in general, and the destruction of selected German factories in particular, would have a devastating effect on the morale of the workers and, by extension, the German people as a whole. During his months back in Britain he had seen such effects as a result of German air attacks and was greatly influenced by them. This concept would be more clearly articulated in the years ahead.

Some would later argue that Trenchard's enthusiasm for strategic bombing developed only after the war, and that he had been opposed not only to strategic bombing but also to a separate Royal Air Force, and the Independent Force that it spawned, while the war was in progress. This is inaccurate. In October 1917, Trenchard proposed the combination of the RNAS and the RFC into a single service under an Air Secretary and an Air Chief of Staff. The following month he stated that 'long distance bombing...ought to be vigorously developed as part and parcel of the Royal Flying Corps'. This call for a strategic air offensive was repeated by Trenchard in a memo of June 1918.[15] Trenchard was aware, however, of the difficulties experienced by the British aircraft manufacturers. Airplane losses in France were so high, production could not keep pace. He did not wish to short the combat units of machines in order to establish the new strategic air force. Frederick Sykes argued a 'margin' of excess aircraft was being produced that would allow the formation of the Independent Force without hurting the combat situation on the Western Front. Trenchard disagreed that such a margin existed. Therefore, Trenchard's reluctance to assume command of the Independent Force can be better understood if one recalls his devotion to Haig and the British Army. In 1918, the ground forces were paramount, and Trenchard neither advocated nor approved of air operations independent of the ground situation, a strategy advocated by Sykes. In addition, as Trenchard himself later maintained, his bombers had not the range nor the mass to carry out effective strategic strikes (barely one-third of bombing missions struck targets in Germany). As a consequence, he objected to the division of limited air resources, some for army operations, some for fleet defense and still others for long-range bombing: 'I believe the air is one'.[16] He saw air power on an evolutionary path and it was unwise to move too far too quickly. Trenchard was not unusual in this regard. In the USA, Billy Mitchell, Ben Foulois and Hap Arnold all made similar intellectual journeys from skepticism to advocacy. The fact that Trenchard refused to accept the exaggerated claims of men like Sykes and Smuts was more a sign of measured maturity than of fickleness.

It seems to be a trait of democracies that after a victorious war their military forces do not simply demobilize, they disintegrate. This was the case in postwar Britain. For the RAF it meant, by March 1919, a drop from a force of some 22,000 aircraft and over 240,000 personnel to only 28 understrength squadrons (about 200 planes) manned by fewer than 30,000 people. The plight of the RAF seemed especially wobbly when Prime Minister David Lloyd George decided early in 1919 to combine the ministries of War and Air into a single unit. Fortunately for the RAF, the man chosen to head this combined ministry – and presumably oversee the demise of the infant RAF – was Winston Churchill. Although a former army officer who had headed the Admiralty during the first year of the war, Churchill possessed an unusually flexible mind and was therefore open on the question of air power. He did not, however, get on well with Frederick Sykes. The latter exacerbated matters by submitting a plan shortly after the Armistice that called for an enormous air force, fully 154 squadrons, exclusive of training units, deployed throughout the empire. In a war-weary Britain strapped for funds, such a proposal was fanciful at best and irresponsible at worst.[17] Sykes was therefore nudged into retirement and Trenchard – who had served with Churchill in India many years before – was brought back as CAS. More than any other single factor, this decision saved the RAF as a separate service. Trenchard well understood the political and economic imperatives of a peacetime budget, and his proposal for an RAF of 24½ squadrons, though pitifully small, was more in keeping with the temper of the times.[18] Trenchard has had many detractors, but few would deny his ability as a bureaucratic in-fighter. Given the weakness and unsettled nature of the RAF, his relatively junior rank, his lack of a strong faction in Parliament, the press or the public, and his poor writing and speaking skills, his ability to get his way with the government and the other services was remarkable.

When funds are slashed there is a tendency for interservice rivalries to

flare as the military arms begin to scramble for their share of a severely
shrinking budget. Postwar Britain exemplified this tendency. In a sense, the
RAF's independent status was partly a millstone around its neck. In the
interwar period it found itself constantly on the defensive against the other
services and the Treasury who saw it as a frail and youthful little brother
easily bullied.[19] It is difficult to determine who threw the first punch, but
relations between Trenchard and his service counterparts, Field Marshal
Henry Wilson and Admiral David Beatty, were stormy bordering on rude.
These two men made no secret of their desire to disband the RAF and
restore its airplanes (few though they now were) back to the army and fleet
from whence they came. For his part, Trenchard fought back by noting the
high cost in sterling and lives of traditional war-making, costs dramatically
reduced through air power. For example, one Air Ministry pamphlet
suggested there were 'certain responsibilities at present assigned to the Navy
and Army which the Air Force is *already* technically capable of undertaking,
and for which it may be found economical in the near future to substitute to
a greater or lesser extent air units for military or naval units'.[20] When the
army and navy continued to push to disband the RAF in the interests of
economy, the CAS responded in a wonderfully Trenchardesque style:

> The Field Marshal wishes to lay axe to the roots, as by doing so he
> thinks he may the easier obtain the fruit. What is wanted in order that
> the maximum amount of fruit may be got for our money is severe
> pruning of the overhead fruitless branches of some of the neighboring
> trees which are at present crowding out the younger and more
> productive growth and thereby preventing its vigorous expansion to full
> maturity.[21]

Given the increasingly heated verbal and bureaucratic sparring, it is
surprising that Trenchard was able to win a major concession from Beatty
and Wilson in 1921. Catching them off guard and appealing to their sense of
fair play, Trenchard convinced them to cease attacking his service for one
year while he attempted to organize his fledgling command and make their
struggle a more equal one.[22] It was a decision the two men later regretted,
because Trenchard used that time to solidify his power, establish the RAF
on a strong organizational and administrative footing, and devise a use for
the air weapon that would ensure its survival as a separate service – air
control of colonial territories.

Administering the world's largest empire was an expensive and labor-
intensive enterprise. Each colony required a garrison of sufficient size to
maintain peace and order. In the aftermath of the war such an expense
caused consternation in the British government. Trenchard therefore
suggested to Churchill that the RAF be given the opportunity to subdue a
festering uprising in Somaliland. Churchill agreed. The results were
dramatic: the RAF chased the rebel ringleader, 'the mad mullah', out of the
area, and Somaliland was pacified at a cost of only £77,000, rather than the

£6 million it would have cost for the two army divisions originally planned. As a consequence, the demand for air control grew, and over the next decade the RAF deployed – with varying degrees of success – to Iraq, Afghanistan, India, Aden, Transjordan, Palestine, Egypt and the Sudan.[23] The strategy employed in these campaigns was to patrol the disputed areas, fly political representatives around to the various tribes to discuss problems and devise solutions, issue ultimatums to recalcitrants if persuasion failed and, as a last resort, bomb selected rebel targets to compel compliance. On the one hand, they encouraged among airmen the development of initiative and a theater-wide perspective, but it may also have given an erroneous impression regarding the psychological effectiveness of bombing. To be sure, these air operations were neither grand nor glorious, but they kept the RAF alive while it sought a more suitable foe.

This foe seemed to present itself in late 1921, when continual arguments between Britain and France over occupation policy, trade and colonial issues bubbled to the surface. For centuries these two countries had been bitter rivals, and more recent cooperation had not yet hardened into goodwill and a meeting of minds. Displeasure with France turned to concern when an intelligence report reached the government that showed a great and growing superiority in French air strength. France was reported to have an air force of 123 squadrons comprising 1,090 aircraft, and there were plans afoot to expand to 220 squadrons of over 2,000 aircraft – nearly ten times the size of the RAF. To make matters worse, 20 of the RAF's 28 squadrons were stationed overseas; a mere two fighter squadrons were charged with the air defense of the Isles.[24] Studies done by the RAF speculated that if half the projected French air force was to strike London it could deliver 100 tons of bombs in the first 24 hours, 75 tons in the second 24 hours and 50 tons each day thereafter. Using the experience of the German air attacks during the Great War as a guide, Britain could expect to suffer an average of 50 casualties for each ton of bombs dropped. This meant that French air strikes would cause over 20,000 casualties in the first week of war. In a maximum effort, those figures would double.[25]

Although British leaders did not believe war with France would occur, they were concerned the capability of their own air force had fallen so far so quickly. In addition, they realized such military weakness could have other negative effects. During the Ruhr crisis of 1922, Harold Balfour stated: 'Mere fear of war in quite conceivable circumstances greatly weakens British diplomacy and may put temptation in the way of French statesmen that they would find it hard to resist'.[26] Trenchard encouraged such thinking, but as one historian put it: 'Trenchard exploited the government's fears but he did not create them'.[27] As a consequence, Parliament moved to greatly expand the RAF by adding 52 more squadrons by 1928, which were specifically designated for the air defense of Great Britain. Fiscal realities would prevent this force actually being built, but its prospect caused the RAF to begin seriously thinking about how best to employ such a sizable air force.

Trenchard's views on the importance of strategic air power had solidified

since the war. This was due to several factors: there was no longer a British
army in Flanders dependent on air power for its survival, aircraft capabilities
had increased, and if a goal of the RAF was to remain a separate service, then
clearly a separate mission was necessary. The possibility of a Continental
menace helped to crystallize Trenchard's thoughts on that mission. Financial
considerations were critical: the war's cost had been enormous and Britain
could not afford a large defense establishment. Trenchard had to prioritize,
building an air force that would suit national security within fiscal
constraints. A force structure that emphasized offensive air power – bombers
– optimized these factors.

The three main beliefs that Trenchard carried with him from the war were
that air superiority was an essential prerequisite to military success; air power
was an inherently offensive weapon; and that although air power's material
effects were great, its psychological effects were far greater. In a speech on
13 April 1923 he fleshed out these ideas:

> in the next great war with a European nation the forces engaged must
> first fight for aerial superiority and when that has been gained they will
> use their power to destroy the morale of the Nation and vitally damage
> the organized armaments for supplies for the Armies and Navies.

He then expanded on the importance of the morale factor: war was a contest
between the 'moral tenacity' of two countries, and 'if we could bomb the
enemy more intensely and more continually than he could bomb us the result
might be an early offer of peace'. Significantly, Trenchard did not claim an
air campaign would by itself bring victory in war against a major European
foe; rather, it would create the conditions necessary 'in which our Army can
advance and occupy his territory'.[28]

Regarding the belief that air power was intrinsically offensive, the CAS
used the example of a football match: you may not lose if you spend all your
efforts defending your own goal, but you will certainly not win. In airwar
the offense not the defense was the stronger form of war. He conceded,
however, that some form of defense (interceptors and antiaircraft guns) could
be useful 'for the morale of our own people'. In a typical bit of British sang-
froid, Trenchard commented: 'Nothing is more annoying than to be attacked
by a weapon which you have no means of hitting back at'.[29] In practical
terms, this meant as many bombers as possible and as few fighters as
necessary. The ratio arrived at was two-to-one. Thus, of the 52 squadrons
designated for 'home defense' by Parliament, fully 35 were to be
bombardment.[30] Of interest, this force ratio seemingly caused little debate at
the time or, indeed, throughout most of the interwar period. Unlike in the
US Air Corps where fighter advocates like Claire Chennault argued
vociferously for a reduced emphasis on the bomber, no such open debate
occurred in the RAF. It was not until the late 1930s and the ascendance of
Hugh Dowding at Fighter Command that Trenchard's fundamental
principles regarding force structure were seriously questioned.

The real key to the concept of strategic air power espoused by Trenchard was the selection of targets. Since the war, he had changed his views on the desirability of attacking enemy airfields in an effort to gain air superiority. Although 40 per cent of the IAF strikes had been against airfields, these attacks had had slight effect. As a result, he now envisioned a great air battle taking place between opposing air forces. When one side gained the upper hand they would then concentrate on paralyzing the enemy nation and breaking its morale. How precisely did he expect the morale of an enemy to break? Like most airmen he was frustratingly vague on this issue. Air power was simply too new, and the possibilities it offered to wage war in a fashion previously impossible were sensed rather than understood. At its worst, such vagueness took the form of an address by Trenchard in October 1928: 'The objectives to be attacked will be centres which are essential for the continuance of the enemy's resistance. They will vary frequently and the air forces will be directed against the one which at the moment is the best for air attack'.[31] In another instance, he maintained that air attack would 'induce the enemy Government, by pressure from the population, to sue for peace, in exactly the same way as starvation by blockading the country would enforce the Government to sue for peace'.[32] When pushed for specificity, Trenchard would refer to 'centres of communication' such as major roads, rail lines and telephone exchanges, as well as munitions factories.[33]

Trenchard was usually inadequate at expressing his strongly held beliefs in an articulate and cogent form. He therefore left it to his staff officers, his 'English merchants', to translate his rumblings into prose. Nonetheless, his subordinates generally understood him and even developed an affection for the old man. The legendary T. E. Lawrence, who sought anonymity and privacy after the Great War, joined the RAF as an 'aircraftman' using the name of Shaw. During his time as a ranker Lawrence kept a diary that was published after his death. In *The Mint* he describes the near reverence with which Trenchard was held in the barracks:

> The word Trenchard spells out confidence in the RAF...We think of him as immense, not by what he says, for he is as near as can be inarticulate: – his words barely enough to make men think they divine his drift: – and not by what he writes, for he makes the least use of what must be the world's worst handwriting: – but just by what he is. He knows; and by virtue of this pole-star of knowledge he steers through all the ingenuity and cleverness and hesitations of the little men who help or hinder him.[34]

Lawrence was certainly not alone in his affection for the Air Marshal. In addition to his staff, Trenchard relied on two other avenues to formalize and institutionalize his beliefs on air power: RAF doctrine manuals and the Royal Air Force Staff College.[35]

In July 1922, the RAF published its first doctrine manual, CD 22, titled simply 'Operations'. To a great extent CD 22, which was issued to all RAF officers in the rank of flight lieutenant and above, echoed the ideas Trenchard had expounded since 1917. It noted that air forces must cooperate with surface forces because often the objective of a campaign was 'the destruction of the enemy's main forces'. It also stressed the importance of morale in war and that victory occurred when so much pressure was imposed on the people they would 'force their government to sue for peace'. Regarding the importance of air superiority, it argued that other targets were subsidiary and should not be attempted 'until a serious reverse' had been inflicted on the enemy air force.[36]

The issue of which targets would most effectively achieve the anticipated effects on morale was, as usual, unstated, although the manual did refer to naval bases, munitions factories and railway junctions.[37] The manual did, however, point out that bombing attacks were to be carried out in accordance with international law. Attacking 'legitimate objectives' in populated areas was permissible, although 'all reasonable precautions' must be taken to spare hospitals and other privileged buildings.[38] This was an interesting paragraph regarding an issue that was to be the subject of much contention in the years ahead. Perhaps not surprisingly, although air policing was a major RAF mission between the wars, it was not something the service wanted to hang its doctrinal hat on – it garnered no glory and generated little force structure. CD 22 contained a chapter titled 'Aircraft in Warfare Against an Uncivilized Enemy', but clearly such operations were considered of far less importance than conventional air warfare. The long-term effects of such air control operations on RAF thinking were mixed.[39]

'Operations' remained official doctrine until July 1928 when it was superseded by AP 1300, 'Royal Air Force War Manual'. This was a more sophisticated effort than its predecessor, discussing air power in a broader sense while at the same time reducing administrative and organizational material. Many of the arguments were the same: war was largely a psychological effort; air power was an inherently offensive weapon; air power would serve as part of a joint force in which all the services would work together to attain the government's objectives; at times, the most effective use of air power was to defeat the enemy's army; and air superiority was crucial to military success. The first major change concerned the sequence of the air superiority battle. Instead of resisting all distractions until the enemy air force was defeated decisively, AP 1300 regarded the strategic bombing campaign as primary, with the air superiority battle as the diversion.[40] This reversal from previous doctrine no doubt reflected a desire to avoid the counterforce battle. The Great War had degenerated into a bloody slugfest between opposing forces; air power was supposed to eliminate not perpetuate that intermediate step to victory.

The most important aspect of AP 1300 was the extent to which it discussed the rationale behind strategic bombing and the selection of targets. The choice of bombing objectives was dependent on five factors: the nature of the war and the enemy; the general war plan of the government; diplomatic considerations; the range of the bombers; and the strength of the enemy air defenses. As a general rule, the manual opined that 'objectives should be selected the bombardment of which will have the greatest effect in weakening the enemy resistance and his power to continue war'.[41] In some cases this meant it would be wiser to attack the 'vital centres' of an enemy country rather than assist armies and navies directly. The vital areas suggested were organized systems of production, supply, communications and transportation:

> If these are exposed to air attack, the continual interruption, delay and organization of the activities of these vital centres by sustained air bombardment will usually be the most effective contribution which can be made by air power towards breaking down the enemy's resistance'.[42]

Of interest, the manual also noted the in-depth understanding that was required of an enemy country. Although not using the term 'economic intelligence', that is precisely what was meant. Such intelligence, hitherto unnecessary in warfare, was now becoming essential.

It is important to note that AP 1300 never referred to the bombing of population centers. All targets suggested throughout the manual were clearly of a military nature. Yet, AP 1300 repeated the now decade-old adage that victory in war was a result of the collapse of civilian morale. How could the will of the people be broken without bombing the people? The formulation supplied by the Air Staff writers was to assert that the bombing of industrial centers would destroy the factories that employed the workers. The loss of work would have a shattering effect on the workforce – presumably due to the loss of a salary and the dislocation involved – that would have a cascading effect throughout society.[43] This was interesting though questionable logic, but it is clear that AP 1300 was advocating a strategy fundamentally different from that proposed by those like Giulio Douhet who advocated targeting the population directly. Although both formulations sought a collapse of morale that would lead to a change in government policy, the method of achieving that collapse was subtly though clearly different.

Unquestionably, the RAF was sensitive on the issue of targeting morale. The nuances in bombing theory noted above were not understood by those outside the service, and the RAF was frequently in the position of having to defend itself against charges of making war on women and children. The air control operations in the Middle East were especially misconstrued as bloody and remorseless attacks against defenseless natives. As a result, the RAF produced studies showing that far fewer people died, on both sides, in air operations than in traditional pacification efforts carried out by ground troops. Looking at colonial campaigns between 1897 and 1923, it was estimated that over 5,000 British soldiers lost their lives at a cost of nearly 1,800 tribesmen. Since the arrival of the RAF, however, friendly casualties numbered a mere dozen men, while native losses were between 30 and 40 killed. Moreover, one report quoted from the 1920 Army directive to its troops in Mesopotamia to illustrate the point:

Villages will be razed to the ground and all woodwork removed. Pressure will be brought on the inhabitants by cutting off water power and by destroying water lifts; efforts to carry out cultivation will be interfered with, and the systematic collection of supplies of all kinds beyond our actual requirements will be carried out, the area being cleared of the necessities of life.[44]

The RAF argued that the traditional method of subduing rebellious villages was to shell them with artillery – a highly indiscriminate use of force. In his memoirs, Air Marshal John Slessor recalled that on one occasion his army counterpart in Waziristan suggested an air strike against a native village. Slessor demurred, stating that such strikes were against government policy. The soldier replied: 'Oh come on, that will be all right, we'll say we shelled it!'[45] A discussion between the Chief of the General Staff of the Indian Army, General Sir Claud Graham, and the air officer commanding in India, Air Marshal John Salmond, over military policy in Afghanistan is also illustrative. Salmond pointed out that the government's policy was to avoid aerial bombing of Kabul and native villages, but Graham argued that Afghanistan 'was not a signatory to the Hague or Geneva Conventions, the Afghans mutilated and ill-treated wounded opponents, they were not a civilised nation and he assumed, therefore, that there were no reservations'. The general concluded, 'Personally, if I were doing the bombing I should not care what the restrictions were . . . In the past they had not used the Air Force ruthlessly enough'.[46] This was hardly a policy of moderation.

Not just air control was criticized as immoral. Air bombardment in general was often seen as indiscriminate and in violation of international laws regarding non-combatant immunity. Repeatedly, RAF leaders decried any such intention. In a strongly worded and lengthy memo to the other service chiefs, Trenchard rejected claims that the RAF was intent on population bombing. Attacking legitimate objectives in populated areas was inevitable, and 'writers on war of every nation have accepted it as axiomatic' that such targets can be struck. Terror bombing was 'illegitimate', but it was a different matter 'to terrorise munitions workers (men and women) into absenting themselves from work . . . through fear of air attack upon the factory or dock concerned'. Trenchard's memo angrily concluded:

I emphatically do not advocate indiscriminate bombardment, and I think that air action will be far less indiscriminate and far less brutal and will obtain its end with far fewer casualties than either naval blockade, a naval bombardment, or sieges, or when military formations are hurled against the enemies' strongest points protected by barbed wire and covered by mass artillery and machine guns.[47]

Another senior air leader, Air Commodore Edgar Ludlow-Hewitt, stated flatly that population bombing was sheer unintelligent frightfulness based on the same kind of false doctrine which, in common with all attempts to win by terrorising civilians, has ended in failure. It is a senseless, inhuman method of warfare which I believe will never succeed against any nation of stamina and spirit'.[48]

Wing Commander Arthur Tedder (later Marshal of the Royal Air Force Lord Tedder) similarly argued: 'Terrorising of enemy people as a whole by indiscriminate bombing does not comply with principles of concentration. It is morally indefensible, politically inexpedient and militarily ineffective'.[49]

It must be pointed out that it was not merely for humanitarian reasons that the RAF opposed bombing other than military targets. Public opinion played a significant role, as did the purely practical matter that urban bombing was inefficient. The amount of high explosive necessary to cause significant damage to a major city was enormous. Given the modest size of the RAF and its bomber aircraft, payloads could be better spent on specific targets. Moreover, Britain felt particularly vulnerable to air attack because its key center of gravity was, unquestionably, London. The concentration of political, financial, social and industrial power in the London area made it the most valuable target in the country. Worse, because it was so close to the Channel it was within easy striking range of airbases on the Continent. The fear of a 'bolt from the blue' against London preoccupied British political and military leaders from the early 1920s on. In 1932, former Prime Minister Stanley Baldwin made his glum prediction that the bomber would always get through. He added his pessimistic assessment that the only way to prevent the destruction of one's cities was to bomb an enemy's even more viciously – Trenchard's the best defense is a good offense approach. In reality, Baldwin was advocating no such thing. In fact, the week following this comment he proposed at the Geneva Disarmament Conference the abolition of aerial bombardment. Obviously, this offer was done as much for strategic reasons as for humanitarian: because of the unusual vulnerability of Britain to air attack it had more to gain from such a prohibition.[50] The point to note, however, is that British political and military leaders had little incentive to push for a city-busting air strategy, and in fact they advocated precisely the opposite.

The other method of articulating and then disseminating air-power concepts throughout the RAF was through the Staff College at Andover. Soon after the war Trenchard realized that in a fundamental sense the RAF would stand or fall based on how well it was run. As a separate service it had to develop, quickly, the capability of organizing and administering its own affairs. As a consequence, he established three major schools in the first three years of peace: a technical school at Halton to train 'aircraftmen' in specific mechanical skills; a cadet college at Cranwell, similar to Sandhurst, for educating young officers; and a staff college at Andover, like the Army's at Camberley, for mid-career officers to teach them staff skills as well as a higher understanding of war. Trenchard referred to Andover, opened in 1922, as 'the cradle of our brain'.[51]

The form used at the Staff College was for the small faculty (originally five officers, all of whom later attained flag rank) to present lectures each morning, which were then discussed in seminar by the students (generally around 30 each year). Reading requirements were not heavy, and students were usually provided with a detailed outline of each lecture to help them prepare. Guest speakers from the government, business or the other services were frequent, and such lectures were often given in the evenings. Tactical air exercises were common, and each student was required to write an essay on his past experiences. The best of these essays were published each year and distributed throughout the RAF – most dealt with air operations in the Great War. As time went on, more students wrote of air control activities in the Middle East. A handful of aircraft were also available to the faculty and staff for refresher practice.[52]

In keeping with the RAF's need for competent staff officers who could work effectively in a joint environment, the curriculum, especially in the early years, emphasized administrative duties, tactics, and the missions and capabilities of the other services. For example, in the second class (1923–24) only about two weeks of the entire year's curriculum were devoted to air doctrine.[53] Interestingly, however, the Staff College's first commandant, Air Commodore Robert Brooke-Popham, taught these lessons himself. The prestige lent to the subject was therefore considerable, and the precedent set was continued by all succeeding commandants prior to the war.[54]

Brooke-Popham had been a successful combat commander in France, so his reputation and seniority gave credibility to Andover. Although some of his ideas seem a bit bizarre today, his views on air power were well thought out and compelling.[55] In his first lecture, the commandant argued that due to industrialization, the growth of democracy and trade unionism, people as a whole were now more directly affected by war. Just as important, they were more able than in the past to influence or even stop a war via the vote or a strike. As a result, 'it is now the will-power of the enemy nation that has to be broken, and to do this is the object of any country that goes to war'.[56] The first step in this process was to win air superiority, but unlike the official doctrine then articulated in CD 22, which seemed to imply this was an end in itself, Brooke-Popham cautioned that gaining control of the air was useful only in that it allowed an air attack on the vital centers. It was their neutralization that brought victory, so air leaders must not lose sight of their true goal. These vital centers would vary depending on the enemy – they might even be his armed forces – but the ultimate objective was to break the will of the enemy.

The lectures on air strategy by Brooke-Popham's successor as commandant, Air Commodore Edgar Ludlow-Hewitt, were quite good. He too realized that air superiority was essential but would have to be fought for. However, bringing the enemy to battle was difficult, because one could not fix the enemy in the sky as was possible on the ground. He therefore argued it was necessary to 'find some way of drawing the enemy to some spot chosen by us'. The method used to coax the enemy into battle was obvious: threaten something vital to his security.[57] Significantly, it was precisely this 'bait' technique that was used by the Allies in 1944 to bring the Luftwaffe to battle when they attacked German aircraft factories and oil refineries.

The Air Commodore also went into some depth on the subject of targeting. Noting that the key areas of an enemy country would vary with circumstances, Ludlow-Hewitt nevertheless identified three main target sets in a modern industrialized country. The first was the commerce, industry and distribution system – to include food, munitions, ore deposits and coal supplies. The second category was transportation nodes, which included not only land systems but also port facilities and harbors. Finally, the industrial workers were of major significance: 'if their morale can be tampered with or can be depleted – if their security can be endangered – their work will fall off in quantity and quality'.[58] Paralleling the doctrine manuals, Ludlow-Hewitt maintained the collapse of morale was more likely achieved 'by crippling his industries, delaying his railways and stopping his ports than by spraying the whole population with bombs'. He noted, however, that the success of the air offensive resulted from selecting the proper targets. This, in turn, required a special intelligence that established an enemy's habits of life, mentality, political system, economic apparatus, transportation systems, commodities flow, etc.[59] Unfortunately, although other air leaders echoed his calls for a robust intelligence network attuned to the needs of air warfare, little was done to establish it prior to the war.

The issue of how popular will would be broken was addressed by others at the Staff College through the interwar years. Arthur Tedder, an instructor in the early 1930s, speculated on the effect to be expected from air strikes on industry:

> men driven off their tools, clerical staffs from their offices, work decelerated and finally stopped. Material ruined and operations interrupted. Consequent delay, and final complete dislocation and disorganization of systems attacked. Spread of panic. Bombardment of one area likely to stop work in others.[60]

This was an air strategy of paralysis not obliteration.

The RAF also carried out a number of exercises during the interwar period. The first such major exercise was held in 1927 and continued most years thereafter until World War II. The scenarios for these exercises were ostensibly defensive in nature – enemy countries like 'Southland', 'Eastland', 'Red Colony', 'Caledonia', etc. were set to attack, usually London, and those attacks must be defeated. Although the air defense observer network, controllers, fighter squadrons and searchlight units received a thorough workout, so too did the bomber units, who attempted to penetrate the RAF defenses and strike London. In general, the purpose of the bombing strikes was to 'break enemy national resistance by intensive air bombardment of the vital points in her economic and industrial system'. More specifically, the targets designated for these bombing units were military objectives that required precise application of force: the 'seat of government', airfields, munitions factories, docks, arms depots, chemical industries and power stations.[61]

RAF strategic thinking ceased being an academic exercise and took on greatly increased significance by the mid-1930s. The rise of Nazi Germany forced air leaders to begin planning for a genuine military threat, not just an inconvenient diplomatic nuisance as with France in the decade previously. As a consequence, the RAF went through a period of frenzied planning and expansion beginning in 1935, which would last the remainder of the decade. Although the Air Ministry and the government tended to focus on these various expansion schemes, the operational RAF went about its business of thinking through the matter of warfighting. This effort culminated in a new edition of AP 1300 which was written during peace but which came out soon after the outbreak of war.

The new manual stressed in the strongest terms yet that the key to war was national will: 'a nation is defeated when its people or Government no longer retain their will to prosecute their war aim'.[62] This will was buttressed by several factors: the armed forces, manpower, the economic system and finances. The purpose of military forces was, therefore, to defeat the enemy forces in battle, starve the people into submission through blockade, or instill a sense of 'war weariness' in the people by disrupting their normal lives. This last path to victory was seen as the true one for air power. As before, the method advanced to effect this disruption was bombing the enemy industrial and economic infrastructure, such as public utilities, food and fuel supplies, transportation networks and communications. It was hoped the destruction of such targets would cause 'a general undermining of the whole populace, even to the extent of destroying the nation's will to continue the struggle'.[63] Note the muted hope that bombing would make a bloody land campaign unnecessary.

There was also an increased emphasis on air defense, and it was finally acknowledged that both active and passive measures were necessary and even desirable. In truth, this trend had been in motion for some years and it was largely imposed on the RAF from without. The argument that the best defense was a good offense fell out of favor as the Luftwaffe grew increasingly powerful from 1935 onwards. Intelligence predictions regarding the size of the German air force, and its superior production rate, forced Britain to re-evaluate its air strategy. At the same time, however, the British economy was still depressed and unable to keep pace with German expansion. In 1937, Thomas Inskip was appointed Minister for the Co-Ordination of Defence with guidance to check the rising defense budget. Although often vilified for his stringent fiscal policy in the face of a looming German threat, Inskip did reorient military aircraft production. Three fighters could be built for every bomber, and given the possibilities offered by the new communications warning net and especially the dramatic breakthroughs in the field of radar, Inskip gave priority to the production of fighter aircraft.[64] The notion that bombers could strike virtually anywhere, at any time, from any direction and achieve tactical surprise was no longer viable: bombers could be detected, intercepted and stopped. The new fighter planes on the horizon, the Hurricane and Spitfire – fast, maneuverable and heavily armed – promised to tip the balance of the air battle once again against the bomber. As a consequence, strong air defenses, combined with hundreds of new fighters, were in place in England by 1940: Air Chief Marshal Hugh Dowding's Fighter Command was ready for the Battle of Britain. The new war manual belatedly ratified these developments.[65]

As in previous manuals, great pains were taken to stress that although the civilian populace was much more involved than ever before in the business of war, it was not, as such, a legitimate target. Area bombing was thus rejected: 'all air bombardment aims to hit a particular target' and in every case 'the bombing crew must be given an exact target and it must be impressed upon them that it is their task to hit and cause material damage to that target'.[66] Nonetheless, even if 'the people' were not targets, 'the workers' most certainly were, because it was they who put the weapons in the hands of the soldiers, and it was they who controlled the actions of the political leaders. The point in attacking certain industries was thus not only to destroy the tools with which the enemy waged war, but to instill such fear in those making the tools they refused to show up for work. Hence, factories should be attacked when it was known the maximum number of workers were present.

This scrupulous regard for precise targeting of specific military objectives was not just for public consumption. The Air Targets Committee at the Air Ministry looked closely at potential target sets in Germany and prepared an extensive list of suitable possibilities. These target categories were specific military objectives: oil, gas, electricity, chemicals, explosives, non-ferrous metals, ferro alloys, the aircraft industry, iron and steel, roller bearings, raw materials, transportation networks and optical glass industries. Seemingly, a possible exception to this list was the inclusion of foodstuffs. But foodstuffs were the traditional objectives of a naval blockade and thus well established as legitimate targets in international law.[67] In addition, in a classified study written in 1938 by the Air Staff and endorsed by the Director of Plans, Air Commodore John Slessor, RAF bombing policy was spelled out. The document noted there were no internationally agreed laws regarding air warfare – conferences convened since the turn of the century had been unable to reach consensus. Consequently, air warfare followed the same rules as war at land and sea. The key legal tenet guiding air leaders was that deliberate bombing of civilian populations was not permitted: 'A direct attack upon an enemy civil population...is a course of action which no British Air Staff would recommend and which no British Cabinet would sanction'.[68]

The Air Staff worried, however, that the respect for law so traditional in Britain was not shared in other countries. Specifically, Nazi Germany, which had driven 'a coach and four through half a dozen international obligations', could hardly be relied upon to keep its word regarding the largely unwritten rules of air bombardment. Britain must, therefore, maintain an air capability that would be effective regardless of laws and agreements: 'expediency too often governs military policy and actions in war'.[69] This parting caveat was prophetic, because it was indeed expediency that would later shape British bombing strategy. But it seems clear that RAF doctrine going into the war had drawn a clear line regarding the issue. It should also be noted that, at the same time, lectures at Andover followed the line described above almost exactly.[70] This position carried over into the war.

The week before Germany invaded Poland, the CAS sent a letter to the Air Commanding-in-Chief of Bomber Command stating RAF policy in the clearest of terms:

> we should not initiate air action against other than purely military objectives in the narrowest sense of the word, i.e., Navy, Army and Air Forces and establishments, and that as far as possible we should confine it to objectives on which attack will not involve loss of civil life.[71]

The following year, during the campaign in France, the CAS reiterated this policy in a classified message to all RAF commanders. Air Chief Marshal Cyril Newall stated that the intentional bombing of civilian populations as such was illegal; it must be possible to identify the objectives struck in advance; attacks must be made with 'reasonable care' to avoid undue loss of civilian lives in the vicinity of the target; and the provisions of international law must be observed.[72] The CAS then elaborated on the thorny subject of what precisely constituted a 'military objective'. He listed several: military forces, works, fortifications, barracks, depots, supply dumps, shipyards and factories engaged in the manufacture or repair of military material, equipment or supplies. Also included were power stations, oil refineries and storage installations, and transportation lines serving military purposes. Following the provisions of international law, the directive concluded that 'provided the principles set out above are observed [regarding the prohibition of deliberately bombing the population] other objectives, the destruction of which is an immediate military necessity, may be attacked for particular reasons'.[73]

To be sure, the motives for such restraint were not completely noble. The years of fiscal stringency had left the RAF with a small and marginally capable force. Although it was up to the task of air control, the mass and sophistication required to mount a strategic air campaign against a major power were not available. The bewildering variety of expansion schemes that began in the mid-1930s to counter Luftwaffe growth only confused matters in the short term by adding the requirement for simultaneous expansion and training in new equipment. As a consequence, despite 20 years of doctrine that emphasized the primacy of offensive air power, the RAF was woefully unprepared to conduct such operations once war broke out. It was one of the first great shocks of the war to discover that Bomber Command was too small, too poorly equipped and too ill-trained to carry out the role scripted for it.[74] Not for the first or last time in air warfare, the technology had failed to keep pace with the doctrine devised to employ it. The RAF was therefore unwilling to throw the first stone when it believed the Luftwaffe had a larger supply of bricks near at hand. In addition, Britain was already acutely aware of the necessity of maintaining the friendship and moral support of the United States. Indiscriminate bombing would quickly sour such relations.[75] Nonetheless, RAF doctrine and policy throughout the interwar years, and indeed for the first year of the war with Germany, consistently stressed the principle of avoiding civilian non-combatants while concentrating on enemy industry. Unfortunately, the propensity of RAF thinkers to link this industrial targeting strategy with the morale of the enemy nation caused untold confusion to outside observers, then and since.

Although RAF policy in the first year of the war followed the guidelines noted above, the pressure of war soon forced changes. France, indeed most of Europe, was now part of Hitler's empire, the British Army had been thrown off the Continent at Dunkirk, Axis forces were moving rapidly across North Africa, German submarines were sinking British shipping in the Atlantic at an alarming rate, London had suffered through the initial stages of the Blitz, and British bombers had suffered such heavy losses in daylight they had been driven to the relative safety of the night. In short, Britain was alone, outnumbered, outgunned and desperate. The choice of Arthur Harris to lead Bomber Command in this dark period was pivotal. He, like Trenchard, was single-minded in his determination. Agreeing that there was no workable alternative, Harris carried out an urban bombing campaign against Germany's major cities as had been directed by Churchill and the Air Ministry. The aim was to destroy German morale by targeting residential areas where the workers lived. Given the abysmal accuracy of night bombing early in the war, such area attacks would have been the result whether intended or not. Like Trenchard in World War I, however, Harris persisted with this strategy – even when greater accuracy became possible in 1944 – with a stubbornness that earned him widespread criticism after the war with the revelation of the destruction leveled on Germany. Unfortunately, Trenchard and prewar RAF leaders have also been tarred with the urban bombing brush. This is inaccurate. Although Trenchard and his successors viewed the collapse of enemy morale as the ultimate goal, the mechanism used to achieve this goal was the destruction or disruption of enemy industry – a legitimate military target under the laws of war. This belief was consistently reflected in the RAF's doctrine manuals, in the courses at the Staff College that its most promising officers attended, and in the prewar guidance of the RAF's senior leaders.

RAF doctrine, which expanded and codified Trenchard's beliefs, was thus a unique strain of air-power theory that combined key concepts of the other two main schools of strategic bombing in the interwar years, those of Douhet and the instructors at the Air Corps Tactical School in the USA. Douhet also believed the ultimate objective in war was to destroy enemy morale, but he preached this was best done by bombing the people directly with gas and incendiaries. The Tactical School at Maxwell Field, Alabama, instead chose to concentrate on breaking the *capability* of the enemy to wage war. Their chosen target to implement this strategy was the industrial infrastructure. Quite simply, the RAF combined these two approaches: they chose the Douhetian objective of morale, but the Tactical School industrial targeting scheme. In the event, none of these three air-power theories proved completely accurate in World War II. But it must be remembered that the airplane was in its infancy and there was very little experience upon which to base air-power doctrine. Airmen thus did the best they could, examining the history of warfare and of air power in the Great War, calling upon their own aviation experience and, most of all, relying on their own logic and imagination unconstrained by temporary technological limitations.

Hugh Trenchard, the 'father of the RAF', sustained his service in its bleak period after the Great War, presented a theory of strategic air power which identified enemy morale as the key target, and then institutionalized those ideas through a series of doctrinal manuals. These precepts were then taught and refined at another of Trenchard's creations, the RAF Staff College. However, his theories proved ill-suited to the conditions that existed in World War II. When thrust into the furnace of total war those theories were adapted and reforged. The goal became unconditional surrender, and the nuances inherent in the doctrine of 'morale bombing' were lost in the process.

NOTES

This chapter originally appeared under the same title in the *Journal of Military History*, April 1996. The article won the Society of Military History's Moncado Award for 1996.

1. For this interpretation see Malcolm Smith, *British Air Strategy Between the Wars* (Oxford: Clarendon Press, 1984); Barry Powers, *Strategy Without Slide Rule* (London: Croom Helm, 1976); Neville Jones, *The Beginnings of Strategic Air Power: A History of the British Bombing Force, 1923–39* (London: Frank Cass, 1987); Anthony Verrier, *The Bomber Offensive* (New York: Macmillan, 1968) and Alan J. Levine, *The Strategic Bombing of Germany, 1940–1945* (Westport, CT: Praeger, 1992).
2. William L. Mitchell, *Winged Defense: The Development and Possibilities of Modern Air Power, Economic and Military* (New York: Putnam's, 1925), 20–1.
3. An excellent discussion of these issues is found in Dennis M. Drew and Donald M. Snow, *Making Strategy: An Introduction to National Security Processes and Problems* (Maxwell AFB: Air University Press, 1988), *passim*.
4. Peter King, *Knights of the Air: The Life and Times of the Extraordinary Pioneers Who First Built British Aeroplanes* (London: Constable, 1989), 314–15.
5. Smith, *British Air Strategy*; Powers, *Strategy Without Slide Rule*; Jones, *Beginnings of Strategic Air Power*; H. Montgomery Hyde, *British Air Policy Between the Wars, 1918–1939* (London: Heinemann, 1976).
6. Lt. Gen. Jan C. Smuts, 'The Second Report of the Prime Minister's Committee on Air Organisation and Home Defence against Air Raids', 17 August 1917, as quoted in Eugene M. Emme (ed.), *The Impact of Air Power* (Princeton, NJ: Van

Nostrand, 1959), 35. It should be noted that few RNAS officers rose to high rank in the RAF. One historian implies that Trenchard thought poorly of the naval aviators based on two events during the war: in March 1916 and again in September 1917 naval aviators refused to fly RFC aircraft because they thought them obsolete and the mission too risky. John H. Morrow, Jr, *The Great War in the Air: Military Aviation from 1909 to 1921* (Washington, DC: Smithsonian Institution, 1993), 167, 174, 236.

7. There are many accounts of these squabbles, and none of the principals emerge looking either statesmanlike or dignified. See especially Hyde, *British Air Policy*; Andrew Boyle, *Trenchard: Man of Vision* (London: Collins, 1962), and Frederick Sykes, *From Many Angles* (London: George Harrap, 1942). Incidentally, also resigning at the same time were Admiral Mark Kerr, Trenchard's deputy, and J. L. Baird, Rothermere's Under-Secretary.

8. 'Future Policy in the Air', 22 September 1916, Trenchard papers, RAF Hendon, File CI/14. This memo was later published as a Royal Flying Corps pamphlet titled 'Offence versus Defence in the Air', October 1917, copy located in Brooke-Popham papers, Liddell Hart Archives, King's College, London, File IX/5/4.

9. Major Sefton Brancker, the deputy director of military aeronautics, made an astounding comment in this regard in a letter to Trenchard in September 1916: 'I rather enjoy hearing of our casualties as I am perfectly certain in my own mind that the Germans lose at least half as much again as we do'. Malcolm Cooper, *The Birth of Independent Air Power* (London: Allen & Unwin, 1986), 75.

10. 'A Review of the Principles Adopted by the Royal Flying Corps Since the Battle of the Somme', RFC pamphlet, 23 August 1917, Brooke-Popham papers, Liddell Hart Archives, King's College, London, File IX/3/2.

11. 'Long Distance Bombing', 28 November 1917, Trenchard papers, RAF Hendon, File I/9. Indeed, fully 85 per cent of the IAF's missions were directed against airfields and railyards.

12 'The Scientific and Methodical Attack of Vital Industries', 26 May 1918, Trenchard papers, RAF Hendon, File I/9; see also 'Memorandum on the Tactics to be Adopted in Bombing the Industrial Centres of Germany', 23 June 1918, Trenchard papers, RAF Hendon, File I/10/4.

13 'Bombing Germany: General Trenchard's Report of Operations of British Airmen against German Cities', *The New York Times Current History*, April 1919, 152. Although a strategy of a geographically dispersed campaign seems to violate the principle of mass, Trenchard believed his forces were too small to cause catastrophic damage in any event, so it was wiser to opt for a psychological effect.

14. A list of all 350 strategic bombing missions conducted between October 1917 and the Armistice, excluding aerodrome attacks, is contained in H. A. Jones, *The War in the Air: Being the Story of the Part Played in the Great War by the Royal Air Force*, 7 vols (Oxford: Clarendon Press, 1922–37), 7 (Appendices), 42–84.

15. 'Memorandum on Future Air Organisation, Fighting Policy, and Requirements in Personnel and Material', 2 October 1917, Trenchard papers, RAF Hendon, File CI/14; 'Long Distance Bombing'; 'On the Bombing of Germany', 23 June 1918, Trenchard papers, RAF Hendon, File I/9.

16. Transcript of interview between Trenchard and H. A. Jones, 11 April 1934, Public Records Office (PRO), Kew, File AIR 8/179. This rationale is also developed at some length by one of Trenchard's aides, MRAF John C. Slessor, *These Remain: A Personal Anthology* (London: Michael Joseph, 1969), 80–5.

17. Sykes, From Many Angles, 558–61; P. R. C. Groves, *Behind the Smoke Screen* (London: Faber & Faber, 1934), 253–9.

18. Trenchard, 'Permanent Organization of the Royal Air Force', 25 November 1919, Brooke-Popham papers, Liddell Hart Archives, King's College, London, File IX/5/9. This document is referred to as the 'Jonah's Gourd memo' because Trenchard equates the wartime RAF with the prophet Jonah's gourd that sprang up overnight, but then died just as quickly the following day.

19. In contrast, one could argue that the US Air Corps' status as part of the Army was an advantage: with little to lose it could play the role of the recalcitrant child constantly agitating and irritating its older siblings.

20. 'The Future of the Air Force in National and Imperial Defence', Air Ministry pamphlet, March 1921, Brooke-Popham papers, Liddell Hart Archives, King's College, London, File IX/5/11, 13–14. (Emphasis in original.) Throughout most of the interwar period the RAF received less than 20 per cent of the defense budget.

21. Memo, Trenchard to Wilson, undated but c. 1920, PRO, File AIR 8/2.

22. Boyle, *Trenchard*, 348–51; B. McL. Ranft (ed.), *The Beatty Papers, Vol. II, 1916–1927* (Aldershot: Scholar Press, 1993), 84; Smith, *British Air Strategy*, 23. Naval air was generally slighted while part of the RAF, and the Admiralty complained their legitimate aviation needs were not being met. They therefore insisted naval aircraft be returned to fleet control. This indeed occurred in 1937.

23. 'Notes on the History of the Employment of Air Power', August 1935, PRO, File AIR 10/1367. The best account of these operations is David E. Omissi, *Air Power and Colonial Control: The Royal Air Force, 1919–1939* (New York: St Martin's, 1990). There are numerous contemporary accounts, but especially see: Flight Lieutenant C. J. McKay, 'The Influence in the Future of Aircraft Upon Problems of Imperial Defence', *Royal United Services Institute (RUSI) Journal*, 47 (May 1922), 274–310; Air Commodore C. F. A. Portal, 'Air Force Co-Operation in Policing the Empire', *RUSI Journal*, 82 (May 1937), 343–58; Squadron Leader J. L. Vachell, 'Air Control in South Western Arabia', *Royal Air Force Quarterly*, 2 (January 1931), 1–9.

24. 'Minutes of Meetings and Memoranda of Sub-Committee on the Continental Air Menace', December 1921–March 1922, PRO, File AIR 8/39.

25. 'Staff Notes on Enemy Air Attack on Defended Zones in Great Britain', 28 May 1924, Trenchard papers, RAF Hendon, File CII/3/177-227. The German attacks had caused 65 casualties per ton of bombs dropped in 'crowded areas' and four casualties in 'sparse' areas. The RAF used the compromise figure of 50. These estimates were proven to be greatly exaggerated during the Luftwaffe's bombing of Britain during World War II.

26. As quoted by Air Vice-Marshal A. S. Barratt in 'Air Policy and Strategy', Staff College lecture, 14 February 1938, RAF Hendon, '16th Staff Course' file.

27. John Ferris, 'The Theory of a "French Menace", Anglo-French Relations and the British Home Defence Air Force', *Journal of Strategic Studies*, 10 (March 1987), 66.

28. Trenchard, 'Buxton Speech', 13 April 1923, Trenchard papers, RAF Hendon, File II/5/1-57.

29. Trenchard, 'Speech at Cambridge University', 29 April 1925, Trenchard papers, RAF Hendon, File CII/3/177-227. The Air Staff reviewed the threat from antiaircraft guns and concluded blithely that it was insignificant. Based on experience in the war, it took over 11,000 shells to down a single aircraft. Not only did that wear out an average of two gun barrels but, adding the cost of ground crews, lights, etc., each plane downed cost the defender over £50,000. Moreover, the Air Staff had seen no improvements in artillery since the war, and opined that any in the future would be more than compensated by increased aircraft speed and altitude capability. 'Notes on Anti-Aircraft Gunnery', November 1926, Trenchard papers, RAF Hendon, File CII/3/177-227.

30. 'CAS Conference Minutes', 10 July 1923, PRO, File AIR 2/1267; 'Air Staff Memo No. 11A', March 1924, PRO, File AIR 8/71.
31. Trenchard, 'Notes for Address by CAS to the Imperial Defence College on the War Aim of an Air Force', 9 October 1928, Trenchard papers, RAF Hendon, File CII/4/1-47.
32. MFR (Memo for Record) by Trenchard, [1923], Trenchard papers, RAF Hendon, File CII/19/1.
33. Trenchard, 'The Employment of the Home Defence Air Force', 3 February 1928, Trenchard papers, RAF Hendon, File CII/4/1-47.
34. T. E. Lawrence, *The Mint* (London: Jonathan Cape, 1955), 95.
35. Another, more informal, avenue for disseminating ideas on air power was through professional journals such as *RUSI* and *RAF Quarterly*. However, it is difficult to determine whether RAF officers, especially senior leaders, ever read such journals. For a useful overview of this secondary source see Robin Higham, *The Military Intellectuals in Britain, 1918–1939* (New Brunswick, NJ: Rutgers University Press, 1966).
36. 'Operations', RAF manual CD 22, July 1922, PRO, File AIR 10/1197, 5. For the publication and distribution of the manual see AIR 5/299.
37. Ibid., 57.
38. Ibid., 58.
39. Ibid., ch. XI.
40. 'Royal Air Force War Manual', RAF manual AP 1300, July 1928, PRO, File AIR 10/1910, ch. VII. It should also be noted that the manual's cover stated that no reference would be made to the use of gas in war due to international 'engagements' on the subject to which Britain had subscribed.
41. Ibid., ch. VIII.
42. Ibid.
43. Ibid.
44. 'The Fallacies of "Inhumanity" and "Rancour",' Staff College lecture, undated, Bottomley papers, RAF Hendon, File B2244; see also 'Air Control: The Other Point of View', Staff College lecture, May 1931, Bottomley papers, RAF Hendon, File B2241, and 'Psychological Effects of Air Bombardment on Semi-Civilized Peoples', 7 February 1924, PRO, File AIR 8/71.
45. MRAF John C. Slessor, *The Central Blue* (London: Cassell, 1956), 66, 132.
46. 'Notes on Conference at Quetta', 2 July 1922, J. Salmond papers, RAF Hendon, File B2592.
47. Trenchard, 'The War Object of an Air Force', 2 May 1928, PRO, File AIR 9/8. A slightly different version of this memo is found in the Trenchard papers, RAF Hendon, File CII/4/1-47.
48. Ludlow-Hewitt, 'Direct Air Action', Staff College lecture, 1928, Bottomley papers, RAF Hendon, File B2274. Of note, Ludlow-Hewitt was the Air Officer Commanding-in-Chief of RAF Bomber Command at the outbreak of World War II.
49. Tedder, 'The War Aim of the Air Force', Staff College lecture, n.d., Tedder papers, RAF Hendon, File B270.
50. This is the major theme of Uri Bialer's *The Shadow of the Bomber: The Fear of Air Attack and British Politics, 1932–1939* (London: Royal Historical Society, 1980).
51. Surprisingly, the role of the Staff College in doctrine formulation and education has not been adequately examined. This gap is partly explained by the paucity of records. Only scattered documents and lectures remain and there is no official history. There is, however, a useful article (based on his Master's thesis) by Allan D. English, 'The RAF Staff College and the Evolution of British Strategic

Bombing Policy, 1922–1929', *Journal of Strategic Studies*, 16 (September 1993), 408–31. In addition, for a good overview see: Wing Commander R. A. Mason, 'The Royal Air Force Staff College, 1922–1972', unpublished manuscript in Staff College library, RAF Bracknell, 1972.

52. Mason, 'The Royal Air Force Staff College', 9–12.
53. As noted, the records of the Staff College (most are located in the archives at RAF Hendon) are sparse. However, there is a file for each year that contains a schedule covering the entire program, and an assortment of lectures that were presented. In truth, there seems to be little system in determining which lectures were preserved; rather, whatever was found was thrown into the file. Nonetheless, reviewing the files for each year gives a reasonable insight into the curriculum.
54. Not all of the commandants' lectures remain but, based on those extant, the best are those of Air Marshals Ludlow-Hewitt (1927–30) and Brooke-Popham (1922–26).
55. Brooke-Popham had a large library of military history and theory (over 600 volumes), which he donated to the Staff College when he left. He was an old-fashioned gentleman, and in 1922 he told his students: 'I hope I shall not be accused of harping too much on the question of horses. I know there are good men who don't hunt and bad men who do, but I am certain that every man is improved by hunting or even by keeping a horse and riding it'. Mason, 'The Royal Air Force Staff College', 6.
56. Air Commodore Robert Brooke-Popham, 'The Nature of War', Staff College lecture, 6 May 1925, PRO, File AIR 69/6.
57. Sir Edgar Ludlow-Hewitt, 'Air Warfare', Staff College lecture, 1928, Bottomley papers, RAF Hendon, File B2274.
58. Ludlow-Hewitt, 'Direct Air Action', Staff College lecture, 1928, Bottomley papers, RAF Hendon, File B2274.
59. Ibid.
60. Tedder, 'The War Aim of the Air Force'.
61. 'Report on Air Exercises, 1932', PRO, File AIR 10/1523. For exercises from other years see also: 1929, AIR 20/157; 1931, AIR 9/64; 1932, AIR 20/172; 1934, AIR 2/1398; and 1935, AIR 9/64. For an overview of several of these exercises see Scot Robertson, *The Development of RAF Strategic Bombing Doctrine, 1919–1939* (Westport, CT: Praeger, 1995).
62. 'Royal Air Force War Manual', RAF manual AP 1300, February 1940, PRO, File 10/2311, I/10.
63. Ibid., VIII/12.
64. Sean Greenwood, ' "Caligula's Horse" revisited: Sir Thomas Inskip as Minister for the Co-Ordination of Defence, 1936–1939', *Journal of Strategic Studies*, 17 (June 1994), 17–38.
65. A new chapter was added to AP 1300 titled 'The Strategic Air Defensive'; see also Smith, *British Air Strategy*, 188–91; Wesley K. Wark, *The Ultimate Enemy: British Intelligence and Nazi Germany, 1933–1939* (Oxford: Oxford University Press, 1986), 35–58.
66. RAF manual AP 1300, VIII/39.
67. 'Air Targets Intelligence Germany: Vulnerability to Air Attack and Lists of Most Important Targets', September 1939, PRO, File AIR 20/284.
68. 'The Restriction of Air Warfare', 14 January 1938, PRO, File AIR 9/84, 22.
69. Ibid., 14; see also Memo, Slessor to CAS, 9 September 1938, PRO, File AIR 2/3222.
70. H. A. Smith, 'International Law', Staff College lecture, 19 June 1939, RAF Hendon, '17th Staff Course' file.

71. Letter, Newall to Ludlow-Hewitt, 23 August 1939, PRO, File AIR 75/8.
72. Message from CAS to all Air Officers Commanding, 4 June 1940, PRO, File AIR 8/283.
73. Ibid.
74. The sorry state of Bomber Command at the beginning of World War II is well documented in Neville Jones, *The Beginnings of Strategic Air Power: A History of the British Bombing Force, 1923–39* (London: Frank Cass, 1987).
75. Memo, Slessor to CAS, 9 September 1938, PRO, File AIR 2/3222.

3

John C. Slessor and the Genesis of Air Interdiction

Most historians of the Royal Air Force state that the theory of strategic bombardment held sway during the interwar period to such an extent that any officer who seemed to argue with that primacy was doomed to obscurity. Initially, I agreed with this interpretation. And then one day I picked up 'Jack' Slessor's Air Power and Armies *and was stunned. This was an unusually erudite and compelling work on the subject of tactical air operations. Yet, Slessor was widely respected in the RAF before, during and after World War II. In 1950 he was named Chief of the Air Staff and promoted to five-star rank. Quite obviously, his outspoken advocacy of tactical aviation earlier had not hindered his career.*

Slessor has not yet had a biographer, perhaps because his detailed and extensive memoirs have saturated the market: The Central Blue *and* These Remain *are exceptionally well written, insightful and detailed. Like all such works, however, there are omissions and interpretations that are in need of correction. More importantly, within these works and in the literature of air power in general, there has been little analysis of his ideas on tactical air power. In my view, his writings on this subject are among the most insightful written prior to World War II.*

John Cotesworth Slessor was one of the Royal Air Force's most brilliant thinkers. Recognized as an authority on air-power doctrine and theory throughout his career, he also served several tours on the Air Staff. In addition, he was an extremely successful operational commander. Slessor was a flight commander in World War I, a squadron commander in Britain and a wing commander in India between the wars, a bomber group commander in the early stages of World War II, and the Air Officer Commanding-in-Chief of Coastal Command during 1943. During his tenure there the German U-boat menace was defeated decisively and many referred to Slessor as 'the man who won the Battle of the Atlantic'. The Air Marshal finished the war as deputy commander of the Mediterranean Allied Air Forces. After the war Slessor served as the RAF personnel chief, as Commandant of the Imperial Defence College and in 1950 he was named Chief of the Air Staff. He retired from that position in 1953 as a Marshal of the RAF.

Slessor was a prolific writer. In addition to two volumes of memoirs, he wrote three books after retirement that dealt with NATO strategy and the role of air power in the defense of Europe.[1] This chapter, however, will look at Slessor's early career, before World War II, concentrating on his writings that deal with the employment of air power in conjunction with a major land campaign, specifically, his seminal *Air Power and Armies*, published in 1936. In emphasizing air operations at the theater level of war Slessor was somewhat unique among his RAF colleagues, who generally wrote either about strategic air power directed against an enemy's major centers of gravity or of narrow, tactical concerns. Although not discounting the importance and even necessity of such subjects, Slessor concentrated instead on how best to use air power as a complement to a field army. In essence, he advocated the rapid accomplishment of air superiority, followed by systematic and relentless attacks against the enemy army's lines of supply – what today would be called an air interdiction campaign. My purpose here is to present a brief overview of Slessor's early career and then explore his ideas on air power as presented in *Air Power and Armies*.

'Jack' Slessor was born in Rhanikhet, India, on 3 July 1897, where his father was stationed in the Sherwood Foresters of the British Army. In 1903 his father retired, the family moved back to England, and Jack was sent to Haileybury public school. Afflicted with polio as a child, he was largely unable to participate in the most physical sports, but he quickly developed a great love for fox-hunting, shooting, fishing and riding. When the Great War broke out Jack attempted to join the army, but was turned down due to his physical limitations. Nonetheless, the young man persevered, imposed on family friends who pulled some strings, and in 1915 he was accepted into the Royal Flying Corps. This experience with the rules of officialdom and their more pragmatic opposite later prompted him to write that 'one of the best possible methods of selection of officers is by selective and controlled nepotism'.[2] It was certainly successful in his case.

Although now in uniform, Slessor's problems were far from over. Pilot training was a hit and miss affair in those early days. He won his wings with a scant 12 hours of flying time, 'having broken no less than four aeroplanes' in the process. The new pilot flew his first operational mission soon after; in October 1915 he was the first British pilot to intercept a Zeppelin over England. Unfortunately, he was never able to get close enough to use his guns and the airship escaped. Not having flown at night before, Slessor completed his exciting first mission by promptly crashing in an unlit turnip field upon landing. The young officer also served in the Sinai and the Sudan, where he received a Dervish bullet in the thigh as well as a Military Cross, and after seeing further combat as a flight commander in France as part of an observation squadron, he returned to England for a tour as an artillery and infantry cooperation officer. The Armistice found him serving as an instructor at the Central Flying School.[3]

After the war Slessor briefly left the service, but four months of leisure convinced him he needed steady employment. He re-entered the Royal Air Force (a separate service since April 1918), and was posted to India. After a

serious car accident followed by a bout of pleurisy and inflammation of the
liver, Slessor returned to Britain to serve on the Air Staff. A year later he
was selected to attend the RAF Staff College at Andover, and upon
graduation in 1925 he was returned to flying duties, this time in an army
cooperation squadron at Farnborough. This was an educational three years
that taught him a negative lesson: the British army was training assiduously
to fight World War I. He would have more to say about that later.

Slessor had by now acquired a reputation as a tactical expert, and in 1927
wrote a lengthy essay, apparently never published, that detailed his thoughts
on army cooperation. His overall message was fairly negative. The RAF
hierarchy was not sufficiently supportive of this mission, so Slessor called for
more squadrons, more aircraft and more training. He also suggested a
reorganization of the units providing this support, giving all administrative
duties to the wing and making the squadrons responsible solely for
conducting operations. In a somewhat humorous display of pique, Slessor
complained that the squadrons were too burdened with administrative
details. Henceforth they should not even be allowed typewriters: they were
symbols of a system; a system to 'render returns and pro-formas and submit
answers to correspondence in quintuplicate'.[4] In 1928, Slessor was sent back
to London for another stint in the Plans Branch of the Air Staff.

The Plans Branch, consisting of two officers, worked directly to the Chief
of the Air Staff, Air Chief Marshal Sir Hugh Trenchard. Clearly, Slessor
deeply respected the old man and soon became one of Trenchard's 'English
merchants' – responsible for translating the Chief's frequently incoherent
rumblings into understandable prose.[5] In this position he helped write
Trenchard's famous 'last will and testament' in late 1929. This controversial
piece, officially titled 'The Fuller Employment of Air Power in Imperial
Defence', called for an expanded RAF at the expense of the other two
services.[6] Trenchard's regard for his young staff officer was high. When told
by the Army chief, Field Marshal George Milne, that the RAF officer
detailed to teach at the Army Staff College was unable to discuss effectively
the broader aspects of air power, Trenchard assured him the next officer
holding that post would be a fine tactician, a strategic thinker and someone
well connected to the Air Staff who would be conversant with current policy.
That officer was to be Jack Slessor.[7]

In 1930, while concluding his tour on the Air Staff, Slessor was tasked to
write a new army cooperation manual. His effort was a document
significantly different in focus and scope from the existing manual. Rather
than providing a simple description of how aircraft should cooperate with the
infantry, cavalry and artillery, Slessor's version presented an overview of the
organization, function and objectives of an army and air force. He then
discussed the command relationships between the two components, noting
they should work together closely and their headquarters should be
collocated. Significantly, noted he that the air commander should be dual-
hatted; that is, he should be both the commander of the air element of the
theater force and also serve as the chief air advisor to the commander-in-

chief. The importance of this thorny issue of command and control would be raised again and again in the years ahead.

Perhaps the most important sections of the new RAF manual were those that explained how air power could cooperate most effectively with land forces in a major campaign. In a clear description of what would later be called air interdiction, Slessor wrote: 'Valuable results may be achieved by carefully organized attack on the enemy system of supply, maintenance and transportation. The more highly organized the enemy is the more vulnerable will he be to actual interference with his supply'.[8]

The manual further noted that when the enemy did begin to retreat due to the combined effects of air and land attack, aircraft could become even more effective, turning a withdrawal into a rout and 'crushing the enemy's power of resistance'. Many of the ideas contained in this manual foreshadowed those Slessor would expand upon over the next few years.

Slessor's tour as an instructor at the Army Staff College between 1931 and 1934 solidified his deep knowledge and understanding of ground operations, and when combined with his combat experience, as well as the tenets of strategic air power learned at Trenchard's knee, it made Slessor an unusually broad and flexible thinker. Although an acknowledged authority on tactical air power, Slessor was also, as Trenchard had promised the army chief three years previously, well versed in the RAF's doctrine regarding strategic bombing. Slessor's challenge was to teach his army students in such a way that they understood all the various roles and capabilities of air power, while emphasizing the area most likely to be of concern to them – tactical cooperation. This required a delicate balance and, as he confided in a letter in mid-1934, he seemed to have succeeded in convincing his army colleagues he was an air-power zealot, while his fellow RAF officers thought him 'too khaki', concluding that if everyone was dissatisfied with him, then he must be on the right path.[9] More importantly, Slessor was responsible for planning Camberley's major exercise for 1934, and he used the opportunity to try out some of his own theories. First, he devised a scenario in which a resurgent Germany had invaded the Low Countries and was in the process of building airfields, presumably for the purpose of bombing England. It was the duty of a British Expeditionary Force to land in the Low Countries, expel the invaders and occupy the threatening airbases. Slessor was also able to convince the army to adopt his command structure which envisioned co-equal air and ground commanders. This exercise, the culmination of his tour at Camberley, was viewed by Slessor with great satisfaction.[10]

At the end of 1934 Slessor left Camberley for another tour in India. While there, he took the lectures he had given at the Staff College, refined them based on his flying experiences in the Waziristan Campaign, where he received the Distinguished Service Order for his performance, and in 1936 published *Air Power and Armies*. This was perhaps the best treatise on air-power theory written in English before World War II.

Unlike Giulio Douhet in Italy, Billy Mitchell in the USA and Hugh Trenchard, who had all begun their careers as army officers, Slessor started off as a flyer in 1915. It may be worth speculating on how the lack of army training and indoctrination during his formative military years – and the concomitant backlash it seemed to incur in many airmen – affected Slessor's outlook on air power. Nonetheless, his close relationship with the army during and after the war, as well as his tour at Camberley, gave him important insights into the subject of air–ground operations. When assessing *Air Power and Armies*, however, it must be remembered, first, who his audience was at Camberley, and second, his admonitions repeated throughout that he is writing about a war in which the British Army has already been committed to a land campaign. Slessor acknowledged that a primary function of air power was strategic bombing, but he intended to deal with

> the actions of the Royal Air Force in one special set of conditions, namely when the Empire is engaged in a war in which it has been necessary to send an Army and Air expeditionary force to fight in an overseas theatre of war.[11]

He would not, therefore, discuss how air operations could be conducted separately from other forces – a common theme of other air theorists at the time – but rather would explain how air and ground forces could operate in concert to achieve a common goal. Indeed, he chastened his readers that 'no attitude could be more vain or irritating in its effects than to claim that the next great war – if and when it comes – will be decided in the air, and in the air alone'.[12]

One of the first things to strike the reader regarding *Air Power and Armies* is that its arguments are based not only on logic – the method employed by most air theorists in the interwar years – but also on history. Noting that experience enables commanders and staff officers 'to be wise before the event', he relied heavily on the history of war, concentrating especially on the Great War.[13] Most airmen of that era showed a disdain for such study, perhaps because it seemed to teach the wrong lessons for air power. Responding to this tendency, Slessor wrote:

> If there is one attitude more dangerous than to assume that a future war will be just like the last one, it is to imagine that it will be so utterly different that we can ignore all the lessons of the last one'.[14]

Typically, he was not as well versed in the history of naval warfare. This is surprising in that the fundamental tenets of sea power are quite similar to those of air power. Both are, at base, forms of economic warfare designed to weaken a country's determination to continue the conflict. One would therefore think that airmen would ground themselves more fully in their naval antecedents, but such is generally not the case. In any event, one of the lessons of the Great War, as indeed had been the case over the previous four centuries, was that the security of Britain demanded that the Low Countries remain in safe hands. London, the industrial, financial, political and moral center of the empire, was a mere hundred miles from potential enemy airbases on the Continent. More than ever before, Britain could not allow a foe to have such an advantage. This was an issue worth fighting for.

Slessor believed the character of war had changed dramatically. Unlike the French, he believed trench stalemate was over. The advent of the tank and airplane meant that the static warfare of the Western Front was an aberration. In the future, war would be dominated by small, maneuverable armies. He thought that Britain's use of a large, infantry-based expeditionary force in the Great War was a folly that should not be repeated and that the British people, he believed, would not tolerate again. The safety of the empire had always depended upon a strong navy, but the army should consist of no more than 12 regular divisions and all of these should be either mechanized or motorized. Clearly, his tour at Camberley had kept him abreast of the latest developments in modern land warfare.[15] In addition, and not surprisingly, Slessor believed air power would play a key, perhaps dominant, role in future war. He saw air power as the third revolution in the history of warfare, behind gunpowder and the machine-gun. However, air was the most important because the first two allowed more efficient killing on the battlefield, 'but AIR may stop men or their supplies arriving at the battle-field at all'.[16] In fact, he saw air power as the antidote to modern weapons of surface warfare.

Keeping with the book's focus of assuming a land campaign, air power's role was 'to assist and co-operate with the army in the defeat of the enemy's army, and of such air forces as may be co-operating with it'.[17] As will soon be clear, this translated into the communications and supply lines of the enemy forces – interdiction – rather than strategic air strikes against the enemy's vital centers. The first requirement for assisting the army, however, was to obtain air superiority, because he was certain ground operations would not be successful without it. In fact, Slessor hinted that achieving air superiority may of itself bring surrender, 'but these are not the conditions which it is the object of this work to examine'.[18] He realized, however, that controlling the air over an entire theater was unlikely and unnecessary due to the immensity of the sky. He therefore stressed the need for local air superiority, but even this was difficult and required constant maintenance. Air superiority was not a phase; it required persistence.

Slessor also emphasized that winning the air superiority campaign demanded initiative. Here he echoed the views of his mentor, Trenchard, by noting the importance of morale. One did not achieve victory by waiting for the enemy but by striking first and hard.[19] Slessor did not advocate the bombing of airfields, which he saw as ineffective and at best a temporary nuisance, nor did he see much utility in defensive air patrols. Such things may be useful, but the primary means of destroying the enemy air force was through air combat. The enemy air force must be brought to battle, but this could be difficult. Unlike armies that had to fight in order to achieve their objective of defeating the enemy army or preventing it from overrunning their country, air forces could avoid battle while still bombing a country's vital centers. Thus, it was not necessary to choose between air superiority and bombardment – both campaigns could be waged simultaneously. This ability to conduct parallel and not merely sequential combat operations was one of the factors that differentiated air power from surface forces. The method suggested by Slessor to bring the enemy air force to battle was to attack objects so vital to the enemy that they must be defended. In essence, he was saying that the bombers would be the bait that would draw enemy fighters into the air where they could be destroyed.[20] Even so, Slessor was ambivalent about the air superiority campaign, arguing on the one hand as to its necessity, while on the other that it should not be seen as an end in itself. There was clearly a line, fine though it may be, between aggressively waging the battle for air superiority, while also avoiding its distractions in order to conduct a more lucrative bombing campaign.

Slessor posited a war in which the British Army was deployed to the Continent to secure the Low Countries from a hostile power. The initial stages of that joint campaign were therefore symbiotic: the army and navy secured a foothold and established airbases, and the air force then protected the surface forces from enemy attack. Once secured, a strategic air campaign against the enemy would be carried out:

> then the ultimate reduction of the enemy nation may (and very likely will) be undertaken, not by the traditional methods of land invasion, or by continued assault upon their armies in the field, but by air measures. That is to say it will become an air campaign, and the task of the army will be simply to protect the air bases.[21]

Unfortunately, Slessor declined to discuss the details of such an air campaign. Instead, he concentrated on the preliminary joint campaign, largely because he believed air power would not stop a major land assault by itself, and hitting strategic targets would not take effect quickly enough to prevent the British Army from being overwhelmed. Therefore, air, land and sea commanders had to cooperate to stop an enemy offensive.

Nonetheless, Slessor's general comments regarding a strategic air campaign were interesting. He was unsure as to which targets were most likely to ensure success; indeed, he recognized that most countries had several centers of gravity, which he defined as 'an organ or centre in a man, an army, or a nation, the destruction or even interruption of which will be fatal to continued vitality'. Although adding the caveat that 'it is difficult to be more definite about a subject which is necessarily so imponderable', there are several interesting aspects to Slessor's discussion. First, he implies that there are vital centers at all three levels of war – the strategic, theater and tactical. He went on to argue that these centers may change over time. Typical key targets at the strategic level were power plants, iron and steel works, chemical factories, transportation hubs and oil refineries. He then remarks, not very helpfully, 'that a book for itself' could be written on the subject. Unlike some, he was careful not to equate strategic bombing with a mechanistic destruction of target sets. Obliteration of an objective was not always necessary; rather, neutralization for a specific time period could be satisfactory. He used the example of a man's windpipe: it was not necessary to sever it, simply interrupt it for a few minutes to achieve the same result. Slessor also was tepid in support of morale bombing. Although stating that 'it must not be imagined that the writer underrates the possibly terrible effects of air bombardment on the morale of the civil population', he saw the reduction of industrial capacity as both more practical and more quantifiable.[22] Finally, he stressed the need for industrial intelligence. Specifically, he called for detailed technical expertise to ensure effective targeting. In one prescient comment he opined that although economic and industrial intelligence were once of only 'academic interest', they were now crucial. In truth, these brief insights into strategic air warfare are intriguing. It is interesting to speculate on what type of book Slessor would have written had he instructed at Andover rather than Camberley.

But we must be content with the book Slessor did write. In it, he focused on the theater – what today is termed the operational level of war – arguing that the neutralization of key nodes at that level would prevent effective operations. On the other hand, he decried those who wished to use air power as 'flying artillery'. It was not a battlefield weapon. Rather, he believed the enemy should be attacked, repeatedly, as far from the battlefield as possible. In this regard, Slessor envisioned air power as the key element in sealing off the enemy's forces and strangling them into submission. In short, he was stating that interdiction should be the primary air mission when cooperating in a land campaign. In this regard he tended to favor supply interdiction (to include material and equipment) over force interdiction (troops and combat vehicles), maintaining that movement by rail and road was virtually impossible in daylight for the side that had lost air superiority. Cutting off all supplies and communications was not likely, but they could be severely curtailed. Moreover, as with strategic air warfare, he argued that paralysis not destruction should be the goal.[23] The precise method of effecting such paralysis was clearly spelled out.

Slessor argued that the new machinery of land warfare required ever increasing amounts of supply, especially petroleum products and ammunition. This would, in turn, require increased reliance on rail transport. Here was an Achilles' heel. In Slessor's view, the railroads, especially the marshaling yards, were highly vulnerable to air attack and therefore were a growing liability to the side that had lost air superiority.[24] In truth, this was a prediction borne out in the spring and summer of 1944 when Allied air power carried out its devastating Transportation Plan, which severely disrupted German rail traffic throughout the northwest theater of operations. Even more spectacularly, Slessor later noted that air superiority, combined with air interdiction of rail lines and major bridges, was decisive in turning back the Germans in the Battle of the Bulge.[25] Of note, he pointedly warned his army colleagues that they must take greater care to protect their own supply lines from enemy air attack. Friendly air superiority could not always be assured.

Significantly, Slessor recognized that effective interdiction required cooperation between air and ground units. He even offered that there were occasions when ground forces should support the air effort – a heretical belief among most ground officers at the time. Finally, he argued – as he had in the army cooperation manual and the 1934 exercises – that air power must be commanded and directed by an airman who was equal in authority to the ground commander. These two individuals and their staffs were to collaborate in the design and implementation of the theater commander's overall plan. Interestingly, he speculated that the theater commander could be an airman.[26]

Although Slessor cautioned against an extensive use of air power in a tactical role, he did offer some guidelines for those occasions when such operations were necessary. As with all air missions, he saw the first requirement as air superiority. Second, even more than in interdiction operations, it was essential for the air and ground commanders to coordinate their efforts closely – their headquarters should be collocated if possible. Because of the proximity of friendly troops, mistakes could not be tolerated. After careful planning, air power could be used tactically in three different situations: in attack to facilitate a breakthrough; in pursuit to turn victory into rout; and in defense to 'putty up' an enemy breakthrough on the ground.

It is clear from Slessor's scarcely veiled hints, as well as his later career and writings, that he was a strategic air-power advocate. Indeed, it is fairly apparent from these hints that Slessor wanted to write about strategic air power but his army audience would have none of it. He was therefore compelled to write a book that assumed a land campaign. The result was an outstanding book with several especially notable aspects: its detailed discussion of air superiority, what it is, how it should be gained and when it is necessary to maintain it; the emphasis on the need for specialized air intelligence; and the detailed discussion of an army's center of gravity – its supply lines. Slessor was arguing that when cooperating in a land campaign, air power was wasted if used merely as a tactical weapon; rather, air power should concentrate on the disruption, destruction and neutralization of enemy armaments and supplies – interdiction. Given his penetrating examination, it is unfortunate Slessor did not write a companion volume on strategic airwar. (As noted earlier, his many writings after World War II are concerned primarily with nuclear deterrence and the situation in Europe.)

In a sense, Slessor's masterful volume served as a transition between the RAF of the post-World War I era and the RAF of the pre-World War II era. The rise of Nazi Germany in the mid-1930s forced air leaders to begin serious planning for a major military threat, not merely the imperial policing operations of the 1920s. As a consequence, the RAF went through a period of frenzied planning and expansion that would last the remainder of the decade. Although the Air Ministry and the government tended to focus attention on these various expansion schemes, the operational RAF went about its business of thinking through the matter of warfighting. Slessor, now an air commodore and the RAF's director of plans, played a key role in shaping RAF policy and strategy in the crucial years between 1937 and 1940.

During the interwar years, Jack Slessor was perhaps the most prescient thinker in the RAF regarding the form future war would take. His major study, though perhaps limited by external factors rather than his own beliefs, is the most balanced and judicious treatise of all those written regarding the new air weapon. The hope of air advocates that land and sea forces would play but a minor role in future war was, of course, not borne out, but Slessor barely hinted at that possibility. Instead, he presumed a major land war with a Continental power. In such a scenario, air power was, at best, *primus inter pares*, and its most important contribution was to gain air superiority and then to interdict the enemy's lines of supply and communication. Given the adolescent state of British air power, this vision of future war was quite realistic.

NOTES

A version of this chapter was originally published under the same title in the *Royal United Services Institute Journal*, August 1995.

1. Slessor's memoirs are *The Central Blue: Recollections and Reflections* (London: Cassell, 1956) and *These Remain: A Personal Anthology* (London: Michael Joseph, 1969). His works on defense policy include *Strategy for the West* (London: Cassell, 1954), *The Great Deterrent* (London: Cassell, 1957) and *What Price Coexistence?* (London: Cassell, 1961).
2. Slessor, *Central Blue*, 6.
3. These events are discussed in Slessor, *These Remain*, 44–58.
4. Sqdn Ldr John C. Slessor, 'The Organisation of Army Co-Operation Units in Expeditionary Forces', August 1927, Public Records Office (PRO), Kew, File AIR 75/2. Of interest, Slessor wrote on the cover of this essay: 'Boom [Trenchard] ticked off about this. I still can't see why'.
5. This is evident in Slessor's character sketch of Trenchard on page 45 in *The Central Blue*.
6. Slessor would later maintain that he thought Trenchard made a serious error in writing this paper, because it unnecessarily provoked the other services. He would have been better off working in his usual fashion – quietly and behind the scenes. Letter, Slessor to Freeman, 11 October 1938, PRO, File AIR 75/42.
7. Letter, Trenchard to Milne, 10 December 1928, Trenchard papers, RAF Hendon, File CII/19/2.
8. 'Employment of Army Co-Operation Squadrons', RAF Manual AP 1176, 1932, RAF Hendon, File 8951, ch. V. For the previous edition (1926), see File 6419.
9. Letter, Slessor to Courtney, 27 July 1934, PRO, File AIR 2/1664.
10. Ibid. See also, in same file, 'Camberley Exercise, 1934' for the wargame scenario; see letter, Slessor to Freeman, 11 October 1938, PRO, File AIR 75/42, for his positive reflections on the tour at Camberley.
11. Wing Cmdr John C. Slessor, *Air Power and Armies* (Oxford: Oxford University Press, 1936), i.
12. Ibid., 214.
13. An example of Slessor's sound knowledge of military history was his lecture on

the Schlieffen Plan of 1914, which is reproduced as the first chapter in *The Great Deterrent*.

14. Slessor, *Air Power and Armies*, x.
15. Slessor was awarded the Royal United Services Institution gold medal for his essay 'Combustion Engines in the British Army', *RUSI Journal* 82 (August 1937), 463–84. Interestingly, Slessor confided to Trenchard that he believed 12 divisions were extravagant, but he did not want to offend his army colleagues. His main purpose in writing the essay was to decry the army's emphasis on traditional infantry divisions. Letter, Slessor to Trenchard, 23 June 1937, PRO, File AIR 75/42.
16. Slessor, *Air Power and Armies*, 200. (Emphasis in original.)
17. Ibid., 1. Further evidence of his broad view of joint operations is given in his essay, 'The Co-Ordination of the Future Services', *RUSI Journal* 76 (November 1931), 752–5.
18. Slessor, *Air Power and Armies*, 28.
19. In today's parlance, Slessor was advocating 'offensive counter air operations' versus the more passive 'defensive counter air operations'.
20. It is worth noting that Slessor scarcely even mentions antiaircraft artillery, which he saw as almost totally ineffective against attacking aircraft. This was a gross miscalculation as the war would soon demonstrate. In addition, like most airmen of his time, he thought escort fighters were theoretically desirable but technically impracticable – another error proven by the war.
21. Slessor, *Air Power and Armies*, 3.
22. Ibid., 65–9.
23. This emphasis on paralysis sounds similar to the sort of thing then being advocated by J. F. C. Fuller and B. H. Liddell Hart. It is likely Slessor was well acquainted with their ideas based on his tour at Camberley.
24. Slessor, *Air Power and Armies*, 137–8.
25. ACM John C. Slessor, 'The Effect of Air Power in a Land Offensive', *RUSI Journal* 93 (May 1948), 268–73. On the other hand, interdiction was less successful in Italy during 1944–45, when Slessor served as Deputy Commander of the Mediterranean Allied Air Forces. Slessor discusses this interdiction campaign, Strangle, in *Central Blue*, 566–77.
26. Slessor, *Air Power and Armies*, 87.

4

Between the Devil and the Deep Blue Sea: Britain's Fleet Air Arm before World War II

Interservice rivalry has long been a continuing fact in the militaries of most countries. The rivalry between air and sea arms have often been the most pronounced and bitter, perhaps because these services seem to be coveting the same basic mission of strategic attack.

I witnessed this rivalry throughout my own military career, and, indeed, beyond it. These periodic bouts of interservice rivalry are generally most likely to occur when defense budgets are cut. That was true during the interwar period as it was also true in the aftermath of the Gulf War. While trying to understand the roots of this rivalry in the armed forces of the United States, I stumbled upon the similar situation in Britain prior to World War II. The fight between the Royal Navy and the RAF over the control of the Fleet Air Arm was protracted and bitter. But, although the arguments behind this battle often sounded trivial, the fundamental issues at stake were significant.

Interservice rivalry between sailors and airmen has existed almost since the invention of flight. In both the United States and Great Britain this animosity reached a high pitch between the world wars. In the United States this was due partly to the incendiary words of men like Billy Mitchell, who was unremitting in his attacks on the navy. Tension was also high due simply to bureaucratic politics: there was money, and therefore force structure, in air power. Whichever service controlled the nascent air assets would have increased power. More significantly, however, rivalry developed due to ideological reasons. This in turn led to disagreements over how sea and air fleets should be employed in war. To a great extent, this debate continues today.

The situation in Britain between the airmen and the sailors was unique. From 1918 until 1937, the Fleet Air Arm (FAA) – the air assets that worked with the fleet and operated from both aircraft carriers and land bases – was part of the Royal Air Force (RAF). Under this arrangement, the pilots, mechanics and radio operators who served in the FAA were trained by the RAF, although a percentage of these individuals were from the Royal Navy

(RN). The RAF was responsible for the design and procurement of the aircraft provided to the FAA, but the Admiralty actually funded these assets and had an input into their selection. While at sea, FAA personnel came under the authority of the ship's captain. This dual control was an interesting experiment that ultimately proved unsuccessful. Indeed, the amount of animus that arose between the RAF and RN over this issue was enormous, even exceeding that experienced in the USA, which is saying something. My intent in this chapter is to describe that experiment and, by doing so, to reveal how the services' separate views as to the conduct of war were the main cause of their mutual animosity. These differing views have changed somewhat over the years, but their basic incompatibility transcends national experience and, indeed, is manifested in the continuing rivalry today between the US Air Force and the US Navy.

When Britain entered World War I it had two air arms. The British Army had an air contingent, the Royal Flying Corps (RFC), and the Royal Navy had an air arm as well, the Royal Naval Air Service (RNAS). The two services jealously guarded their infant air assets from each other, but as the war progressed, critics pointed to the inefficiency and duplication of maintaining two separate systems for design, procurement, production, training, logistical support and military operations. Matters came to a head in 1917 when German bombers began raining their loads on England, which was largely powerless to prevent them. The public outcry against these attacks was so intense, the government of Prime Minister David Lloyd George was forced into action. He appointed a special committee, headed by the South African general Jan Smuts, to look into the matter of air power generally and air defense specifically.

After five weeks, Smuts issued reports concluding that the problems of waste and duplication, as well as air defense, could be solved by the formation of a new Cabinet-level department, the Air Ministry, and placing under it a new military service. This Royal Air Force would be comprised of the personnel and assets of the RFC and RNAS. His recommendation was accepted and the RAF was born on 1 April 1918.

The Army and Navy were not amused, and when the Armistice was signed they looked forward to returning to the situation prior to 1 April – they expected the return of their air arms. In a letter to Winston Churchill, who was the new Secretary of State for War and Air, Admiral Sir David Beatty, the First Sea Lord, wrote that in the formation of the RAF, 'the Government in arriving at this decision never questioned the principle that a naval unit of the fighting fleet must be manned, administered and controlled by the Admiralty'.[1] He was confident Churchill would do the right thing to solve this problem.

This was not an unrealistic hope. When Lloyd George appointed Churchill to his post it was widely assumed that his guidance included the abolition of the upstart Air Force – the crisis had passed; it was time to return to normality. Such was not to be the case, for Churchill looked favorably upon the infant RAF. Although thwarted on one flank, the soldiers and sailors moved on another. Over the next six years, the two senior services were instrumental in pushing for a series of government boards and committees to look into the issue of air power and whether or not a separate service was necessary. Admiral Sir Ernle Bradford declared the Navy's strategy baldly, 'we have at last started to officially attack the Air Ministry'.[2] The fora convened to study the issue included the Balfour Sub-Committee of 1921, the Geddes Committee of 1922, Balfour again in 1923, the Haldane Inquiry of 1924 and the Colwyn Committee of 1925. The seemingly endless succession of such investigative commissions, all of which eventually concluded in the RAF's favor, prompted the chief of the RAF, Air Marshal Sir Hugh Trenchard, to explode in exasperation: 'all of my time and energy are frittered away in meeting these incessant attacks, and I cannot get on with my real work, which is vital to the Empire's safety'.[3]

Although the victor in these endless engagements appeared to be the RAF, the long-term trend was decidedly less so. Cleverly, the Admiralty constantly sought ways to increase their power over the FAA by focusing on details. As a result, the correspondence between the two services throughout the 1920s is marked by interminable squabbles over issues such as the percentage of FAA aviators who actually wore naval uniforms, whether or not RAF aircraft mechanics had to perform traditional seamen's duties while they served on board ships, who should sign the annual performance reports on the airmen while at sea, whether radio operators should be officers or enlisted personnel, and the quotas allotted to the Admiralty for the RAF training schools. In these rather mundane but crucial matters the Navy's position held sway and for good reason. Most of the actual operational activities of the FAA occurred at sea, so it was only logical that Navy interests would take priority. The Admiralty was well aware of the implications of these maneuvers. As Captain Murray Sueter put it, 'we will make it [the FAA] more naval rather than more aerial'.[4] The RAF resented what they saw as a steady encroachment on their territory, but there was little to be done.

In the 1930s, the debate between the RAF and RN became more substantive due to the emergence of real enemies: Germany, Japan and Italy. This caused both services to think far more seriously about how they actually intended to fight another war, rather than how they should best organize and manage their forces in peacetime.

The heart of the problem between the sailors and airmen centered on their views of war. Although there are radical differences to be sure, in some ways sea power and air power are similar, and this leads to direct competition over scarce resources in order to perform the same mission. At base, both are a form of economic warfare. Sea power, through the instruments of blockade, embargo and sea control, attempts to isolate an enemy country, deprive it of raw materials and strangle its trade. It is hoped that the resultant damage to the economy will break the will of the enemy leadership and lead to surrender. Naval doctrine proposed to accomplish this strangulation by following the theories of Alfred T. Mahan, whose books on sea power had an enormous impact on Admiralty thinking. Mahan stressed the absolute necessity of command of the sea. Until such command was achieved, a nation would always be at risk from an enemy fleet that could disrupt its sea lanes and deprive it of needed resources and trade. In order to gain command of the sea, it was therefore necessary to destroy the enemy's main battle fleet. This climactic engagement between the battleships of the opposing fleets was not only necessary, it was desirable, and the sooner it occurred, the better. The RN should thus seek out its enemy counterpart as quickly as possible and bring it to battle. Once the enemy fleet was destroyed, Britannia would rule the waves. This would not only mean security for Britain itself but would result in the slow but inexorable strangulation of the enemy. Because the Navy's view of strategic operations focused on the battle fleet, naval aviation was merely an adjunct to that fleet. Aircraft carriers existed for the purpose of protecting the battleship flotilla while it carried out its primary naval functions. The RAF followed a different star.

Strategic air attack is similar to sea power in its intent: to so disrupt the economy of an enemy country that the will of its people to continue would fail and surrender would result. It was not expected that such an air campaign would substitute for land or sea operations; rather, it would make those operations far easier and less costly. Significantly, however, whereas sea power as a strategic weapon is generally employed indirectly – the sinking or interdiction of ships at sea that bring supplies and resources to an enemy country – air power promises to destroy the enemy industries directly and thus more rapidly. The difference is important because it will determine how military forces will be employed to effect this economic dislocation.

Trenchard and other strategic bombardment advocates saw the airplane as a revolutionary weapon that allowed the direct attack of an enemy's heartland. It was hoped this would preclude the need for an extended, bloody land war of the kind that had killed over ten million soldiers in the Great War. More importantly, airmen believed that such a bombardment campaign could have immediate effects, unlike the 'slow motion' results of a naval blockade. In sum, the Navy saw itself as an inherently strategic force, with air power's role as a supporting element to the battle fleet. Airmen also saw themselves as an inherently strategic force, but one in which the airplane itself was the chief weapon. As the Air Minister phrased it in 1922:

> The foresight of earlier generations gave us the mastery of the sea; it is now ours to ensure for our successors the mastery of the air. Progression not retrogression must be our aim, and we should beware lest our judgment be influenced by the outworn shibboleths of an era which is passing.[5]

It should also be noted that when the Admiralty looked out on a hostile world their gaze fell on the naval power of the Pacific, Japan. The German and Italian fleets, although a concern, inspired less worry than a Japanese move on Hong Kong or Singapore. For the RAF, on the other hand, the primary threat lay in Europe with the German Luftwaffe. Therefore, not only did the two services have different views on the nature of war, they differed on who they imagined Britain's primary enemy was to be.

The fundamental differences between the conduct of sea warfare and that of air warfare had a crucial operational implication. Both sailors and airmen recognized the importance of achieving air superiority. Air Marshal Geoffrey Salmond expressed this concept in the strongest possible terms: 'The culmination of all air operations is the supreme air battle and no supreme sea battle can take place without the strategical supremacy of the air having been attained'.[6] In this view, attaining air superiority was clearly a primary objective of an air force at the beginning of a war; without it, traditional military operations at sea, on land or in the air would be far more costly. Moreover, this air superiority should be total. Given the ubiquity of the airplane – its ability to be in many different places very quickly – the enemy's entire air force had to be destroyed to ensure safety everywhere.

Sailors disputed such a view. They cared little whether an enemy had an air force over its key cities; they weren't going there anyway. Instead, the seamen needed mere localized air superiority. They needed protection over the fleet. This difference of opinion was important because it related directly to the key issue of unity of command. If the RAF's view of air superiority was adopted, then unity of command demanded that all available air assets, including the FAA, should be used to gain victory in the air battle.[7] The RN, on the other hand, insisted that unity of command meant that it had to control the FAA to ensure local air superiority over the fleet. In essence, the issue was seen as one of winning the war versus winning the battle. Airmen attached great strategic significance to the air superiority battle, but sailors viewed it as merely a segment of a larger naval campaign that would be decided by the guns of the battleships.[8] It is useful to note here that naval airmen, to say nothing of the Admiralty, were not yet proposing that naval air power could be used as an extension of the Navy's traditional method of strategic economic warfare. That concept would come much later, but in the meantime, another problem was brewing.

It is frequently the case that interservice rivalry is particularly intense in an era of fiscal austerity. Hard decisions regarding what gets funded and what does not invariably lead to special pleading and raw nerves. Interwar Britain was no exception. The Great War had nearly flattened the country's economy, and the Great Depression that followed a decade later only made things worse. As a result, when disarmament talks began at Geneva in 1932, the British government saw an opportunity to cut defense costs. If Britain could safely disarm, or at least place upward limits on the size of the defense establishment, savings would result, and the economy would be given a medicinal shot. What part of the defense establishment should be cut? Because of its junior status, eyes turned primarily to the RAF.

Between 1932 and 1934 when the Geneva Conference sat, a number of proposals were put forward by the British government, as well as other participants, to place severe restrictions on aircraft quantity, size, weight and performance characteristics. It was even suggested that all aerial bombing be prohibited. The RAF was once again in a fight for its life. As a result, the Air Ministry drew up less fatal alternatives to serve the needs of the disarmament imperative while also saving its skin. Regrettably, but not surprisingly, the RAF offered up 'its' naval air assets as a sacrifice in the cause of peace. Although this proposal was in keeping with the RAF view of war noted above, it was obviously a political bombshell. The Admiralty reacted indignantly. They had always suspected that the RAF was less than totally committed to the FAA and this dastardly proposal confirmed it. The Admiralty suggested instead that the FAA be enlarged, due to its importance to the fleet and hence national security, at the expense of the RAF's bomber elements.[9] In the event, the disarmament movement collapsed: Hitler's Germany had no intention of disarming; they intended to rearm and quickly. The RAF and the FAA were both saved, but the ill will the disarmament talks generated between the services lingered.

Matters continued to lurch shakily on over the next few years. As the Hitler menace became increasingly apparent, Britain began its slow, painful and occasionally fitful drive to rearm. In 1936, the government of Neville Chamberlain was concerned about this rearmament – the Depression lingered and economy was still essential. It therefore appointed Sir Thomas Inskip to oversee the military services. Inskip was an unusual choice for the position of Minister for the Co-Ordination of Defence. He was colorless and not well known. One wag noted that his appointment to such a high post was the greatest surprise since the Emperor Caligula had named his favorite horse as one of Rome's consuls.[10] Nonetheless, Inskip took control quickly and made his weight felt.

One of the first items on his agenda was a complaint from the Navy that the FAA was being mismanaged by the RAF because the airmen were perennially unresponsive to Admiralty needs.[11] Inskip decided to look into the matter. To the amazement of all, on 21 July 1937 he announced that he was most concerned that relations between the Admiralty and the Air Ministry 'have not been conducive to the best results'. He was not one to assign blame, but nonetheless had concluded that returning the FAA to the Navy would be 'a more natural order than the present system'.[12] The Navy was delighted by this unexpected turn of events, while the RAF was flummoxed. The Air Minister immediately complained to the Prime Minister, stating that Inskip's charter was solely to look at questions of broad strategic principle. Instead, he had made a major organizational change without warning and without even giving the RAF a chance to make its case on the subject.[13] Chamberlain let the decision stand. Although the land-based FAA assets, which later became Coastal Command, remained with the RAF, the sea-based air power, the bulk of the FAA, returned home after nearly two decades.

In truth, despite the RAF's rhetoric and vitriol, Inskip had made the appropriate decision. The FAA *was* mismanaged and deficient. Its standard aircraft were the Swordfish and Sea Gladiator, obsolete biplanes that would not have lasted five minutes against front-line aircraft. Moreover, not only was it deficient in quality but the FAA was deficient in quantity, ranking a distant third behind the naval air arms of the United States and its main potential adversary, Japan. What had gone wrong?

The fact of the matter is, the RAF *had* neglected its naval air assets. Given its doctrine of strategic attack and its focus on a continental war in Europe, combined with the chronic shortage of funds, this should not be surprising. The RAF's preoccupation with other matters is well illustrated by its own 'War Manual'. When AP 1300 was first published in 1928, its table of contents listed a chapter 11 titled, 'Aircraft in Co-Operation With the Navy'. But the chapter was missing; a simple sentence on an otherwise blank page stated bleakly, 'In the Course of Preparation'. One would have thought the RAF could have devised something to say about FAA operations in the ten years it had owned them. This could hardly have been reassuring to the Admiralty. In contrast, the chapter on cooperation with the Army was the second longest of the manual. Obviously, the RAF *had* given thought to an air campaign against a land power.

Another venue for airmen to express their views on air operations, specifically FAA operations, was in professional military journals. The *Royal Air Force Quarterly*, established in 1930, was the official publication of the Air Ministry, but in the entire decade of the 1930s only four articles appeared dealing with the subject of the FAA. One of these articles dealt with flying boats – a dead-end technology; a second argued that carrier-based aircraft were inherently inferior to land-based aircraft – an appraisal sure to warm the hearts of the admirals; a third was a brief overview of the FAA written by a naval officer; and the last was a prescient piece that argued the need for escort carriers for convoy protection – a need soon revealed in World War II. This was not much to show for a decade of thought.

Another highly respected publication was the *Royal United Services Institute Journal (RUSIJ)*. It was not affiliated with a particular service and thus contained an eclectic balance of articles by personnel from diverse backgrounds. Numerous items concerning the FAA appeared in its pages during the interwar years – all were written by naval officers and most were critical of the RAF's stewardship of the FAA. For example, in 1923 *RUSIJ* awarded its annual gold medal for the top essay to Captain A. H. Norman, RN, for his provocative article on why the RAF should be abolished. The second place prize that year went to Lieutenant Commander G. N. W. Boyers, RN, for his essay on why the FAA should be returned to the Admiralty.

The situation was even more stark in *The Naval Review*. Throughout the 1920s and 1930s it contained several articles each year on the FAA; virtually all were critical of the RAF. More importantly, these various essays, as well as those in *RUSIJ*, were generally articulate and reasoned. Clearly, naval airmen were thinking seriously about their profession; there was little evidence their RAF counterparts were similarly intellectually curious about theirs.

There were other reasons why the FAA was not in adequate shape. It is the duty of military officers to assess the threats facing their country and then devise military structures and strategies to meet those threats. As noted, the thinking of the RAF and the RN, as well as that of the British Army, was significantly different on this score. The Navy expected to fight primarily in the Pacific against another sea power, but also to fight against a Germany that had shown a predilection for submarine warfare. In both cases, the Navy needed an FAA attached to the battle fleet. The RAF, on the other hand, planned to fight Germany. The first step in that conflict would entail an air superiority battle, which *might* require the assistance of the FAA. While air dominance was being achieved, the RAF would simultaneously conduct a strategic bombing campaign against the enemy's heartland; the FAA would play little or no role in that effort. For its part, the British Army expected another Continental war that would require, as in 1914, a British Expeditionary Force deployed to France. That BEF would need the support of the RAF to ensure success. Although soldiers would have liked more air assets devoted to them, they were reasonably satisfied with what they expected to get from the RAF. They had early on left the fight against the infant air service, had accepted them on equal terms, and learned to work with them effectively.

The problem with the services' views was their largely mutually exclusive nature. All of the services believed their vision of future war was the most accurate and that they would have to bear the brunt of the fight. Yet, none of the services thought they were receiving sufficient funds to accomplish their essential tasks. Given the relative weakness of the British defense establishment between the wars, and the economy that supported it, something was bound to give. In this case, everything gave. The sadly ironic part of this dilemma was that all three services were correct, on both counts. Britain *would* have to fight major sea, air and land wars against powerful opponents, worldwide. *And* they would have insufficient resources to do so.

It must also be noted, however, that the Navy itself was partly to blame for the deficiencies in the FAA. Because of the emphasis within the RN on the battleship, little priority was given to aviation, specifically the aircraft carrier. For example, the construction of the aircraft carrier *Courageous* was delayed five years, and *Ark Royal*, which was intended to be the most advanced carrier in the world, was delayed a full six years, not being commissioned until 1938. Naval aviation had few effective advocates within the sea service, and one reason for this was that there were virtually no naval aviators of senior rank. Promotion in peacetime was slow, and the FAA was so young there had been insufficient time for naval aviators to climb the ladder to high rank. Thus, aviators had little voice in the decision-making process. This was both regrettable and unnecessary. In the US Navy the problem was recognized and solved by allowing more senior officers to transfer to the air branch and still occupy major command positions. As a result, Ernie King and 'Bull' Halsey, already respected seamen, earned their wings as captains, but then went on to command large air units.[14] Having such men in key senior positions was absolutely crucial to the formation of an effective naval strategy in World War II. Because the RN did not take such an approach, however, they had only one flag-officer who wore wings at the start of the war.[15]

In addition, the RN did in fact control the purse strings of the FAA. Had the Admiralty wished, it could have insisted on the procurement of modern ships and aircraft to field a first-rate air arm. It was the Navy, after all, that bought the Swordfish and Sea Gladiator for its carriers. Likewise, it was the Navy that delayed carrier procurement while also building small and marginally useful aircraft carriers like *Furious* that could accommodate a paltry 18 planes. And it was the Navy that refused to allocate funds for the construction of escort carriers – despite the experiences of the Great War and the German submarine menace.

Finally, it must be admitted that many senior naval officers were dedicated members of the 'gun club', advocates of the great battleships that would soon be revealed by the war as obsolescent. One of these men, Admiral Sir Tom Phillips, so denigrated the importance of aviation – he called it 'poppycock' – that he waved off attempts to incorporate its use with the ships under his command. He thought they were not needed. In December 1941 he would stand on the bridge of his flagship, the battleship *Prince of Wales*, when it, along with the battlecruiser *Repulse*, were sunk by Japanese aircraft off the coast of Malaya. They had no air cover. Note, this occurred more than four years after the Navy had regained control of the FAA.

The case of Admiral Phillips notwithstanding, it was not that the RN was insufficiently air-minded. It was convinced of air power's importance. Indeed, it loved the air force so much it wanted one of its own. The real issue was who would control the air assets and to what end would they be used. Unfortunately, the RN was so busy fighting to regain control of the FAA, they neglected to plan for its use in the event the fight was won.

The interwar years were marked by a prolonged and bitter struggle between the RN and the RAF over the control of air power at sea. Although the bureaucratic and political nature of this infighting was often petty – and both sides were equally at fault – these organizationally based squabbles should not mask the deeper issue of what precisely was to be the role of naval air power. The Navy and the Royal Air Force had different ideas on that subject. They therefore believed, not illogically, that in order to be sustained in their views they must be in complete control. Any sort of divided rule would result in compromise, dilution and mediocrity – mediocrity of equipment and also of ideas regarding the employment of that equipment.

By the end of World War II, the situation had changed for both the Royal Navy and the US Navy. The aircraft carrier had displaced the battleship as the backbone of the fleet. As the war in the Pacific approached its end, the Japanese fleet was largely defeated. The mission of the US carriers increasingly turned to support for amphibious operations and, surprisingly, attacking strategic targets on land. The advent of nuclear weapons completed the Navy's metamorphosis in the years that followed: with not an enemy fleet in sight during the Cold War, it focused on nuclear strike, both by ballistic submarines and by nuclear-armed aircraft. In short, the Navy took up strategic bombing. Not surprisingly, this aggravated tensions with the Air Force. For the past five decades these tensions have occasionally flared up, especially during times of fiscal austerity. Over the course of the past eight decades the views of the sailors and airmen have grown surprisingly close, which is perhaps why the strains remain so prevalent.

Interservice rivalry has scarcely diminished since the era between the wars. To an extent, this is both good and desirable. It fosters competition, especially in the realm of ideas. As complex, dangerous and risky as war can be, professional officers must constantly seek ways to wage it more effectively and efficiently. But competition can be taken too far. Between the world wars the fight for control of the FAA became ensnared in petty arguing and animus. The important differences between the RAF and RN regarding the conduct of war and the role of air power in war, became masked and pushed aside by the squabbling. So much energy, both physical and mental, was put into the fight, the actual object over which they were fighting – air power at sea – was largely ignored. As a consequence, the FAA entered World War II in sorry shape. Rather than the FAA being trapped between the devil and the deep blue sea – as many sailors believed – it was instead caught between a rock and a hard place, and suffered grievously as a result. The lesson for today is that military officers in all of the services should continue to debate the best way to approach the use of force in military conflicts. But while doing so, they must remember that the goal is increased national security and not mere organizational ascendancy.

NOTES

A shorter version of this chapter appeared under the same title in the *Royal United Services Institute Journal*, October 1999.

1. Letter, Beatty to Churchill, 17 July 1922, AIR 8/17. (All documents designated 'AIR' are located in the Public Record Office in Kew, London.)
2. Quoted in Geoffrey Till, *Air Power and the Royal Navy, 1914–1945* (London: Jane's, 1979), 35.
3. Letter, Trenchard to Baldwin, 4 February 1926, AIR 8/79.
4. Quoted in Till, *Air Power and the Royal Navy*, 114.
5. Memo by Secretary of State for Air to the Cabinet, 'The Relations Between the Royal Air Force and the Navy', August 1922, AIR 19/97.
6. Memo, G. Salmond to Air Ministry, no date, but presumably sometime in 1921, AIR 8/17.
7. Air Staff memo, 'Answer to Naval Staff Memorandum', 22 June 1923, AIR 19/96.
8. Air Staff memo, 'Navy Control of Shore-Based Aircraft', 12 February 1936, AIR 9/2.
9. Air Staff memo, 'The Limitations of Seaborne Air Forces', 20 October 1931, AIR 8/135; Memo by the First Sea Lord, 'Policy in Regard to the Limitation of Naval Armaments', 11 January 1932, AIR 8/135.
10. Sean Greenwood, '"Caligula's Horse" Revisited: Sir Thomas Inskip as Minister

for the Co-Ordination of Defence, 1936–1939', *Journal of Strategic Studies*, 17 (June 1994), 18.

11. 'Fleet Air Arm Enquiry, Admiralty Paper F', 4 June 1936, AIR 8/211.

12. Air Staff memo, 'The Navy and Its Relation to the Fleet Air Arm and Shore-Based Aircraft', 26 July 1937, AIR 19/23; Admiral Sir Roger Keyes, 'The Riddle of Defence: Men, Money and Machines', *The Sunday Times*, 22 November 1936, in AIR 9/5.

13. Letter, Swinton to Chamberlain, 22 July 1937, AIR 19/23.

14. King won his wings 27 years into his career, at age 47, in 1928. Halsey had already served for 30 years when he became an aviator in 1934 at age 52. Both went on to become fleet admirals.

15. Till, *Air Power and the Royal Navy*, 45.

5

The Impact of Technology and Design Choice on the Development of US Fighter Aircraft

When working on my Master's degree at the University of Colorado, I approached my favorite professor, Dr Denys Volan, and asked if he would agree to mentor me in an independent study on Napoleonic warfare. Dr Volan, who had been an official Air Force historian for a number of years, responded that he knew little of Napoleon, but he would be willing to guide a study in air power. I agreed, somewhat reluctantly, and my academic focus was thus unexpectedly and quickly set.

One of the issues we discussed over bourbon in his study was the influence of doctrine within the Air Corps prior to World War II. Volan had always been skeptical of claims that doctrine was so powerful and pervasive that it had determined the Air Corps' force structure. I therefore began to look at technology as a possible alternative influence. I now realize that the philosophy of technological development is a separate academic discipline in its own right. Nonetheless, it did seem to me, and still does, that doctrine is insufficient in addressing the fundamental question: Given our policy of isolationism and defense within the US between the wars, why did the US enter World War II with the best offensive bombers – the B-17 and B-24 – and mediocre defensive fighters – the P-39 and P-40? Technological imperatives seem to provide an answer.

The United States had the best long-range, heavy bombers in the world at the beginning of World War II, but its standard pursuit aircraft were inferior to those of the other belligerents. This seems unusual considering that the strategic posture of the United States between the wars was one of defense, not offense. Fighters, which were seen as strategically defensive weapons, should have had a higher priority than offensive bombers. The reason for this disjunction is usually attributed to doctrine: Air Corps leaders saw the future of their service as integrally joined with bombardment. Hence, although national policy was defensive, Air Corps doctrine was offensive.

The basic principles of US air power were articulated by Billy Mitchell and a group of crusaders who followed him. They argued the airplane was a revolutionary weapon because it offered unique capabilities in war. The key to enemy resistance had always been the 'vital centers', those major industrial, economic, political and population areas that sustained the nation. In order to defeat an enemy, these vital centers had to be captured or destroyed. For centuries, however, these centers were protected by armies and navies. In order to capture Paris, for example, one first had to fight one's way through the French Army. Air power offered an alternative. Operating in the third dimension, aircraft could fly over enemy armies to strike directly at a nation's vital centers, thus obviating the need for a bloody preliminary clash of armies. In the aftermath of World War I, such promises were enticing. Air power, specifically the long-range bomber, was hailed as the weapon of the future. The doctrine of the US Army Air Corps was written according to such precepts.

However, the United States had retreated into an isolationist shell after the war and was in no mood for talk of long-range bombers waging war on distant lands. Air leaders were thus faced with a dilemma: how could they build an offensively oriented air arm when the American public thought only of isolation and defense? Major General Benjamin Foulois, Chief of the Army Air Corps from 1931 to 1935, devised an ingenious, if not ingenuous, solution:

> Up to this time my air staff planners had been stressing the need for bombers in offensive operations and had gotten nowhere with the General Staff. Discouraged, they came to me and I could see only one way out: 'Stress defense, not offense, and stress reinforcement of the Hawaiian Islands', I told them, 'and maybe that will work'. It did, and the climate became more favorable as we dropped the word 'offense' from our justification papers. Thus, historians will note that our plans continually stressed the defense of our coasts and our overseas possessions from that point in time on. As I saw it, if we could get bombers that could carry bigger bomb loads and fly greater distances this way, what difference did it make what words we used?[1]

Using such subterfuges the Air Corps developed heavy bombers like the B-17 and B-24 and formulated a doctrine for their employment in future wars.[2]

There is another interpretation. Lagging American pursuit aircraft in 1941 was due also to technological and economic reasons. Pursuit, as opposed to bombardment, demands high performance by the very nature of its mission. However, in the 1920s and 1930s the technology needed to produce a maximum-performance airframe and engine either was not yet available or was not sufficiently supported by the major aircraft manufacturers in the United States.

The nation was in the midst of the Great Depression and companies were loath to take risks. Instead, they concentrated on enterprises that were safe, conservative and promising the greatest return on their investment. In aeronautical terms this translated into large, reliable, economical and durable multi-engine airliners. Not coincidentally, Air Corps bombardment aircraft closely resembled their commercial cousins. Small, fast, high-performance pursuit aircraft were expensive, and there was no commercial counterpart to the military pursuit plane. In short, they were bad business. As a result, aircraft and engine designers tended to avoid the needs of pursuit and concentrate instead on those of bombers and airliners.

This chapter will discuss airframe and engine development between the World Wars. It hopes to show that for various technological and economic reasons, as well as related design decisions, the requirements of maximum performance were slighted. As a result, pursuit aircraft, which demanded maximum performance, lagged behind in the decades between the World Wars.

MONOCOQUE METAL CONSTRUCTION

A 'monocoque' aircraft structure is one in which the outer covering, rather than an internal framework, carries all or a major part of the stresses. In nature, the ideal monocoque structure is the eggshell. Such a design is difficult to build, however, so aircraft designers resorted to semi-monocoque designs with some internal bracing. This provided superior strength and a noticeable saving in weight. However, airframe design had to undergo an evolutionary process to reach the stage of metal monocoque construction.

In World War I aircraft, the standard airframe construction consisted of doped fabric stretched over a wooden frame. The load was carried by the frame and the covering was merely for aerodynamic purposes. The strength of this structure was limited by the strength of the wooden frame, and it was not unusual for an aircraft to have the wings crumple when in a dive.[3] The introduction of a metal frame provided an increase in structural strength. Although the Germans had employed this technique in the Junkers J aircraft, some of the Stakken R planes and the late-model Fokkers, in the US Army this step was not taken until 1921 when the Air Service built the PW-1.[4]

The introduction of metal wing spars and ribs also increased the dependability of airfoils. Because a piece of wood's quality is determined by the tree it comes from, it is difficult to predict its strength beyond general considerations. On the other hand, metal is uniformly similar, so its strength and endurance can be tested to within 5 per cent. As a consequence, airframe builders had to use large amounts of wood of considerable thickness to ensure strength and survivability. This condition became more prevalent as aircraft increased their speed. In fact, over 200 mph an aircraft with a wooden framework weighed more than one of metal framework, for although wood has a lower specific weight, more of it must be used to guarantee the same strength.[5]

The next step was to substitute wood for fabric in covering the fuselage and wings. This move toward a semi-monocoque design was important. Wood as a covering meant the framework could be reduced in size and weight, with the skin now absorbing some of the stress. One of the most successful aircraft to use this principle was the Fokker Trimotor of the late 1920s. The era of wood-covered aircraft was fairly short, however, because of the crash of a Trimotor that killed the famous Notre Dame football coach, Knute Rockne. It was determined the accident was caused by the failure of a wooden wing spar that had rotted.[6] As a result, wood began to pass from use and a corresponding impetus was given to metal construction.

The first significant attempt to use metal skin was made by Hugo Junkers in 1915. Adolph Rohrbach followed with an all-metal aircraft in 1919, but it was many years before the use of metal became widespread. The first operational all-metal fighter in the United States was the Boeing P-26 of 1933.[7]

One of the reasons for the tardiness in adopting metal in aircraft structures was the slow progress of metallurgy. Aluminum was undesirable because of its low strength. Steel and other ferrous materials were sufficiently strong, but too heavy. The ideal solution was duralumin, an alloy of aluminum, copper, manganese and magnesium that combined the strength of the ferrous metals and the lightness of aluminum. It was seven times heavier than wood but had vastly greater strength.[8] It was also easier to fabricate and manufacture. With this discovery, metal was more financially viable and, in effect, it became lighter than wood. The effect on military aircraft development was dramatic.[9] The first US military planes to use this design, the P-26 and YB-9, resulted in a significant performance jump over their predecessors. Although there were other reasons besides metal causing this performance leap, it provided the stability and strength necessary to make practical innovations like cantilever wings and retractable landing gear.

CANTILEVER WING DESIGN

A fully cantilevered wing is one that supports its own weight and is internally braced by the use of a lateral wing spar. The alternative to cantilever design is a wing externally braced by struts or cables.

The cantilever was invented long before it came into popular use. Perhaps the most notable of the early attempts at internal bracing was the Fokker D.VII, whose upper wing was semi-cantilever – that is, a great deal of internal bracing was used – but struts were still necessary. Anthony Fokker maintained the struts used on the D.VII were not needed but were added as a psychological prop to the pilot, who might become disconcerted at seeing no visible means of support.[10] Even so, it was many years before his design was incorporated into a production fighter in the USA. Engineers recognized the importance of the Fokker design but they did not fully understand its principle. The first American production-line pursuit aircraft with fully cantilevered wings were the Seversky P-35 and Curtiss P-36 of 1937. By contrast, the first production bomber was the Martin B-10 of 1933.

A main advantage of the cantilever wing was a reduction in drag which had resulted from the struts and wires. There were two problems to be overcome in order to achieve this gain in aerodynamic efficiency. First, the cantilever wing's sole reliance on internal bracing required extremely strong lateral spars to support the wing during the violent stresses of combat. If wood was used the structure would be prohibitively large and heavy. Metal provided the strength to make the cantilever wing practical.

The second *perceived* problem with the cantilever wing was the mistaken belief that the increased thickness of the wing, which was necessary to accommodate the large wing spars, would actually incur more drag than the externally braced type. It was feared this extra drag would cancel out the advantage gained by removing struts and cables.[11] This was an erroneous belief. The cantilever wing was a breakthrough in technology, allowing all types of aircraft to achieve greater airspeed without changing the power output of the engine. But pursuit was tardy in the performance race, as we shall see.

RETRACTABLE LANDING GEAR

The use of a retractable undercarriage that would fold into the fuselage or wing root was a relatively old concept, but was slow to gain acceptance. The first retractable gear was probably on the Wiencziers monoplane of 1911, but it was not practicable at the time and virtually all aircraft through World War I had fixed undercarriages.[12]

As speeds began to increase, retractable landing gear began to take hold. The racing aircraft of the 1920s used the device frequently. Successful commercial aircraft like the Boeing *Monomail* incorporated it in 1929, as did the Lockheed *Orion* in 1931. In fact, by 1933, a transport airplane with a fixed gear appeared 'ante-diluvian'.[13]

The reason for slowness in adopting retractable landing gear was the standard one: designers did not appreciate the gains that would outweigh the disadvantages of increased weight and complexity. The art of streamlining was in a fairly rudimentary state in the early 1920s, and engineers did not realize how significantly fixed gear increased drag. In fact, it accounted for 10 to 15 per cent of the total drag of a single-engine aircraft.[14]

As was often the case in the 1920s and 1930s, the military were a step behind the airlines in accepting the new device. In the case of bombardment, this step was a small one. The Boeing YB-9, accepted by the Air Corps in 1933, was the first American bomber to use retractable gear. The Martin B-10, also with retractable gear, was introduced the same year.

Pursuit was slow to follow. The Boeing P-26, which appeared at approximately the same time as the new bombers, was fitted with wheel pants to cover its fixed gear, which was further braced by wire cable. The result was ironic. The skies were filled with transport aircraft and military bombers with retracting undercarriages, while the newest Air Corps fighter, which needed this innovation most, had antiquated wheel pants on fixed gear. Not until 1937 were fighters with retractable gear produced in quantity:

the Seversky P-35 and Curtiss P-36. Once again pursuit was left at a disadvantage by faulty design decisions that did not incorporate the latest innovations already used by bombers with such success.

THE NACA COWL

The use of a cowling over an aircraft engine to cover its irregular contours was desirable to reduce drag. Serious attempts were made in the 1920s to design effective cowls, but problems were encountered with engine cooling.[15] Merely fitting a cowling around air-cooled cylinders disrupted and reduced the air flow to such an extent that effective engine operation was impossible.

A compromise was reached when a partial fairing and spinner were installed on a radial engine that covered the crankcase and propeller hub but left the cylinders exposed to the cooling air stream. An example of this method was Charles Lindbergh's *Spirit of St Louis*, which had such a fairing installed over its Wright Whirlwind engine.[16]

In 1927, engineers of the National Advisory Committee for Aeronautics (NACA) developed a cowl that helped solve the problem of cooling while at the same time streamlining the air flowing over the power plant section. The key to the success of the NACA device was the series of baffles built inside the cowling and around the cylinders, which channeled the air for effective cooling; the air was then directed into the slipstream with minimal disturbance.[17] This was such an important discovery that, in 1929, it won for NACA the Collier Trophy, awarded annually for the greatest aviation achievement in the United States.

At approximately the same time, engineers in Great Britain, led by Hubert Townend, developed a similar device. The Townend Ring utilized the same principle but was not as large or as inclusive as the NACA. Rather, it was a ring that covered the circumference of the cylinder heads but did not extend backwards to the fuselage like the NACA. Not too surprisingly, the Townend Ring was initially favored because it did not seem as radical, and it was felt it would affect the cooling process less seriously.[18] Consequently, although the Townend Ring was not as efficient as the NACA cowl, it was still used for many years. In addition, the NACA cowl was initially rejected by pilots who complained of the poor visibility incurred. Many aviators thought it imperative to see between the cylinders, especially during final approach and landing. In fact, the first US Army airplane fitted with a NACA cowl was involved in a fatal midair collision. The surviving pilot blamed the accident on the poor visibility caused by the new cowl, leaving a strong impression on other Army pilots.[19]

Despite these apparent disadvantages, engineers soon realized that if they truly desired to maximize speed and minimize drag, they would have to utilize the cowl. Its efficiency was unquestioned. As speed doubles drag quadruples, so high speed demands streamlining. The NACA cowl eliminated 50 per cent of the engine drag previously associated with uncowled radial engines, and for a pursuit plane this equates to a 6 to 10 per cent increase in speed.[20] Even commercial aviation recognized the import of the NACA cowl; its installation on the DC-3 saved an estimated five cents per mile.[21] In fact, in 1933 NACA computed the cowl saved both military and commercial aviation nearly $5.3 million per year in fuel, oil and maintenance costs. When a Lockheed Air Express set a speed record in 1929 the pilot wired: 'Record impossible without new cowling. All credit due NACA for painstaking and accurate research and generous policy'.[22] What was most gentlemanly, NACA had not even taken out a patent on its new device.

Although the ultimate advantage lay with the pursuit plane, once again it was late in incorporating the changes. The P-26 with its Townend Ring, to say nothing of its open cockpit, fixed landing gear and braced wing, was not as streamlined at its contemporary, the B-10. The importance of this distinction can be seen on the DC-3 where the streamlining that resulted from the cantilever wings, retractable gear and NACA cowl meant an increase in cruising speed of 50 per cent, without an increase in engine horsepower.[23] To further illustrate, a NACA cowl was fitted to a Curtiss AT-5A in 1928 and, solely as a result of the decreased drag, the top speed was raised from 118 to 137 miles per hour, the equivalent of an extra 83 horsepower. By way of contrast, the Townend Ring when fitted to that airplane gave a boost of only 11 miles per hour.[24]

Although these structural and aerodynamic innovations were important, the real key to better aircraft performance centered on power plant development. Given a powerful enough engine, even a brick can be propelled through the air, but the most advanced airfoil is still but a glider without a motor.

ENGINE DEVELOPMENT

When studying the development of aircraft piston engines one pattern shows itself clearly: the cyclical nature of the supremacy of the radial and the in-line engine. The question of which type is superior had been asked since the Wright Brothers but was never resolved until the advent of the jet engine obviated its importance. The rivalry saw one type gain temporary superiority, forcing the other to produce an innovation that would, in turn, put it back on top temporarily.

The first occurrence of this rivalry was in 1903 after the Wright Brothers' historic flight. The Wrights had used an in-line, water-cooled engine of their own design that developed a minimum amount of power – just enough to keep them airborne for short periods of time. Samuel P. Langley, another early air pioneer, had attempted powered flight the same year but had been unsuccessful. The engine used in his abortive attempt was a water-cooled radial engine of exquisite design. The Langley engine was one of the finest ever built. However, its design was not emulated and the in-line version of the Wrights was used almost exclusively for a number of years thereafter for the pragmatic reason that the Wrights had flown and Langley had not.[25]

As Europe plunged into World War I, a new type of aero engine blazed temporarily across the scene. The rotary engine became very popular in the early years of the war because of its compactness, freedom from vibration, light weight and ease of cooling.[26] Since no engine of any type was very powerful, a premium was placed on light weight and small size. The ascendancy of the rotary was short-lived, however, because of inherent weaknesses that could not be overcome. The unique feature of the rotary was that the entire row of cylinders rotated around a stationary crankshaft. This produced a tremendous amount of torque that tended to rotate the entire aircraft – a problem solved by the strong arm of the pilot. Also, it was difficult to build an engine in which all the parts rotated but the crankshaft. Because of this, an especially heavy price was paid in oil consumption, which the rotary managed to sling out at a rate of up to one-quarter that of the fuel.[27] The chief problem of the rotary, however, lay in its excessive drag. The rotating cylinders caused a great deal of windage loss, about 25 per cent more than if they were stationary as in the simple radial design, and this resulted in reduced speed.[28] Since radial air-cooled engines had severe overheating problems, designers began returning to the water-cooled engine about the middle of World War I. The result was the highly successful design of the Swiss engineer Marc Birkigt, the Hispano-Suiza, used in several French and British aircraft.[29] This engine was so superior it set the standard for many years to come.

The American Liberty engine of World War I fame was also a water-cooled motor patterned after the Hispano-Suiza, only of 400 horsepower.[30] After the war, the Liberty and the Hispano (which was produced in the United States by the Wright Company) were the standard engines used in the USA for several years. The only new development immediately following the war was the Curtiss water-cooled types designed for racing planes. These engines developed into the highly successful D-12 model that gave stiff competition to the Liberty and Hispano and eventually displaced them.

In 1925 an event occurred that had a great effect on the engine industry. Frederick B. Rentschler, vice president of the Wright Aeronautical Corporation, left with several colleagues and joined Pratt & Whitney to establish an aero-engine branch. One of his new engineers was George J. Mead, who felt certain air-cooled radials had a number of inherent advantages that had not been fully exploited, the most important of which was light weight. The dry weight of the air-cooled and water-cooled engine was approximately the same for engines of equal horsepower, but when the weight of the accompanying water, radiator and pipes was included in the water-cooled type, the weight different was sizable. Therefore, with engines of equal power, an airplane with an air-cooled engine would, theoretically, go faster than one with a water-cooled engine. Other factors working to the advantage of air cooling were simplicity, ease of start in cold weather, less torsional vibration, lower cost, ease of maintenance, compactness and, an important consideration for military aircraft, there was less danger of failure due to enemy fire in combat.[31] The result of Mead's effort was the Wasp, one of the most successful engines ever built, which sired a whole series of outstanding aero-motors.

The Navy desired this engine type because it was especially suited for carrier-based airplanes that had to take off in short distances and be small enough to store below decks. Significantly, the Navy did not attempt to develop any liquid engines after 1933, and there were no liquid-cooled aircraft used by the Navy during World War II.[32]

However, liquid cooling made a dramatic comeback in the early 1930s due largely to the influence of the Schneider Trophy Race, international sea plane contests held annually that saw the development of the fastest aircraft in the world. The engines powering these racers could now truly be called liquid-cooled because ethylene glycol (Prestone) was added to the water, resulting in a higher boiling point of the solution, thus allowing less fluid to accomplish the cooling. The reduced frontal area resulting from the decreased size of the radiator was enormous, approximately 50 per cent.[33] This was such a dramatic improvement it immediately put liquid-cooled motors back in competition with air-cooled. After the performance of the British and Italian sea plane racers, the liquid-cooled engine vaulted into ascendancy in Europe. As a result, the Air Corps encouraged various companies to start work on liquid-cooled engines.

This was a momentous decision. There were then no companies in the USA with experience in this area; the manufacturer of the highly successful D-12, Curtiss, had left the arena to concentrate on airframe development. Consequently, the two major firms, Pratt & Whitney and Wright, began development in what was for them a new field. Three other smaller firms, Lycoming, Continental and Allison, also began work on the same problem. Of the five concerns, only Allison was able to develop a successful product. After a few years, both Pratt & Whitney and Wright abandoned their efforts.

There is some question as to whether the engine builders undertook this development on their own initiative, or whether they were pressured into doing so by the Air Corps.[34] Regardless, it was an error. There were simply not enough funds available during the Depression to allow a company to adequately develop two different types of engines. The diversion of energies at the two major engine factories in the United States to liquid-cooled motors meant a corresponding reduction in research on air-cooled types. This situation is particularly ironic because these efforts were fruitless. It should be emphasized that the motives behind this decision were entirely progressive: engineers believed it to be the correct action to ensure technological superiority. Even so, hindsight shows it to have been an unproductive and unfortunate digression.

By the end of World War II, the two types of engines were roughly compatible in performance once again. At this point, jet turbines began to dominate the scene and further development of the piston engine was terminated, leaving only the violent contentions of partisan advocates as to which type was superior.

The importance of engine development to pursuit cannot be overemphasized. For a fighter to be superior to a bomber it must have a light but very powerful engine. The success of a fighter is judged in terms of speed, acceleration, agility and rate of climb. A bomber does not require the same degree of performance in these factors, but must be capable of long range, a heavy payload capacity, durability and reliability. Consequently, if engine performance lagged in the years prior to World War II, it was the pursuit that suffered the most, not bombardment.

CYLINDER DESIGN

Put simply, the cylinder is composed of the barrel in which the piston slides up and down, and a head that rests on top of the barrel and encloses the combustion chamber. The design of the cylinder presented problems because it had to be as light as possible so the overall weight of the engine would be kept to a minimum. Since most engines had anywhere from eight to two dozen or more cylinders this was an important consideration. What made design so difficult, however, was the cylinder also had to be extremely strong and capable of withstanding very high temperatures and pressures.

In 1915, engineers determined that cylinder barrels must be of steel so they would not wear out, but the cylinder heads should be made of aluminum because it was light and had three times the heat conductivity of steel.[35] This arrangement seemed to work fairly well until high-power engines were built at the end of World War I. Increased power resulted in increased heat and pressure. When a cylinder design is scaled up, the heat generated increases by the cube of the enlargement factor, but the surface area and ability to dissipate heat increase only by the square of the enlargement factor. Thus, if cooling is adequate before scaling up, it will be inadequate afterward.[36] This problem was solved by better design of cooling fins on the cylinder heads. These fins exposed more surface to the airstream, which cooled the heads at a more efficient and rapid rate.[37] Even so, cooling was a challenge for the technicians and, as noted earlier, water-cooled engines became popular at this time partly because of it.

Metallurgical advances also played a part. New types of aluminum alloys were developed that could withstand greater heat and dissipate it at a faster rate. These refinements were so effective, the pressure within the cylinders was doubled by the end of World War II without causing any further difficulties in cylinder cooling.[38] By then, air-cooled cylinders were just as efficient in heat dissipation as liquid-cooled cylinders.

The importance of cylinder-head development should be stressed. As the power of engines increased, the heat generated within the engine increased also. Until a method was found to modify cylinder heads so they could withstand the additional heat and stress, the amount of power generated was restricted. Pursuit needed bigger engines. Until cylinder design improved, high-powered engines were not practical. But as engines improved due to better cylinder design, they required better fuel to run them.

THE IMPACT OF HIGH OCTANE GASOLINE

One of the most important breakthroughs made in high-powered aircraft engines was the development of high-performance gasoline. For successful use in internal combustion engines, gasoline must have the highest possible resistance to 'knock' or 'ping' caused by the gasoline in the engine detonating before the introduction of an electrical spark from the spark plug.

As a gas is compressed its temperature rises – much like a bicycle pump tube that becomes hot after a few pumps. If a poor grade of gasoline is used – one with a low 'knock rating' – this heating tendency may be enough to explode the mixture. This is extremely harmful to an engine because of the tremendous stress it puts on the interior parts. For example, if the piston is on the upstroke when detonation occurs, the detonation will attempt to push the piston back down, while at the same time the crankshaft is attempting to push the piston up. If detonation is allowed to continue it may blow the engine apart; at the very least it will cause severe overheating. Therefore, a gasoline with a high resistance to detonation is a necessity.

Basically, the internal combustion engine is an air pump. The power generated by this pump is proportional to the amount of air it can induct, mix with gasoline and explode. The more air pumped, the more power the engine will develop. Probably the easiest way to increase the amount of air is to enlarge the size of the cylinders. However, there is a limit to engine size before weight and bulk make in impractical for airplane use. The other obvious solution is to take in the same amount of air, but then to compress it more than before so its kinetic energy rises – a process called supercharging. When this super-compressed air is combined with fuel and ignited, it gives a corresponding increase in power. The difficulty with this solution is the increased danger of premature detonation. This condition limited the compression ratio of early engines. With the conventional automobile gasoline used up to the mid-1920s, the highest compression ratio obtainable was about 5.5:1. The problem was to improve the quality of gasoline so this ratio could be raised to 7:1 or higher before detonation occurred.[39]

Earliest work in this field was done during World War I by Harry R. Ricardo and Charles F. Kettering.[40] They discovered that some chemicals significantly improved gasoline's knock qualities. Tetraethyl lead (TEL) offered the best and most practical means of improving gasoline. Although the increased performance the new gasoline presented was enticing, the price was prohibitive. In 1930, the Army contracted for 100-octane gasoline – the minimum quality used by US pursuit planes during World War II – at a cost of $30 per gallon. In 1933 it was down to $4 per gallon and by 1935 had declined further to $2 as high-octane gasoline became necessary to keep pace with engine development in other countries. It was not until just prior to the outbreak of the war, however, that the price of 100-octane gasoline was reduced to a reasonable amount – about 13 cents per gallon.[41]

The airlines were even more dilatory than the military in adopting leaded gasoline, because they considered it an unnecessary luxury. The standard airliners of the 1920s were not designed to make use of the higher compression ratios the TEL allowed.[42] Just as in an automobile, it is wasteful to use a higher grade of gasoline than the engine is capable of using efficiently. To truly realize the benefits the high-grade fuel offered, the airlines would have had to replace old engines with newer models – an expensive proposition. Not until the early 1930s were engines on the new DC-2 and Boeing 247 designed to use these new fuels. Even then, the higher-performance gasoline was used only for takeoff and climb; once leveled off at cruise altitude, the pilot switched to a different fuel tank and used less expensive gasoline.[43] In 1944, the airlines were still using only 90-octane gasoline, while the military were using at least 115-octane.[44]

Because the airlines would not use the higher-octane gasoline, military aircraft were its only consumers, and since it was required in such limited quantities, the price was high. There was little incentive to build a high-powered engine with a large compression ratio if few would be willing to operate it because of the excessively high price of gasoline. If this gasoline had come into standard use sooner, engine development would have been given a significant boost.

As it was, the new fuel had an enormous impact. In 1937, George Mead declared: 'The improvement in fuels has without doubt been the greatest single aid in bettering engine performance during the past 10 years'. Similarly, noted engineer S. D. Heron maintained that high-octane fuels had doubled the power of engines of a given size.[45] To give one example: the Rolls-Royce Merlin II engine in 1939 used 87-octane gasoline and developed 1,030 hp. In 1942, the same engine was run with 100-octane gasoline and the compression ratio was increased to take advantage of the higher-performance fuel – the Merlin II now developed 1,440 hp.[46]

In summary, there was not a single viable liquid-cooled engine produced in the United States during the decade of the 1930s. In fact, this inactivity lasted from the demise of the Curtiss D-12, about 1927, until the war in Europe had already begun and the Allison engine was available for use in a production aircraft, the P-40. During those intervening years, the air-cooled radial reigned supreme in the United States. In no other major nation was this the case. However, the dearth of liquid-cooled engines was not necessarily condemnable. American air-cooled radials were the best in the world and powered not only all Navy aircraft but also numerous Army planes. As noted earlier, the relative merits and advantages of the two types have been an oft-debated issue. However, the question of which type was superior is not only unanswerable but also irrelevant. It was not essential that both types of engine be developed simultaneously, especially if such a policy retarded the overall development of one or both types. That is what happened in the United States.

Pratt & Whitney and Wright Aeronautical were the two major engine firms in the United States during the 1930s; both were building exclusively air-cooled engines. For reasons that are unclear, both attempted to build liquid-

cooled engines and did so in earnest. Since the companies were not able to
expand facilities because of the Depression, some other function of their
operation had to be reduced. This function was the large, air-cooled radial.[47]
The significance of this diversion of effort can be seen when it is realized
that Pratt & Whitney's new design, the 2,000 hp. Double Wasp, was the
chief victim. The P-47 airframe was simply a scaled-up version of the P-35,
which had been in production since 1937.[48] The delay in producing the P-47
was caused by the non-availability of the engine charted to power it, the
Double Wasp. The melancholy note to this story is that all attempts by Pratt
& Whitney and Wright to build a feasible liquid-cooled engine were fruitless
and the project was finally abandoned, two years too late.

Another important factor was the apathetic attitude of commercial
aviation to the development and improvement of aviation gasoline. As
noted, the airlines were reluctant to exploit this technological breakthrough,
because they could not foresee an economic advantage. Because the airlines
would not back this project, the only remaining customers were the
aeronautical departments of the Army and Navy. Unfortunately, with
scarcity of funds endemic in the service, innovations could not be adopted
in sufficiently large quantities to allow the manufacturer to turn a
reasonable profit, a fact that was a serious deterrent to high-powered engine
development.

CONCLUSION

It has been the purpose here to illustrate the great importance of technology
and design decisions on the development – or non-development – of pursuit
aircraft in the 1920s and 1930s. This effort has resulted in a corresponding
decrease in the value attached to doctrine. It is possible technology played as
large a role as, or perhaps even larger than, that of the doctrine expounded
by many Air Corps leaders in the 1930s.

Pursuit lagged behind in the years prior to World War II also because the
engine and airframe performance necessary to build a superior fighter was
not sufficiently developed or appreciated. The performance and motivation
required to produce a superior bomber were present, however, because the
capabilities required by the bomber were different from those needed in
pursuit. Fighters needed the best speed, the best acceleration, the best rate
of climb and the best ceiling; but the bomber was not dependent on these
qualities for successful mission accomplishment. Consequently, whenever a
decision was made that caused delay in the development of maximum
performance, it retarded pursuit.

An example of this is the situation encountered in the liquid/air power
plant rivalry. The question as to which type is superior is irrelevant because
during the war *both* types were developed into functional engines more than
satisfactory for pursuit aircraft. Unfortunately, this rivalry curtailed work on
air-cooled radials in favor of liquid-cooled engines. This decision – regardless

of who was responsible for it – caused definite retardation of achieving maximum performance.

The case of the P-26 is also instructive. Due to a number of technological miscalculations resulting in poor design choices, the P-26 evolved as a disappointing fighter compared to the bombardment aircraft developed at the same time. All of the innovations holding forth the promise of an exceptional pursuit plane were wasted. If the P-26 had incorporated cantilever wings, retractable landing gear, NACA cowl, enclosed cockpit and been powered by a high-performance engine using high-octane gasoline – all of these innovations were available at the time – it would have been a vastly improved airplane. The failure to adopt new technologies was unfortunate, but the motives behind these choices were based on what appeared as sound, logical computation. Nowhere in these events did doctrine play a significant role.

The second reason for the slow growth of high-performance aircraft concerns the aviation manufacturing industry. It was not a healthy business prior to World War II. The size of the industry was small by US standards, and a large consumer market did not exist; thus, competition was especially fierce. During the crucial years of US aviation development, the country was in the throes of the Great Depression. When scores of businesses were collapsing, expansion was largely illusory and it was considered an accomplishment for a company merely to survive. As the chief executive of United Aircraft later commented, Pratt & Whitney, a United subsidiary, was in constant danger of closing throughout the 1930s, and only the influx of French orders in 1938 saved the company. He added that the entire aircraft industry in 1938 had only 36,000 workers – less than the number employed in the knit hosiery industry.[49] Similarly, Robert Gross of Lockheed hesitated in 1939 when approached about larger aircraft orders. It was not uncommon to lose money on aircraft contracts, but a small loss on a small order could be absorbed. However, a small loss on a large order would be catastrophic.[50] This atmosphere was certainly not conducive to radical innovation and liberal investment. Military aviation presented calculated risks to a manufacturer, dictating caution.

As a result, it was wise for the manufacturer to make his products as competitive as possible to the largest number of prospective buyers. Although the company braving the risks and producing the best or most powerful machine could probably be assured of a military market, its product would probably not be popular to a commercial sector that placed a premium on economy, durability and reliability. Maintenance and material costs were major factors in the airline industry and equipment minimizing these costs was more desirable than what was deemed unnecessarily high performance. The most obvious example of this desire was high-octane gasoline. It was essential to pursuit aircraft, but it was looked upon as a needless luxury by the commercial and private sectors. As a result, the development of high-octane gasoline was limited to the efforts of a very few companies.[51]

The US aviation industry was not receptive to the high level of research and development that pursuit aircraft required. On the other hand, these

same conditions fostered the advance of multi-engine bombardment aircraft
that did not require the same plateaus of performance and that were readily
adaptable to commercial use.

It should also be noted these influences were peculiar to the United States.
The press of war rearmament in Europe caused an acceleration of design. In
Britain, this development centered on the Spitfire and Hurricane, pushed by
the government in 1937 for island defense. In Germany, the experience of
the Spanish Civil War spurred tactical innovation, leading to accelerated
evolution of the highly successful Bf-109. The USA had no such compelling
national threats or experiences that fostered high-performance fighter aircraft
development in the late 1930s, so the forces of the market held sway.

This leads to the conclusion that although doctrine played a significant
role to the detriment of pursuit because of the permeation of bomber
doctrine among Air Corps personnel, the influence of technology and the
decisions made to employ that technology were also of major importance. US
fighters between the World Wars did lag behind in performance relative to
bombers, but the reasons for this are more complex than a simplistic charge
of doctrinal myopia.

NOTES

This chapter is from my Master's thesis an adaptation of which has already been
published under the same title in the *American Aviation Historical Society Journal*,
Spring 1991.

1. Benjamin D. Foulois and C. V. Glines, *From the Wright Brothers to the
   Astronauts* (New York: McGraw-Hill, 1968), 227.
2. Bear in mind, Billy Mitchell's most famous book was titled Winged *Defe*nse, not
   Winged *Offe*nse.
3. N. J. Hoff, 'A Short History of the Development of Airplane Structures',
   American Scientist, July 1946, 370.
4. Lt E. W. Dickman, 'Metal Aircraft Construction', 14 February 1927, Wright-
   Patterson AFB Museum Files (WPMF), 1; G. W. Haddow and Peter M. Grosz,
   The German Giants (London: Putnam, 1962), 75, 93, 102–4; Peter Gray and
   Owen Thetford, *German Aircraft of the First World War* (Garden City, NJ:
   Doubleday, 1970), 430–1; Peter M. Bowers, *Boeing Aircraft Since 1916* (London:
   Putnam), 67.
5. Victor W. Page, *Modern Aircraft* (New York: Norman W. Henley, 1927), 167–8;
   Tre Tryckare, *The Lore of Flight* (Gothenburg: Tryckare & Cagner, 1970), 73.
6. Edward P. Warner, *Technical Development and Its Effect on Air Transportation*
   (York, PA: Maple Press, 1938), 28; Henry Ladd Smith, *Airways: The History of
   Commercial Aviation in the United States* (New York: Knopf, 1947), 332.
7. Gray and Thetford, *German Aircraft*, 154–6; Dickman, 'Metal Aircraft
   Construction', 3; Hoff, 'Airplane Structures', 372. The Junkers J-1, of which
   over 200 were built, was so durable it remained in service in Spain until 1956.
   Theodore von Kármán, *The Wind and Beyond* (Boston, MA: Little, Brown,
   1967), 78.
8. Page, *Modern Aircraft*, 219; David J. Perry, *Aircraft Structures* (New York:

McGraw-Hill, 1950), 181. One author maintains the only reason Britain switched from wood to metal construction was that they were running out of trees. Tryckare, *Lore of Flight*, 73. It should also be noted that in the United States the spruce industry generated during the war for aircraft construction had grown to enormous proportions. There were thousands of acres of trees set aside, five large sawmills, 30 million feet of lumber, four railroads with engines and equipment, automobiles, trucks and even a hotel. It took 28 years to liquidate these war surplus stocks. Maurer Maurer, *Aviation in the US Army, 1919–1939* (Washington, DC: GPO, 1987), 10.

9. Marcus Langley, *Metal Aircraft Construction* (4th edn, London: Pitman and Sons, 1942), 4–5; Benjamin S. Kelsey, *The Dragon's Teeth? The Creation of United States Airpower for World War II* (Washington, DC: Smithsonian Institution, 1982), 22–3.

10. Gray and Thetford, *German Aircraft*, 98–104. In addition, the D.VII and the D.VIII monoplane had wingtip flutter problems. Although this was eventually solved by improved aileron design, many thought the real culprit was the cantilever wing. As a consequence, the concept was slow to gain support among pilots and engineers.

11. Warner, *Technical Development*, 28; H. J. Stieger, 'Cantilever Wings for Modern Aircraft', NACA Technical Memo No. 538, August 1929.

12. Charles H. Gibbs-Smith, *Aviation: An Historical Survey from its Origins to the End of World War II* (London: HMSO, 1970), 193.

13. Warner, *Technical Development*, 22; Joseph P. Juptner, *US Civil Aircraft*, vol. 5 (Fallbrook, CA: Aero Publishers, 1971), 63.

14. 'The Airplane: General Discussion of Materials Used in Aircraft Construction', 1928, WPMF, 51; T. J. Baker, 'Landing Gear: Past, Present and Future', speech given to the Society of Automotive Engineers (SAE), April 11–14, 1949, copy in Air University Library.

15. Robert Schlaifer and S. D. Heron, *The Development of Aircraft Engines and Fuels* (Cambridge, MA: Harvard University Press, 1950), 679; Ronald Miller and David Sawers, *The Technical Development of Modern Aviation* (London: Routledge & Kegan Paul, 1968), 62.

16. Fred E. Weick, 'Drag and Cooling with Various Forms of Cowling for a "Whirlwind" Air-Cooled Engine', NACA Technical Report No. 313, 1929, 171. Of note, the partial cowl used by Lindbergh reduced the engine drag by 23 per cent, but according to the studies done by Weick, a NACA cowl would have reduced it by 60 per cent.

17. Donald H. Wood, 'Design of Cowlings for Air-Cooled Aircraft Engines', *SAE Journal*, December 1941, 581.

18. Schlaifer and Heron, *Aircraft Engines and Fuels*, 679; Miller and Sawers, *Modern Aviation*, 62; Warner, *Technical Development*, 17.

19. Schlaifer and Heron, *Aircraft Engines and Fuels*, 680; John V. Becker, *The High Speed Frontier* (Washington, DC: NASA, 1980), 141.

20. Warner, *Technical Development*, 14; Weick, 'Drag and Cooling', 171; George W. Day, *Frontiers of Flight: The Story of NACA Research* (New York: Knopf, 1948), 114.

21. Warner, *Technical Development*, 14.

22. Memo, 'Economic Value of the National Advisory Committee for Aeronautics', 16 February 1933, John F. Victory papers, US Air Force Academy archives (USAFA), box 59, folder 1.

23. Miller and Sawers, *Modern Aviation*, 48.

24. 'R&D Contributions to Aviation Progress', Joint DOD-NASA-DOT Study,

March 1972, located in WPMF, 111–17. The Martin B-10 was flight-tested with both a Townend Ring and a NACA cowl. With the former, the top speed was 190 mph and the landing speed was 95 mph. With the NACA, however, top speed climbed to 225 mph and the landing speed decreased to a much safer 65 mph. Michael D. Keller, 'A History of the NACA Langley Laboratory, 1917–1947', 203, unpublished study located in the Victory papers, USAFA, box 67. The B-10 was such an outstanding design its builder, Glenn Martin, was awarded the Collier Trophy in 1932.

25. For a detailed discussion of Langley and his engine see Robert B. Meyer, *Langley's Aero-Engine of 1903* (Washington, DC: Smithsonian Institution, 1971).

26. C. Fayette Taylor, *Aircraft Propulsion: A Review of the Evolution of Air Piston Engines* (Washington, DC: Smithsonian Institutions, 1971), 15; S. D. Heron, *History of the Aircraft Piston Engine* (Detroit, MI: Ethyl Corporation, 1961), 6.

27. James M. Laux, 'Gnome et Rhone – An Aviation Engine Firm in the First World War', *Aerospace Historian*, Spring 1980, 19. One engineer noted the rotary operated on pure castor oil – a powerful laxative. As a result, rotary-powered aircraft were liable to make unplanned emergency landings. Herschel Smith, *A History of Aircraft Piston Engines* (Manhattan, KS: Sunflower University Press, 1986), 63.

28. Schlaifer and Heron, *Aircraft Engines and Fuels*, 125.

29. Most notably, the Spad XII and S.E. 5 were powered by Hispanos.

30. The Liberty engine is a story in itself. It was the first engine in the world to surpass the power-to-weight ratio of the 1903 Langley engine. Smith, *Aircraft Piston Engines*, 50. The venerable Liberty powered the first US aircraft to cross the Atlantic, the first to make a nonstop flight across the United States, and the first around-the-world flight. For an excellent description and history of this remarkable motor see Phillip S. Dickey III, *The Liberty Engine, 1918–1942* (Washington, DC: Smithsonian Institution, 1968).

31. Smith, *Aircraft Piston Engines*, 97; L. J. K. Setright, *The Power to Fly* (London: Allen & Unwin, 1971), 171. Water-cooled engines were seen as particularly vulnerable to ground fire because one round through the radiator or water pipe would incapacitate the engine.

32. Setright, *Power to Fly*, 67; E. E. Wilson, 'The Trend of Aircraft Engine Development', *Journal of the Society of Naval Engineers*, February 1926, 137; Kelsey, *Dragon's Teeth?*, 30–5.

33. Schlaifer and Heron, *Aircraft Engines and Fuels*, 667; A. M. Jacobs, 'An Improved Cooling System for Aircraft Engines', November 1929, WPMF, 401. The Supermarine S-6B racing plane, forerunner of the Spitfire, was the most famous of the Schneider Trophy winners. In 1931 it set a world speed record of 379.1 mph. The engine powering the plane was a Rolls-Royce power plant that eventually developed into the legendary Merlin.

34. Schlaifer and Heron say the Air Corps 'requested' Pratt & Whitney to develop liquid engines, *Aircraft Engines and Fuels*, 283. Alexander de Seversky, designer of the P-35, said the Air Corps was 'obsessed' with liquid-cooled engines and insisted he develop them. Alexander P. de Seversky, *Victory Through Airpower* (Garden City, NJ: Doubleday, 1943), 235–7. Noted aircraft designer Grover C. Loening agreed with Seversky's interpretation in a letter to the author, 20 September 1974.

35. Charles Chatfield and C. Fayette Taylor, *The Airplane and Its Engine* (New York: McGraw-Hill, 1928), 104.

36. Smith, *Aircraft Piston Engines*, 4.

37. C. Fayette Taylor, 'The Design of Air-Cooled Cylinders', *Aviation*, June 1925, 634–7.

38. Schlaifer and Heron, *Aircraft Engines and Fuels*, 671.

39. Wilson, 'Aircraft Engine Development', 132; Page, *Modern Aircraft*, 299; 'The Use of Commercial Low-Test Automobile Gasoline in Aviation Engines', Air Service Information Circular No. 216, April 1921, WPMF.

40. Taylor, *Aircraft Propulsion*, 65.

41. Charles G. Forbes, *Aviation Gasoline Production and Control*, Army Air Forces Historical Study No. 65, 1947, 3; Schlaifer and Heron, *Aircraft Engines and Fuels*, 605; Setright, *Power to Fly*, 202; E. R. Irvin, 'Aviation Gasoline', Air Corps Information Circular No. 660, 25 August 1931, WPMF, 2.

42. Earle A. Ryder, 'Valuation of Better Fuels', *SAE Journal*, August 1945, 441.

43. Setright, *Power to Fly*, 200; Miller and Sawers, *Modern Aviation*, 99; Smith, *Aircraft Piston Engines*, 120.

44. Miller and Sawers, *Modern Aviation*, 95.

45. George J. Mead, 'Aircraft Power Plant Trends', *SAE Journal*, October 1937, 462; Schlaifer and Heron, *Aircraft Engines and Fuels*, 558.

46. Setright, *Power to Fly*, 197.

47. United Aircraft Corporation, *The Pratt & Whitney Story* (Hartford, CT: United Aircraft Corp, 1950), 116.

48. The P-47 was much larger than the P-35, but both are of the same basic shape. The real difference was in the engines of the aircraft. The P-35 was powered by a Pratt & Whitney R-1830 that developed 1,050 hp; the P-47 by a Pratt & Whitney R-2800 that developed 2,000 hp. Gordon Swanborough and Peter M. Bowers, *United States Military Aircraft Since 1908* (London: Putnam, 1963), 454, 461, 477.

49. William P. Gwinn, 'Technology – The Key to Survival', *Aerospace Historian*, March 1975, 36–7. I. B. Holley, Jr. phrased it succinctly: 'After the long drought of the Depression years, however, most aircraft firms in the postwar years were reluctant to expand for fear of excess capacity, which threatened to impose crippling overhead costs when there were no more high-volume orders'. I. B. Holley, Jr., 'A Detroit Dream of Mass-Produced Fighter Aircraft: The XP-75 Fiasco', *Technology & Culture*, 28 (July 1987), 579.

50. Kelsey, *Dragon's Teeth?*, 15. Gross went on to state that if he made large profits, he would probably be investigated by Congress.

51. This was especially true after the Vinson-Trammel Act of 1934 which placed strict limits on the profits a company could enjoy from a military contract. Elsbeth E. Freudenthal, 'The Aviation Business in the 1930s', in F. R. Simonson (ed.) *The History of the American Aircraft Industry: An Anthology* (Cambridge, MA: MIT Press, 1968), 102.

6

Clipping the Bomber's Wings: The Geneva Disarmament Conference and the Royal Air Force, 1932–34

While in the Public Record Office, London, researching the doctrine of the RAF, I stumbled upon a number of large files dealing with disarmament. Not overly informed on the subject, I began picking through the files to get an idea of their content and scope. I was amazed to discover how serious an issue that disarmament had been during the interwar period. More specifically, I was stunned to come across proposals put forth by the British government at the Geneva Disarmament Conference of 1932–34 to abolish all aerial bombing. The RAF vigorously protested the actions of its government to no avail. For various reasons, the disarmament conference, and the entire peace movement in general, collapsed by 1935, and Europe instead began rearming for the next war, soon to come.

The more I dug, the more I began to see similarities with the recent past and indeed the present. People and governments then as now hungered for peace and relief from onerous defense expenditures. Reality, and an ever-changing and often hostile world, often intrude on such dreams. The debate of whether arms cause war or their lack of them invites it is as relevant today as it was 75 years ago.

'When the dogs of modern war are unleashed, it is too late to muzzle them; if one pack starts muzzled, it will be eaten by the others.'
Lord Thomson, 1928

The decade following World War I is generally seen as the most trying time in the history of the Royal Air Force (RAF). Rapid demobilization cut the most powerful air arm in the world back to a skeleton organization of two dozen squadrons barely able to maintain a semblance of proficiency, much less serve as an effective fighting force in a major war. Created as a separate service during the crisis atmosphere generated by German air attacks in the Great War, the RAF seemed destined for disbandment as soon as peace had been attained. Due to the financial straits the British government found itself in after the war, and confronted by an army and navy that objected to the very existence of the RAF, the air service was in a parlous position. But Air

Chief Marshal (ACM) Sir Hugh Trenchard, the RAF's Chief of the Air Staff (CAS), devised a mission of 'imperial policing' in which aircraft were used in the colonies to maintain order. Aircraft were quite successful in this role, while also being remarkably cost-effective compared to ground forces, the traditional method of imperial control.[1] Although not a glorious mission, imperial policing kept the RAF alive, allowing it to develop an organization, a tradition and a doctrine which were to become essential in World War II.

In truth, imperial policing only saved the RAF for the first postwar decade. In the 1930s, an even greater threat than the British Army, Royal Navy and government budget cutters appeared to threaten the existence of the fledgling air service. Between 1932 and 1934 a disarmament conference was held in Geneva under the auspices of the League of Nations. The major powers wanted to reduce tensions and armaments, hoping thereby to increase their security. Although all weapons, as well as military personnel, were slated for cuts, the representatives at Geneva took a special interest in air power. Serious attempts were made to prohibit aerial bombing and, indeed, to outlaw military aircraft altogether. Great Britain was in the forefront of this movement. Although the RAF protested angrily and vociferously, the British Foreign Office nonetheless submitted a series of proposals during the Geneva Conference that, if ratified and carried out by the participants, would have meant the end of the RAF. This chapter will detail the air disarmament offers put forward at Geneva and the RAF's attempts to deflect them. In the end, despite the logic and coherency of the airmen, they came within a hair of losing. And it was not the clarity or common sense of their arguments that saved them.

Article VIII of the Versailles Treaty stated: 'The Members of the League recognise that the maintenance of peace requires the reduction of national armaments to the lowest point consistent with national safety, and the enforcement by common action of international obligations'.[2] The victorious Allies failed to live up to this disarmament provision. Instead, they continued to maintain sizable military capabilities, while at the same time keeping Germany in a position of military inferiority, which, in turn, meant she was incapable of forcibly protesting against any of Versailles's terms. Although disarmament conferences were held in 1921, 1927 and again in 1930, they dealt mainly with naval matters – an issue of relatively minor concern to Germany.[3] The Kellogg-Briand Pact of 1928, which renounced war as an instrument of policy, certainly sounded noble but it had no enforcement mechanism.

As time wore on, the lack of progress increasingly began to chafe on the Germans. Typically, for example, in a burst of goodwill occasioned by the signing of the Locarno Pact in 1925 fixing the western borders of Germany, the League of Nations established a Preparatory Commission for the disarmament conference, which would finally fulfill the dictates of the peace treaty. Its charter was to draw up an agenda. Unfortunately, because there were 59 countries involved, progress was slow. After seven years it appeared that the only thing that could be agreed upon was that Germany must remain disarmed. That is, although the other powers would *discuss* their own disarmament, they insisted the strictures of Versailles be maintained. Germany was outraged, so this was hardly an auspicious beginning. In effect, although the Allies set up a democratic government in Weimar, they continued to treat it with hostility and fear. This treatment played into the hands of German extremists on both the right and left, who criticized those in power as toadies and weaklings. Had the Allies granted concessions to Germany – perhaps had they merely lived up to the terms of Versailles – the moderates would have been strengthened and thus better able to withstand the assaults of the extremists.[4] The world could have been far different.

Sympathy for Germany was in short supply in Europe, however, especially in France. Sharing a border with Germany that had been breached twice in the past half-century, France was not in a trusting mood. French fear, which resulted in an inflexible policy that emphasized France's own strength coupled with German weakness, and ensured by a European security system directed against Germany, only exacerbated tensions. These tensions rose further when, in March 1931, the Germans and Austrians announced plans to form a Customs Union. The Allies, especially the French, were quick to condemn this move as a violation of the Versailles Treaty which forbade union between the two countries. Germany was forced to back down and retract its plans, causing further resentment. Worse, the Great Depression was having a severe impact on Germany – already burdened with reparations payments – and by early 1931 it had five million unemployed. Ominously, in the elections of April 1932 the Nazis gained in strength.

There were other concerns felt by the various European powers. Britain was truly shocked and fearful of the air weapon. The 'bolt from the blue' was the term usually used to describe a surprise air attack on Britain. Hundreds of aircraft carrying thousands of tons of bombs would lay waste the major urban centers of the country, especially London itself. This type of fear was prevalent virtually worldwide – Billy Mitchell in the United States and Giulio Douhet in Italy expressed similar sentiments. But this fear was particularly strong in England. For centuries, the island had been secure behind its watery borders guarded by the invincible fleet. The airplane stripped away that aegis, and for the first time since the eleventh century the country was at the mercy of an invader – from the sky. This sense of violation was particularly powerful to a people who had felt secure for so very long.

The fear that gripped the British population and its leaders during the interwar period was partly due, ironically, to the airmen themselves. The exaggerated hype with which they speculated on the horrible nature of future airwar boomeranged on them. The public was regaled with stories of how cities would be gassed and burned, with millions of people fleeing in panic to the countryside:

> There will be undisciplined flight from London, disintegrating to the
> public transport facilities, and dislocating to the food supply...Large

sections of this self-evacuated population will be soon existing in a state of semi-starvation, and lawlessness will add its quota to the upheaval. Of those who remain, either by choice or constraint, some will have their sanity strained to the limit. Others will cower in the assigned shelters . . . One cannot fly from flying![5]

When asked how a country could defend itself against such an onslaught, airmen offered little comfort. The best defense was a good offense; stopping an enemy air attack was virtually impossible, so the only hope was to bomb the enemy worse than he was bombing you. Not unnaturally, many began to question the efficacy of a weapon truly that awful.[6] British political leaders were genuinely frightened of air attack, and Geneva was to be their opportunity to eradicate this emerging evil.

In truth, all war was hell, and the traditional methods of warfare were far more deadly than air attacks had been in the Great War. The Royal Navy claimed, not modestly, that 762,736 German civilians had died as a direct result of their naval blockade during and after the Great War.[7] The great killer in the war, however, was artillery which claimed the majority of the ten million soldiers who died in the war.[8] Yet, calls for bans against blockades, embargoes, sieges and artillery barrages were seldom heard. Perhaps it was the newness of the air weapon that so frightened people. Unlike traditional warfare on land and sea, which man had endured for millennia, airwar brought new and different terrors. Moreover, because of its recent appearance it was seen as more capable of being controlled. The genie was not yet completely out of the bottle. As a consequence, discussions regarding the control of air power tended to dominate at Geneva.

In preparation for the Conference, in June 1931 the British Chief of Air Staff, Air Chief Marshal Sir John Salmond, laid out his recommendations regarding air disarmament. He began by noting that the RAF was then only the fifth largest air force in the world (behind France, the Soviet Union, Italy and the United States), and its military aircraft stationed at home (478) were fewer than half the number the French had on the Continent (1,021). He therefore strongly urged the maintenance of parity: either the RAF should build up, or the French should build down. The need for parity was due to several reasons; one was the great vulnerability of London to air attack: 'The capital is to a unique degree the heart, arsenal, and treasury of the Empire . . . one-third of our total national resources are concentrated in and around it. It is an immense target in a dangerously exposed position'. Because the city was a mere 15 minutes flying time from the coast, Britain's air defense had to be ready for immediate action. Unfortunately, time, space and numbers favored France. This imbalance was made worse by Britain's inferior position in civil aviation: 'owing to our climate, the small distances in these islands, and the excellent existing communications',[9] civil aviation did not develop as quickly as it had in other countries – France then had eight times as many civil airliners. Because civil aviation and the aircraft and engine industries that supported it were seen as integral components of air power, Britain's weakness in this area was compelling.

Added to this was the French and Italian advantage regarding their aircraft stationed overseas. Because their colonies were mostly in North Africa, French and Italian aircraft could quickly be returned home in the event of a crisis. RAF aircraft stationed in the Middle East did not have such a capability. Salmond also noted that due to its doctrine for air-power employment, France had far more army cooperation aircraft. Though not technically offensive aircraft, they could easily be so used in an emergency. As a consequence, France's potential superiority in the air was even greater than the numbers indicated. The combination of these factors meant *numerical* parity for Britain was not really *effective* parity. In order to compensate for France's inherent advantages, the RAF needed either a greater number of equal-performance aircraft, or an equal number of aircraft with higher performance. The latter was more desirable and so Salmond strongly resisted any attempts to limit the horsepower on aircraft engines. To do so would lock in a permanent condition of British inferiority in the air.[10] The RAF felt it had already disarmed enough, but if further cuts were necessary it stressed quantitative disarmament in overall numbers of aircraft rather than qualitative (performance) restrictions.

The following month, Salmond wrote another memo noting that the use of a maximum horsepower limit on aircraft engines was not only undesirable from the British point of view, it was also totally impractical. There would simply be no way to verify such a restriction. In addition, the CAS argued against budgetary limits as a basis for disarmament. It was too difficult to validate such criteria but, more importantly, given the unique financial systems, resource bases, accounting methods and acquisition processes of the various powers, it was nearly impossible to compare them with any degree of validity. He wrote almost plaintively, 'in the view of the Air Staff, we have carried unilateral disarmament too far'.[11] Salmond concluded that further disarmament, or even further restrictions on the RAF, would be a great mistake.

The Secretary of State for Air, the Marquis of Londonderry, sounded a similarly cautious note. He stated that there was an almost surreal tone to the speeches emanating from the Preparatory Commission in Geneva. The talk of peace and brotherhood, although edifying, was of concern. It was time to come back to earth and recognize reality. If ever there needed to be an example of such reality, Londonderry referred to the Japanese invasion of Manchuria then taking place, in complete disregard of the League Covenant:

> When a Great Power has made up its mind on a certain course of action, which will involve it in accusations of a breach of the Covenant and of the Kellogg Pact, it is certain that it will not be deterred from its course of action by such a minor matter as a theoretical breach of the Convention.[12]

It would soon be apparent that the rest of the British Cabinet did not share his views.

The Disarmament Conference was formerly convened at League Headquarters in Geneva on 2 February 1932. In a grim omen, reports were then reaching Europe of Japan's vicious attacks on Shanghai. Thus, it seemed the time was especially propitious for serious discussion regarding disarmament. Unfortunately, the Preparatory Commission's draft agenda was vague in the extreme, merely calling for disarmament to levels to be determined by the countries participating – seven years of wrangling had produced little consensus. In response, therefore, a variety of proposals were offered by the major powers to achieve these drawdowns. The French called for strong guarantees from the League to act in common against an aggressor. They hoped to achieve this partly with an international police force under League control, which would control all heavy bombers, submarines and mobile heavy artillery. This demand for collective security was to be their most consistent and insistent demand throughout the Conference.[13] Surprisingly, the French plan never mentioned the word disarmament. The United States' proposal emphasized continued surface fleet tonnage limits, the abolition of submarines and the protection of civilian populations from bombing. Japan wanted a reduction in the weight of battleships and the size of their guns, was ambiguous regarding submarines and called for the abolition of air bombardment. Italy aggressively sought the abolition of all capital ships, submarines, aircraft carriers, tanks, heavy artillery and bombardment aircraft. The Soviet Union echoed the sentiments of Italy. Britain urged the abolition of submarines and conscription, and was willing 'to support any changes which will really contribute to a reduction in armaments'.[14] In an acerbic speech that grated on many of the participants, the German delegate rejected the Preparatory Commission's draft because it did not go far enough in demanding worldwide disarmament as called for by the Versailles Treaty. In truth, other than pious platitudes regarding the goodness of disarmament, the only thing all countries could agree upon was the abolition of chemical and biological warfare, which had already been outlawed by the Geneva Protocol of 1925.

It immediately became clear that despite attempts to speak of them individually or in isolation, all armaments were tied together. One country's air arm tried to compensate for weakness on land or sea – or vice versa. For example, the Italians were weak in sea power, so anticipated that land-based air power could dominate the Mediterranean instead, which would also be significantly cheaper. As a result of such disparate views and goals, it was soon obvious why it had taken seven years for the Preparatory Commission to establish an agenda; and the same arguments were to be re-fought once again. Almost immediately, the Conference became bogged down in technical details over definitions and methods of quantification. One observer later stated that it seemed that several participants were intent on deliberately dragging their feet. Elections were soon to be held in Germany, France and later that year in the United States. All were hesitant to move too quickly pending the results of those elections.[15]

One of the more thorny issues that illustrates these difficulties concerned the question of what were offensive and what were defensive weapons. The British Foreign Minister, Sir John Simon, pushed through a resolution for the technical committees at the Conference 'to select those weapons whose character is the most efficacious against national defence or most threatening to civilians'.[16] This was an unwise move and led the participants into a hopeless morass. Where you stood on this issue definitely depended on where you sat. For example, to Germany the submarine was a defensive weapon used to defend against the British surface fleet, which it viewed as an offensive weapon and agent of a starvation blockade. The British, on the other end of the hunger weapon, saw it differently. To them, the airplane was defensive, but to the Germans it was offensive.[17] The United States argued that its surface fleet was the first line of defense, but the Japanese viewed it as a tool of imperial aggression. The United States also maintained that aircraft carriers, due to the limited carrying capacity of their aircraft and the fact they were the 'most vulnerable' of all surface ships, were inherently defensive; whereas Italy, who possessed no carriers, labeled them offensive.[18] The list goes on. Not surprisingly, after more than three months, the land, sea and air committees concluded that it was impossible to distinguish between offensive and defensive weapons, concluding opaquely: 'all air armaments can be used to some extent for offensive purposes, without prejudice to the question of their defensive uses'.[19] To confuse matters further, the US, UK and French delegations maintained that those air armaments 'most efficacious for offensive purposes were at the same time the most efficacious for defense'.[20]

Although the technical committees were mired in details, an opportunity for agreement presented itself in late April when the principals met in Geneva. US Secretary of State Henry L. Stimson arrived in Geneva and was joined by British Prime Minister Ramsay MacDonald and German Chancellor Heinrich Brüning. The chancellor put a quite moderate proposal on the table: he wanted *Reichswehr* enlistment reduced from 12 years to six (to spur enlistment and also to build a larger pool of trained reservists); an increase in the size of the army from 100,000 to 200,000; 'samples' of weapons denied Germany by Versailles but then possessed by the other nations (tanks, heavy artillery and military aircraft); and although its existing obligations would remain, they would be based on a new convention and not the hated Versailles Treaty.[21] Stimson and MacDonald were amenable, but the French premier, whose concurrence was crucial, had been unable to attend the meeting due to illness and also the climax of his own re-election campaign. Matters would have to wait just a bit. Unfortunately, André Tardieu was defeated at the polls that very week, and the new premier, Edouard Herriot, would not be available for consultations for at least a month. Brüning was forced to return home to Weimar empty-handed. As a consequence of his failure, he was immediately sacked by President von Hindenburg in favor of Franz von Papen, a far less conciliatory and sagacious statesman than Brüning. The moment had passed.[22]

This situation was not entirely to the dislike of the British military, who maintained a tenuous, and temporary, uneasy alliance to impede the talks. Given the severe financial straits during the decade following the Great War, all the services thought they were unprepared for an emergency that might arise and were therefore loath to reduce still further. They were, however, quite willing to abandon their compatriots if they thought it was to their benefit. On 20 October 1931, Salmond recommended a 'drastic limitation' in naval aviation, arguing that due to the high visibility of aircraft carriers they were easy to monitor and verify, thus making them perfect subjects of limitation.[23] Not surprisingly, the Royal Navy was incensed and insisted instead on a buildup of naval air, at the expense of the RAF if necessary.[24] The key proposals put forward early in the Conference came from France, and they were not to the RAF's liking.

For over a year, the French had suggested that bombing be prohibited outside a certain distance from the front lines. The RAF rejected this idea because it assumed the next war would indeed *have* a front line. This implied a static war as on the Western Front in the Great War. If the next war was one of maneuver and fluidity, however, attempting to legislate the exact point where bombs could be dropped and where they could not seemed impossible. Such a prohibition on bombing had important worldwide implications and was seen as totally unworkable for several reasons:

(1) It would render the air defense of Britain most difficult;
(2) It would 'prejudice' the use of bombing in the colonies;
(3) The defense of Iraq against an outside aggressor would be impossible without air power;
(4) Aircraft would be unable to defend overseas possessions, such as Singapore and Aden, from seaborne attack;
(5) It was unreasonable so long as artillery bombardment remained permissible;
(6) 'Real rules' governing the definition of 'military objectives' would be more difficult to formulate; and
(7) There was a far better alternative at hand: simply to forbid the bombing of the civil population.

In addition, a ban on all bombing, which had also been suggested, was virtually unenforceable, especially given the existence of civil aviation. The logical conclusion to such a total ban – that flight itself would have to be denied – was absurd. The airplane was a reality: it could not be wished away.[25] These arguments were to be trotted out time and again by airmen over the next year, but with little result. The RAF's position was not shared by the Foreign Office. Indeed, the hint that the only solution was the abolition of flight – meant as an absurdity by the airmen – was actually contemplated by Simon. In the event, he fell back on the position that the abolition of bombing was both desirable and possible.[26]

Under the influence of Stanley Baldwin, the former prime minister who at the time of the Geneva Conference was Lord President of the Council, the

British government, early in 1932, began serious discussions of a prohibition on all bombing. The RAF, understandably, was appalled, but their fears were soon confirmed. On 13 May, Baldwin met with Hugh Gibson, the chief US delegate, and expressed his concerns. Baldwin murmured that 'he felt the course we were now following was straight toward the destruction of our civilization and something radical had to be done about it unless we were all going down together'. He therefore stated that 'he had in mind some radical proposals, including the total abolition of all military aviation, including pursuit and observation aircraft; an end to subsidies of civil aviation; and the abolition of aircraft carriers'. There was, however, no mention of a collective security pact to allay French concerns – as events would prove, a serious omission. Baldwin wanted the United States to consider his plan.[27] That indeed occurred, but President Herbert Hoover had a plan of his own.

In an attempt to break the impasse that had been in place for several months, and also help his re-election chances, on 22 June President Hoover proposed severe reductions in naval tonnage, and an abolition of tanks, heavy artillery and bombardment aircraft.[28] Although a dramatic offer, Hoover's plan similarly made no mention of a security arrangement that would placate French concerns. As a consequence, it too was doomed to failure.

France's position was increasingly seen as intransigent, especially by the British. Yet, Paris was absolutely sincere in expressing its fear of a German resurgence. After all, Germany's population was nearly twice that of France, and it had a far greater industrial capacity. If its fetters were removed, Germany would quickly outstrip France. The depth of this concern was poignantly summed up by the French premier, Edouard Herriot, in a conversation with the British Foreign Minister on 26 November 1932:

> He felt charged with responsibility for the lives of millions of French people. He had to meet that responsibility and it made him tremble...In 6 hours Germany could be in Paris. Unfortunately, there was no ocean between Germany and France. If given the Atlantic and Pacific, we would see how reasonable he could be.[29]

Clearly, French fears were deep and, as later events would show, justified.

In Britain, Baldwin, Simon, Sir Philip Cunliffe-Lister (Secretary of State for the Colonies), J. H. Thomas (Secretary of State for Dominions Affairs), Sir Maurice Hankey (Secretary of the Cabinet) and the War and Navy Offices were strongly committed to air disarmament. Though opposed by Londonderry and Sir Samuel Hoare (Secretary of State for India), they were lonely voices and the majority had their way. Simon ordinarily attended the Geneva talks but, due to a busy schedule and poor health, he had his Parliamentary Under-secretary, Anthony Eden, fill in for him in mid-1932. Eden was even more determined to limit air armaments than his superior, and in response to Hoover's proposal he delivered, with obvious relish, a White Paper on 7 July 1932, in which the British government called for the prohibition of all bombing 'save within limits to be laid down as precisely as possible by an international convention'. The paper also called for a prohibition against aerial attacks on the population, weight limits on military and naval aircraft, and a reduction in numbers of military and naval aircraft.[30] This was serious business.

The following day, Salmond wrote of his 'deep misgivings' over Eden's proposal. He was especially concerned that a prohibition on bombing, including legitimate military targets, was in the offing, and he saw this as dangerous. If a country is fighting for its survival, 'it is inconceivable that any threatened nation would observe an agreement which has nothing in logic or common sense to recommend it'. He continued that any government that showed scruples about attacking the enemy's armed forces and war material because it was located some arbitrary distance from the front lines 'would be instantly swept from office'. He was convinced bombing would occur in war; therefore, the most logical approach was to concentrate on defining 'military objectives' so as to reduce the danger of civilian suffering. He hastened to add that he was opposed to bombing of the civilian population: 'No military advantage is likely to accrue to a country which employs its bombing aircraft to terrorise rather than to disarm its opponent'. He feared, however, that if there were no rules whatsoever regarding the definition of legitimate targets, in the event of war countries would simply degenerate into a policy of indiscriminate bombing.[31] This was to be a regrettably accurate prediction. In response, Londonderry wrote the CAS that logic was beginning to take a back seat to politics: the government was fearful of becoming diplomatically isolated from the United States, which clearly favored total abolition. He concluded, 'I am bound to say that I think the whole situation is rather a gloomy one'.[32] Things were about to get a shade darker for the airmen.

At a Cabinet meeting the following week, Simon suggested an *unconditional* ban on bombing but Londonderry strongly protested, so the Cabinet agreed to leave the issue for future discussion.[33] Nonetheless, when two weeks later, on 23 July, the Conference went even further and Eduard Beneš of Czechoslovakia (he was also the Rapporteur of the Conference) proposed that *all* aerial bombing be prohibited, the British delegation concurred, 'subject to agreement with regards to means to make observance of this rule effective'.[34]

Londonderry was most exercised over Simon's agreement to the Beneš Resolution. In a pointed memo he stated that because of the limited progress of the Conference, his colleague had unilaterally decided to exceed the directions of the government: 'I feel compelled to point out, first, that the air policy envisaged in this resolution is entirely different from the only air policy which has been specifically approved by the Cabinet'. He went on to state that the departure from specific directives placed the defense of the Empire in 'grave danger'.[35]

British security was absolutely dependent on bombing aircraft, because air defenses could not be assured by fighters alone.[36] Defense of Empire possessions was even more dependent on bombing aircraft due to their effectiveness and efficiency: 'No other country has made such extensive use of air power, and to no other country is air power so essential'. Turning to one of the airmen's pet irritants, he utterly rejected claims of air power's inhumane nature: 'On the contrary, there is overwhelming evidence that it has resulted in saving countless lives, both British and native, which would otherwise have been sacrificed in punitive expeditions and costly tribal wars'. Londonderry viewed with disdain the naive assumption that mere promises were sufficient to ensure security. When war broke out and a country's survival was at stake, there was no possible justification for assuming prior promises of restraint regarding a prohibition on bombing would be observed. Such promises merely gave an 'illusion' of security; it was a 'paper pact'. It was time for the government to face some 'honest realism' or the consequences could prove 'fatal to the safety of this country and the Empire as a whole'.[37] In a letter to his wife, Londonderry summed up the airmen's disgust by noting:

> It is really like a man sitting on the bough of a tree, sawing it off and being surprised that he has fallen on the ground...However, I am quite in a minority here in this pacifist and sentimentalist atmosphere and I feel most out of place discussing these fatuous doctrines every day'.[38]

Londonderry's arguments had little effect on Simon and Baldwin. The Beneš Resolution was agreed by the government. After recovering from the shock of what was in effect a death sentence, the RAF responded by attempting to move back to its earlier and safer position of focusing on quantitative air disarmament and the defining of appropriate military objectives. This approach seemed to offer at least the possibility of being observed in war.[39]

An internal memo expressed the anger and frustration of airmen at the time. It noted that in 1919, the RAF was the strongest air force in the world but it was allowed to disintegrate. And now there were proposals to reduce it to total impotence. Clearly, the RAF had internal as well as external enemies: 'The Foreign Secretary [Simon] is directly responsible for the appalling muddle in which we now find ourselves'. The result of these misguided peace efforts would be war, with 'infinite suffering, loss of life on both sides, and vast expenditure'. Although arguments for parity were always couched publicly in terms of France, she was not the real threat: '*At the stroke of the pen Germany, who is today helpless in the air, will be overwhelmingly our masters, since German civil aviation already far outnumbers our own*'.[40] Though they did not realize it at the time, it was to be this fear of German air dominance, and the coercive power it contained, that so hobbled Britain's leadership at Munich in 1938.

More diplomatic but no less irritated, Londonderry would later write Simon personally and complain that the British delegation at Geneva (read Eden) was deliberately ignoring the directives of the government. Pointedly, the Air Minister stated: 'your subordinates persistently attempt to vary the emphasis of the British declaration in a sense which will tend to commit the

British Government to the policy of the abolition of aerial bombardment or of all air forces and the internationalisation of civil aviation'. Londonderry must have known that Simon concurred with Eden's actions. He therefore concluded with a warning:

> It is impossible for such a situation to continue, and for your time and mine to be occupied in securing that your staff do not misinterpret a perfectly clear and most carefully drafted document. If your people persist and go public, I will as well and that will only cause us all great embarrassment and hurt the cause of disarmament.[41]

Salmond himself was becoming increasingly frustrated with his civilian superiors. As a consequence, when he saw he was getting nowhere with the prime minister or Simon, he went to the French delegate and asked them to oppose the British government's proposal. Prime Minister Ramsay MacDonald got wind of Salmond's outrageous conduct, but rather than sack him, he merely looked the other way and later declined to elevate him to the peerage.[42]

Over the next few months, Londonderry continued to battle with the Cabinet, arguing it was 'quite time an attempt was made to get the temperature down at Geneva into the realm of practical politics'. He could not believe the government was prepared to do something so foolish as to unilaterally disarm even further, in the face of obvious danger. Once again, he called for an attempt to define 'military objectives' more rigorously. Reflecting the unreality deplored by Londonderry, Sir Philip Cunliffe-Lister suggested at one Cabinet meeting that all airline pilots worldwide be required to sign a solemn oath stating that in time of war they would not fly for a military purpose. Admiral Sir Ernle Chatfield seconded the idea, even suggesting that any pilot caught in violation of this oath would be treated as an outlaw and hanged. Londonderry was beside himself; mercifully, the proposal died.[43]

Fortunately for the RAF, the devil of the details was to raise its head once again. The main stumbling block to an agreement on the abolition of aerial bombing concerned the status of civil aviation. It was apparent early on that restraints on military aircraft were meaningless if civil aircraft were allowed to develop unimpeded. It was a small step to go from a large airliner or cargo plane to a military bomber. In time of crisis, a large bombing force could thus be developed virtually overnight by simply nationalizing a country's airline industry. This was especially troubling for Britain given its small airline fleet. Londonderry reminded the Cabinet that if all military aircraft were indeed banned, then civil aircraft would become the measure of power. In an analogy designed to catch their attention, the Air Minister noted that if all warships were scrapped then whoever had the largest merchant fleet would rule the seas – militarily and economically.[44] The same would be true in the air, with disastrous results for Britain. Nonetheless, the government seriously entertained the idea of international control, as did the French. The

Germans, however, were opposed, which was not surprising given the strength of their national airline, Lufthansa – the only air power Germany was permitted by Versailles. To underscore this point, the German Chancellor, General Kurt von Schleicher (von Papen's successor), once asked disingenuously if the internationalization proposal also meant Britain was willing to put its merchant fleet under international control so as to avoid its use during war.[45]

Similarly, the United States, so eager to prohibit bombing, did not support restrictions on civil air. The US delegate, Hugh Gibson, noted that his country's immense size absolutely required a large airline fleet to tie it together. There were over 11,000 privately owned aircraft in the United States – more than in Europe – but fewer than 100 were capable of military use. Thus, he was unmoved by arguments that the civil aviation sector must be constrained lest it be used in war. Sarcastically, he commented that tales of civil aircraft darkening the skies 'to deal death and destruction' were more the province of H. G. Wells and Jules Verne, not sober politicians. The United States would not support *any* restrictions on its civil aviation.[46] The status of civil aviation proved an impossible problem to resolve. This was fortunate for the RAF, because it prevented agreement on the more serious bombing prohibition.

Despite the high-sounding phrases and radical proposals, progress remained elusive. The French remained adamant that any solution had to include guarantees for its security before France would agree to release the Versailles restrictions on Germany. This was unacceptable to Germany, and on 29 August it announced that it was leaving the Conference 'until such time as the other Powers shall accept the principle of her equality of rights'.[47] What Germany wanted was parity with France, but knew that such a demand would be a political bombshell. As a result, Germany used the euphemism of 'equality of rights' throughout the Conference to signify its demand that it be treated not as a conquered nation with no voice in its future, but as an equal great power. This obdurate stance, in turn, merely strengthened the fear and paranoia in Paris. The Conference was rapidly unraveling. And so in early October, the four major powers – France, Britain, the United States and Italy – met and agreed to Germany's demand for equality of status, in return its resumption of talks in Geneva. Germany consented.

In a further attempt to get the talks back on track, on 10 November Stanley Baldwin gave one of his most famous speeches, often quoted regarding air power. Hearkening back to the apocalyptic visions offered by the airmen themselves, Baldwin stated that the bomber will always get through. 'The only defence is offence', he posited, and this meant 'You have to kill more women and children more quickly than the enemy if you want to save yourselves'.[48] Although some have misinterpreted this as advocating such a policy, Baldwin was actually pointing out what he saw as the futility of air warfare. If this was what air power brought to war, then he wanted it abolished altogether. Indeed, that is exactly what Baldwin was calling for.

Salmond was deeply offended by this speech because it implied air power made war on women and children.[49] As noted earlier, airmen believed with much passion, and logic, that air power was crucial in restoring an element of humanity and discrimination to traditional forms of war.

Germany returned in January, but it was to be a temporary reprieve for the disarmament process, because later that same month Adolf Hitler became Chancellor. The German position became more intransigent almost immediately. On 8 February, the War Minister, General Werner von Blomberg, instructed the Foreign Minister, Constantin von Neurath, to oppose 'under all circumstances' an extension of an arms truce. However, it was important that some other country object first, 'since our intention to rearm would thereby be manifested too soon'.[50] To punctuate this outlook, Neurath in turn instructed his chief delegate at Geneva, Rudolf Nadolny, to ensure that the proposal for an extension of the armaments truce failed, but to make it appear it was due to France's refusal to disarm, rather than because of Germany's insistence on rearming.[51] Unaware of German schemes, Britain plowed forward in the hope of keeping the delegates talking at Geneva, if for no other reason than the realization that the end of the Conference would guarantee Germany's rearmament.[52]

Germany was back but, given its mood, it was likely that unless some fairly dramatic proposals were in the offing, it would not be there for long. Britain obliged by suggesting that the air forces of all the powers be reduced to the British level – about 900 front-line aircraft. In addition, all countries would then reduce their air forces by a further one-third. Finally, Britain suggested that military aircraft be reduced to a maximum allowable weight, 'the lowest figure upon which general agreement can be obtained'. There was, however, a catch: 'pending examination of this proposal, Germany would refrain from claiming the right to possess military or naval aircraft'.[53]

Because the other countries were still in disagreement, little progress was made. At a Cabinet meeting on 7 March 1933, Baldwin stated with some passion that he was primarily concerned with the safety of the country, and he saw two great dangers to that safety – aerial bombing and German rearmament. A ban on bombing might forestall German rearmament, especially in the air, and so he was willing to trade the RAF to remove both of his fears.[54] Salmond could see which way this train was headed. Aware that the Prime Minister was anxious for movement and was about to make a personal and dramatic appeal, Salmond beseeched him to reconsider. The CAS once again told his superior that the abolition of bombing aircraft was unwise. It was impossible to defend the country with fighter planes alone: 'the only effective method is by counter-attack'. Salmond understood the intention of a prohibition was to protect Britain from a knock-out blow, but such hopes were illusory. Switching arguments, he then noted the proposed ban would even allow enemy warships to approach the British coast and shell it with impunity, as the RAF would not be allowed to retaliate by bombing them.[55] As usual, his arguments were wasted.

The following week, in a major attempt to break the deadlock, Prime

Minister Ramsay MacDonald traveled to Geneva and, on 16 March 1933, personally proposed further cuts. MacDonald noted that although in principle he would like to see military aviation abolished, he realized that it would be impractical due to the existence of civil aviation. Therefore, he suggested instead maximum limits of military aircraft for each country.[56] Large countries such as France, Italy, Japan, the Soviet Union and the United States would be allowed 500 military planes. Mid-sized countries – Czechoslovakia and Spain – could have 200, and small countries would be allotted 25 to 50. Ominously, Germany was not on his list. In addition, the Prime Minister offered a prohibition on aerial bombing 'except for police purposes in certain outlying areas'.[57] This caveat, inserted to permit the use of aircraft in imperial policing duties, was regarded with raised eyebrows by virtually everyone.

The addition of the qualifying phrase regarding imperial policing was suggested by the Air Ministry but supported, at least initially, by the army. The use of aircraft in the Middle East to maintain order over vast distances had proven not only successful but also extremely economical. The army, who had previously performed such duties and who would again if air policing was banned, did not relish such operations or their expense.[58] Indeed, if one of the avowed purposes of the Conference was to reduce spending on armaments, then air policing was clearly desirable. Nonetheless, Britain found itself in the awkward position of advocating a prohibition on the bombing of its enemies but not of its own subjects. The irony of this position was not lost on the rest of the world. At this point the army and navy switched sides, and, feigning reluctance, announced they supported the abolition of all bombing, even in the colonies, if that was necessary to secure agreement. It was obvious that if such a total ban was indeed promulgated the RAF would disappear, the army cooperation aircraft would return to army control and the Fleet Air Arm would revert to the Admiralty.[59]

The United States supported the MacDonald proposal, but as time wore on it seemed less and less likely of general acceptance. Collective security had still not been addressed, so the French demurred. On 16 May, in an attempt to generate some momentum for the initiative, President Roosevelt wrote an impassioned letter to the heads of state of the major powers. Calling on them to sweep aside 'petty obstacles and petty aims', he suggested doing away with all offensive weapons and agreeing to a worldwide non-aggression pact.[60] Ten days later, the United States followed up with a call for 'a total and unconditional abolition of aerial bombardment'.[61] Of great significance, Roosevelt further noted that the United States would agree to 'consultation' in the event of a breach of Kellogg-Briand. Moreover, he stated that in the event of clear aggression against a League member, the United States would not interfere with economic sanctions if imposed by the League.[62] This was a tentative, but nonetheless real, move away from a strict policy of isolation. Quick to see this significance, Eden wired Simon on 30 May and suggested a total abolition of military and naval aircraft, 'in combination with measures of international co-operation in respect of civil aviation to prevent its use for military purposes'.[63] For the first time, the two Anglo-Saxon powers seemed willing to do more than simply propose disarmament: they might be willing to play a role in some unspecified collective security arrangement. The French, typically, asked for more, countering with a cumbersome and unworkable plan to disarm slowly over an eight-year period, while Germany was to wait for her planes and tanks. Hitler was hardly likely to accept such a scheme and promptly rejected it as more of the same foot-dragging. Once again the RAF was saved by the intransigence of its ally and its adversary.

It was becoming apparent to some air officers that the RAF was being marginalized in government circles. In October 1933, Air Marshal Edgar Ludlow-Hewitt wrote ACM Edward Ellington, who had taken over as CAS in April, that the policy of disagreeing with the government in a strong and vocal manner was getting nowhere. Indeed, it was counter-productive in that the Cabinet was now tending to discount whatever the airmen said. Ludlow-Hewitt summed up the problem: the government believed the British people wanted an agreement above all else and, if it was not achieved, they would elect a different government. It was the nature of things in a democratic society that domestic politics could often drive vital matters of national security. The solution was simply stated but difficult to execute: 'it is time to avoid frontal assaults. We must find a means of getting round the flank'. His suggestion was to take the case to the people and try to convince them of the nature of the danger emanating from air attack and, more importantly, that the antidote to this threat was *not* unilateral disarmament in the air. He concluded by suggesting a letter-writing campaign by air-minded individuals to the newspapers and to key politicians.[64] Such a tactic would not be necessary.

On 14 October 1933, the German delegate claimed that the major powers were continuing to stall on the promises they had made at Versailles, at a number of conferences since then, and indeed, in their promise of the previous December regarding equality of rights. As a result, Germany had no option but to withdraw from the Conference. This time it was for good. To punctuate the decision, Germany withdrew from the League of Nations at the same time.[65]

Although the Conference continued to stumble along, talk of disarmament was rapidly becoming irrelevant as major changes swept Europe. Since the Conference had begun in February 1932, the heads of governments in Germany, France, Italy and the United States had changed hands. In February 1933, Japan, angered at condemnation over its intervention in China, pulled out of the League but remained at the Conference. Its status was obviously ambivalent. In June 1934 the Conference adjourned, permanently.

What had gone wrong? In one prescient post-mortem, Allen Dulles, a member of the US delegation, wrote:

> Up to the present the attempt has been made to settle disarmament as a technical question. This has failed and probably was doomed to failure from the beginning, since from the European angle the disarmament question is linked up with major political and territorial issues'.[66]

In short, Dulles was noting that Europe attempted to treat disarmament as an end in itself; whereas, for example, Germany was demanding the linkage of disarmament – or rather her own promise against rearmament – to a serious modification of the Versailles Treaty. Typically, Winston Churchill, who had been leery of the Conference from the beginning, stated succinctly: 'It is the greatest mistake to mix up disarmament with peace. When you have peace you will have disarmament'.[67]

Throughout the Conference the position of the RAF was an extremely difficult one. Seemingly, there was a conflict between what was best for Britain and what was best for the RAF. British security would certainly have been advanced if all military aircraft were banned and civil aviation was placed under strict international control. On the other hand of course, such a circumstance would have meant the demise of the RAF. How to support the cause of peace while at the same time supporting your service? The solution was neither as foolish nor as duplicitous as some might think. The RAF was absolutely committed to the security of the country. The most appropriate method of ensuring that security was another matter. Banning military aircraft was viewed by the RAF as an impossibility. The Germans had been forbidden an air force by Versailles and had been under close scrutiny since then. Yet, there were subterfuges, both overt and covert. Lufthansa was one of the largest, most modern and most efficient airlines in the world, employing thousands of mechanics and pilots. The German army, though limited to 100,000, had a cadre of airmen constantly assigned to the staff – Field Marshal Hans von Seeckt and his successors knew the ban on an air force would not last forever, and when it was lifted there must be a doctrine and organization for its use.[68] In addition, gliding was a popular sport in Germany, with thousands of participants, and German glider designs were among the best in the world.[69] Covertly, the Germans arranged with the Soviets in the Treaty of Rapallo of 1922 to cooperate in the design and manufacture of military aircraft, the formulation of doctrine for its effective employment, and the joint training of pilots and mechanics. The RAF was aware of all these activities and their significance. Indeed, as early as 1926 there were published newspaper accounts in England which detailed Germany's illicit air rearmament.[70] If Versailles was so easy to sidestep, how could new agreements be any more effective?

If air disarmament was the key to the Conference, then civil aviation was the key to air disarmament. But attempts to limit commercial aviation were futile. This was business and a lucrative one at that. Attempting to restrict this activity would tend to reward the less efficient and well-organized airlines, while punishing those companies that were powerful and growing.[71] Moreover, the bureaucratic and legal obstacles to such a scheme were immense. The argument most frequently advanced by the RAF, however, was that it was impossible to build large passenger and cargo aircraft in such a way as to make them unsuitable for military purposes. Thus Britain, with a relatively small airline structure and base compared to the United States, France, Italy or even Germany, could well find itself at a hopeless disadvantage if indeed it disarmed but at the outbreak of war all other countries nationalized their considerable airline assets.

In short, airmen could argue, with the purest of motives, that British security was dependent on a strong RAF. If, after all, a country violated Kellogg-Briand and the League of Nations Charter in order to go to war, they were hardly likely to hesitate at breaking the ban on the use of aircraft for military purposes.

It would thus seem that, enticing as the thought of de-inventing the airplane was, or even of clipping the bomber's wings, thereby returning to Britain its safe, insular status, more reasoned judgment recognized that such thoughts were pipe dreams. Air power could not be wished away. The dangers it presented to national security had to be addressed and dealt with; hence, the RAF's constant calls for more practical solutions: quantitative disarmament and the definition of military objectives, with rules limiting air power to the attack of such targets.

Given that Britain had only the fifth largest air force in the world and was particularly vulnerable to air attack, British politicians were eager to limit air armaments, thus increasing their security. The popular term used to express this security was parity. But calls for parity were disingenuous: Britain had no intention of building up to her rivals; she wanted them to disarm to her level. That was unlikely.

In retrospect, it is clear that although such a Conference was increasingly necessary, it was, paradoxically, less likely to produce results as time went on. The world's major nations were beset by domestic concerns and needed relief from the pressing costs of defense. Yet, each country also had security agendas that required military strength. Germany wanted equality of treatment with the other powers, but this meant either its own rearmament or the disarmament of its neighbors. Indeed, when the world spoke of disarmament at Geneva, they were really talking about France, for it was France who had the most potent military forces. But the latter was unwilling to disarm and was adamantly opposed to German rearmament unless the other nations – the League in general or more specifically the United States and Britain – would guarantee its security by formal treaty. This position was clearly articulated by André Maginot, the French War Minister, in July 1931:

> If the nations...agree to achieve a form of mutual assistance represented by a coalition of their united strength against all aggressors, we should be the first to accept a reduction of our military forces, nay, more, to reduce them still further. But if this indispensable guarantee is not offered...then we have reached the extreme limit of disarmament'.[72]

The Anglo-Saxon powers were reluctant to extend such open-ended commitments. Baldwin once remarked to the US ambassador that Britain had paid a very dear price in the Great War for having honored a commitment to Belgium. It was now reluctant to make any more such promises.[73] And the United States was not yet ready to emerge from its isolationist shell. Japan, miffed over past slights by the West, was in an uncooperative mood, especially given her own troubles in China. Disarmament was not an option for it at that time. Mussolini's Italy was similarly beginning to flex its muscles, and although its biceps were to prove less robust than advertised, it was certainly not a force to be ignored in the mid-1930s. One country was virtually ignored, the Soviet Union. Its calls for total, worldwide disarmament, coupled with what was seen as a violently aggressive ideology that threatened the entire world, were seen as mere propaganda not to be taken seriously.[74] But its latent strength and the enigma of its intentions increasingly concerned world leaders as the decade wore on.

The entire issue of disarmament was integrally tied to the security and tranquility of the mind of Europe as a whole. One demanded the other, but which should come first? Simon and other doves were so sincerely devoted to the chimera of peace they were willing to accept its form over its substance – a Kellogg–Briand Pact was a declaration of intent, as was the League Charter. Never mind that the powers continued military operations in their colonies and that Japan invaded China and the League did nothing. The powers *said* they wanted peace and that was good enough. When reading through the diplomatic correspondence between Geneva and London it appears that a search for an agreement, any agreement, had become an end in itself. The British wanted something in writing to show for their efforts, regardless of how viable such a document would be.

When it came to the Geneva talks, the powers realized this was probably the last chance for a lasting peace – at least one that was legislated. Hence, the tenacity with which the Conference was pursued and proposals tendered. A peace built upon mutual strength – as existed in Europe after World War II – was seldom imagined *before* World War II. Disarmament, especially in the form of a blanket condemnation and prohibition of aviation in general and bombardment in particular, was seen as a symbol of the desire for peace. The plans were unworkable and to modern observers seem almost reckless in their naiveté. Did they truly expect that countries would build aircraft, perhaps even military 'defensive' aircraft, but when war came and their survival was at stake they would refrain from using them? Apparently so.

We tend to see the 1920s as the time of greatest danger to the RAF as an institution, but the decade following was no easier. In the 1920s, the RAF was saved by the air control mission; in the 1930s it was saved by Adolf Hitler and Japanese aggression. The threat to the institutional survival of the RAF was real. Although it is easy to look back in hindsight and believe that the arms race leading up to World War II was inevitable, it certainly did not seem so at the time. There were several instances during the Conference when consensus indeed appeared to be coalescing around proposals to outlaw military aircraft or at least aerial bombardment. It was one of the ironies of the situation that the government of Heinrich Brüning gave way to the right and Franz von Papen, followed by Schleicher. While, at the same time, the conservative government of France's André Tardieu yielded to a more conciliatory Edouard Herriot. Had both of these key countries had moderate governments simultaneously the outcome at Geneva might have been different. Alternatively, if Britain or the United States had been more willing – at the outset of the Conference rather than at its end – to take an active interest in the affairs of the Continent in the form of a mutual security arrangement, that too might have pushed through an agreement. At one point or another during the Conference virtually all the smaller countries, but also the major powers, publicly stated their support for a total ban on aerial bombing. The United States, UK, Germany and the Soviets went so far as to call for a ban on *all* military aircraft. Indeed, in a draft text of 22 September 1933, the Conference called for 'the complete abolition of military and naval aircraft, which must be dependent on the effective supervision of civil aviation to prevent its misuse for military purposes'. If such supervision could not be ensured, then all military aircraft would be limited to three tons unladen weight. Significantly, a limit of three tons unladen weight would have meant the abolition of all aircraft larger than a fighter plane.[75]

Within Britain itself, the RAF was all too aware that its survival hung in the balance. Perhaps the most powerful politician in Britain was Stanley Baldwin, and he was committed to disarmament, with an especially pronounced proclivity against air power. Similarly, the Foreign Secretary and his Under Secretary, Simon and Eden, were of like mind on these issues. Indeed, the entire Cabinet, with the exception of Lord Londonderry and Sir Samuel Hoare, were decidedly 'anti-air force'. Moreover, the army and navy had been maneuvering to eliminate the RAF since 1918, and could be counted on to lend their support to all calls for aerial limitations. It is illustrative and typical that the senior British military representative at Geneva, an army general, later sniffed that he would have been more than willing to do away with all aircraft, military and civilian, if that was what it would take to secure an agreement: 'The world was a very good place before aeroplanes came and we got on well enough without them'.[76] Similarly, the US ambassador to Britain reported a conversation with Royal Navy officers in October 1932: 'As a family confidence Admiralty said that their naval studies resulted in conclusion that abolition of aviation bombing would be advantageous to them in all surface ship operations, laughingly admitting that this conclusion was not reached through collaboration with aviation personnel'.[77] Small wonder the airmen believed themselves under siege.

In the event, the disarmament movement collapsed. For the rest of the decade Britain, reluctantly realizing that its weakness was more of an invitation than an insurance, began to rebuild its air strength. It was a slow and painful process but it was done, if only just in time. The RAF was barely ready for war in September 1939, but if its wings had indeed been clipped at Geneva, the efforts would have been futile.

NOTES

This chapter originally appeared under the same title in *War in History*, July 1999.

1. For a good overview of these operations, see David E. Omissi, *Air Power and Colonial Control: The Royal Air Force, 1919–1939* (New York: St Martin's, 1990).
2. Fred L. Israel (ed.), *Major Peace Treaties of Modern History, 1648–1967*, 4 vols (New York: McGraw-Hill, 1967), II, 1277.
3. It should be noted that the 1921 meeting was called by President Warren Harding, the 1927 conference by President Calvin Coolidge, and the 1930 naval conference by Prime Minister Ramsay MacDonald; none was sponsored by the League.
4. The German anger with which she viewed her unequal treatment, and the pressure of public opinion for not being able to rectify this insult, is well summarized in a note to the British Foreign Secretary from the German Foreign Secretary dated 27 July 1931. E. L. Woodward and Rohan Butler (eds), *Documents on British Foreign Policy, 1919–1939*. Second Series, Vol. III, 1931–32 (London: His Majesty's Stationery Office, 1948), 483–6.
5. Air Commodore L. E. O. Charlton, *War From the Air: Past, Present, Future* (London: Thomas Nelson, 1935), 172–3.
6. Samuel Hoare, 'A Note on the Knock-Out Blow', C.P. 44 (32), 25 January 1932, AIR 8/142, Public Records Office (PRO), Kew, Britain. (Hereafter, all documents preceded by AIR or CAB are from the PRO.)
7. A. C. Bell, *A History of the Blockade of Germany, 1914–1918* (London: His Majesty's Stationery Office, 1937), 672. It should also be noted that the blockade was not lifted until after Germany signed the Versailles Treaty in June 1919, seven months after the Armistice. One RAF study noted that the blockade 'in sober truth, killed more men, women and children of the civilian population than are likely to be killed by bombs in any future war'. 'Restriction of Air Warfare', [1934], AIR 8/203. This was an accurate prediction. According to the authoritative US Strategic Bombing Survey commissioned by President Roosevelt, 305,000 German civilians died from air attack in World War II – less than half the number who starved to death as a result of the naval blockade of 1914–19. The United States Strategic Bombing Survey, *Overall Report (European War)*, 30 September 1945, 1.
8. John Terraine, *The Smoke and the Fire: Myths and Anti-Myths of War, 1861–1945* (London: Book Club Associates, 1980), 132.
9. ACM Sir John Salmond, 'The Basis for the Limitation of Air Armaments – Metropolitan and Overseas Quota', D.C. (P) 36 and 37, 8 June 1931, AIR 8/128. Most of the same arguments are repeated in an interesting memo by Arthur Portal to the CAS, 23 January 1933, AIR 8/136. Portal would later be the CAS during most of World War II and would thus have had to live with any limitations agreed at Geneva.
10. Ibid.
11. Memo by CAS to the Cabinet, D.P.C. (31) 11 and 12, 17 July 1931, AIR 8/126.
12. Memo by Secretary of State for Air, 'Convention to Improve the Means of War', 2 January 1932, AIR 8/124.
13. French concerns were fueled by the fact that Japan flagrantly invaded a fellow League member, China, in 1931; yet, the League had not even attempted to impose sanctions on Japan, much less take unified military action against it. Why, therefore, should France expect the League to come to its defense in the event

of German aggression? For the full text of the French address, see *Records of the Conference of the Reduction and Limitation of Armaments. Conference Documents*, 3 vols (Geneva: League of Nations, 1936), I, 113–16.

14. 'The Disarmament Conference', *Royal United Services Institute (RUSI) Journal*, LXXVII (May 1932), 385–91. For the texts of the proposals of the various countries, see *Conference Documents* as follows: Germany (119–22), Italy (123–4), Soviet Union (124–37), United States (139), Japan (143) and UK (144).

15. Maj. Gen. A. C. Temperley, *The Whispering Gallery of Europe* (London: Collins, 1938), 189; *Foreign Relations of the United States (FRUS), 1932, Vol. 1: General* (Washington, DC: Government Printing Office, 1948), 50–1.

16. Temperley, *Whispering Gallery*, 190.

17. Actually, Germany's position was quite consistent. They argued, not illogically, that all weapons denied them by Versailles must, by definition, be offensive. Problem solved. It should be noted that Austria and Hungary – also disarmed after the war – tended to vote with Germany at Geneva.

18. 'The Disarmament Conference', *RUSI Journal*, LXXVII (August 1932), 623–9; memo by CAS, 'The Practicability of Drawing a Distinction between Offensive and Defensive Weapons', 2 September 1931, AIR 8/124. A detailed account of these discussions can be found in *Records of the Conference, Minutes of the Air Commission, February 27th–June 24th, 1932*.

19. *Records of the Conference, Minutes of the Air Commission*, 24.

20. Ibid., 17.

21. Francis P. Walters, *A History of the League of Nations* (London: Oxford University Press, 1952), 506.

22. *FRUS, 1932, I*, 108–12.

23. Memo by CAS, 'The Limitation of Seaborne Air Forces', R.A.I. 4, 20 October 1931, AIR 8/131.

24. Memo by the First Sea Lord, 'Policy in Regard to the Limitation of Naval Armaments', 11 January 1932, AIR 8/135.

25. 'Note by CAS to the French Proposals', August 1931, AIR 8/132; memo by Secretary of State for Air, C.P.183, 3 June 1932, AIR 8/134; memo by CAS [July 1932], AIR 8/149.

26. 'Cabinet Meeting Extract', 12 July 1932, AIR 8/134.

27. *FRUS, 1932, I*, 124.

28. Ibid., 212–14. One observer also noted that Hoover tended to favor Germany over France at Geneva for the pragmatic reason that there was no French vote in the United States; there was, however, a sizable German vote. John W. Wheeler-Bennett, *The Pipe Dream of Peace: The Story of the Collapse of Disarmament* (New York: Morrow, 1935), 208.

29. *FRUS, 1932, I*, 477–80.

30. Woodward and Butler, *British Foreign Policy*, III, 612–13; H. Montgomery Hyde, *British Air Policy Between the Wars, 1918–1939* (London: Heinemann, 1976), 281–2. In his memoirs, Simon unconvincingly attempts to shift the blame for this position on the opposition Labour and Liberal parties, arguing they would not allow rearmament, even if the prime minister had proposed it. Viscount Simon, *Retrospect* (London: Hutchinson, 1952), 179–81. Eden, on the other hand, argues in a somewhat peculiar fashion that Britain was already so weak in the air, further limitations would probably be to her relative advantage. Anthony Eden, *Facing the Dictators* (Boston, MA: Houghton Mifflin, 1962), 33.

31. Letter, Salmond to Londonderry, 8 July 1932, AIR 8/140. It is illustrative of this concern that unrestricted submarine warfare – which had brought the United States into the war in 1917 – was banned by the Washington Naval Treaty of 1922,

of which the United States was a signatory. Nonetheless, on 8 December 1941, the United States ordered just such a submarine campaign to be conducted against Japan. In the blast of war, paper agreements are often the first to fall. J. E. Talbott, 'Weapons Development, War Planning and Policy: The US Navy and the Submarine, 1917–1941', *Naval War College Review*, 37 (May–June 1984), 53–70.

32. Letter, Londonderry to Salmond, 18 July 1932, AIR 8/140.

33. 'Cabinet Meeting Extract', 12 July 1932, AIR 8/134. Simon admitted to the French, US and Italian delegations on 20 June that he personally supported a total prohibition. It appears he had made up his mind and would so vote his conscience at Geneva despite the instructions of his government. Woodward and Butler, *British Foreign Policy*, III, 542.

34. Woodward and Butler, *British Foreign Policy*, III, 613–17. Much to the irritation of the RAF, all nations had an equal vote at Geneva. Small countries with no air forces were more than willing to vote for limitations on air armaments, so the RAF was almost always outvoted in the Air Commission meetings by the likes of Estonia, Finland, Bulgaria and Bolivia.

35. Memo by Lord Londonderry to Cabinet, C.P. 272 (32), 30 July 1932, AIR 8/138.

36. It is useful to note that the concept of the best defense is a good offense is the underpinning of deterrence theory, upon which nuclear strategy in the modern world is based. For the past four decades, the nuclear powers have had virtually no defense against a nuclear attack from intercontinental missiles; they rely on their strong retaliatory forces to deter any such attack.

37. Memo by Lord Londonderry to Cabinet, C.P. 272 (32), 30 July 1932, AIR 8/138.

38. Hyde, *British Air Policy*, 283.

39. An attempt had been made to define the meaning of 'military objectives' at the Hague in 1923. A formula was devised but was so narrow as to be impractical, excluding such targets as rail lines and steel mills. As a consequence, not a single country ratified the convention. Nonetheless, it seemed at least theoretically to be the most promising approach. For the Hague Commission of Jurists see M. W. Royse, *Aerial Bombardment and the International Regulation of Warfare* (New York: Harold Vinal, 1928), ch. 6. Of note, such definitional issues continue to bedevil negotiations. For an excellent and detailed discussion of modern attempts to address the issue of military objectives, see W. Hays Parks, 'Air War and the Law of War', *The Air Force Law Review*, 32 (1990). 1–226.

40. 'First Impression on Sir John Simon's Latest Paper', October 1932, AIR 8/142. (Emphasis in original.) See also memo by Gp Capt J. T. Babington, 'The Interpretation of HMG's Air Policy by the UK Delegation at Geneva', 11 February 1933, AIR 8/150.

41. Letter, Londonderry to Simon, 14 February 1933, AIR 8/157. Of interest, when in early 1934 Sir Robert Vansittart replaced Eden at Geneva, the airmen were delighted. In one humorous letter to the CAS, a staff officer noted that the more Vansittart learned about air power the more supportive he became: 'and in view of the length of the letters he has inflicted upon you it appears that he does not mind paper and is capable of digesting it'. Letter, Bullock to CAS, 15 June 1934, AIR 8/171.

42. John Laffin, *Swifter Than Eagles: A Biography of Marshal of the RAF Sir John Salmond* (Edinburgh: William Blackwood, 1964), 219. Laffin further states, unconvincingly, that Salmond indeed should have received the peerage anyway because his actions saved the RAF.

43. 'Cabinet Meeting Minutes', D.C. (M) (32), 15 September 1932, AIR 8/148; Ministerial Committee for Disarmament, 'Meeting Minutes', 20 February 1933, CAB 27/505.

44. Memo, Londonderry to Cabinet, D.C. (M) (32) 35, 21 February 1933, AIR 8/147. See also, 'The Proposed Abolition of Military and Naval Machines and of Bombing from the Air, and the Control of Civil Aviation', D.C. (M) (32) 37, 24 February 1933, AIR 8/147.
45. E. L. Woodward and Rohan Butler (eds), *Documents on British Foreign Policy, 1919–1939*. Second Series, Vol. IV, 1932–33 (London: His Majesty's Stationery Office, 1950), 243. When discussing civil aviation in the Air Commission, Germany took the interesting position that such matters did not really apply to itself because it had no military air force that could be augmented in time of war by civil airliners. *Records of the Conference, Minutes of the Air Commission*, 28.
46. *Records of the Conference, Series B: Minutes of the General Commission*, 273.
47. 'The Disarmament Conference', *RUSI Journal*, LXXVII (November 1932), 839; Edward W. Bennett, *German Rearmament and the West, 1932–1933* (Princeton, NJ: Princeton University Press, 1979), 53–4, 430.
48. Baldwin quoted in Eugene Emme (ed.), *The Impact of Air Power* (Princeton, NJ: Van Nostrand, 1959), 51–2.
49. Hyde, *British Air Policy*, 285.
50. *Documents on German Foreign Policy, 1918–1945*, Series C, Vol. I: Jan. 30–Oct. 14, 1933 (Washington, DC: Government Printing Office, 1957), 37–8. The armaments truce was a resolution agreed to by League members that they would initiate no steps to 'prejudice the preparation of the Disarmament Convention'. In other words, members would not begin rearmament while conducting the disarmament talks. The resolution was due to expire on 1 March 1933. *Records of the Conference, Conference Documents*, 419.
51. *Documents on German Foreign Policy*, 42–4.
52. Woodward and Butler, *British Foreign Policy*, IV, 513.
53. 'The Disarmament Conference', *RUSI Journal*, LXXVIII (February 1933), 162.
54. 'Cabinet Meeting Notes', 7 March 1933, AIR 8/158.
55. Letter, Salmond to MacDonald, 12 March 1933, AIR 8/149.
56. The senior British military advisor to the Conference, Maj.-Gen. A. C. Temperley, later stated that MacDonald was old and not well. At one point in his speech, the prime minister staggered and began speaking incoherently. MacDonald later admitted he had 'lost consciousness' for 30 seconds or so and had no idea what he had said. Temperley, *Whispering Gallery*, 240.
57. Woodward and Butler, *British Foreign Policy*, IV, 558–65; 'The Disarmament Conference', *RUSI Journal*, LXXVIII (May 1933), 400.
58. 'Cabinet Conclusions', 10 May 1933, AIR 8/159; letter, Londonderry to Simon, 11 May 1933, AIR 8/145. In a somewhat amusing note, ACM Edward Ellington wrote a colleague that 'it is a pity that at times like this there are not some Hindu tribes on the frontier to give trouble'. Presumably that would bring the Cabinet to their senses. Letter, Ellington to Steel, 29 September 1933, AIR 8/145.
59. Ministerial Committee for Disarmament, 'Meeting Minutes', 7 March 1933, CAB 27/505. Actually, a year earlier the Admiralty had already voiced support for a total ban on bombing. 'Measures of Reduction of Armaments which the Admiralty are Proposing as Support at the Disarmament Conference', 1 April 1932, AIR 8/146. This was after Salmond's misguided call to cut the number of aircraft carriers noted above.
60. *FRUS, 1933, I* (1950), 143–5.
61. Ibid., 169.
62. Walters, *League of Nations*, 546–9; *FRUS, 1933, I*, 150–1.
63. E. L. Woodward and Rohan Butler (eds), *Documents on British Foreign Policy,*

1919–1939. Second Series, Vol. V, 1933 (London: Her Majesty's Stationery Office, 1956), 287.

64. Minute, Ludlow-Hewitt to Ellington, 25 October 1933, AIR 8/151. Note: When John Salmond retired, his place as CAS was to be taken by his elder brother, ACM Geoffrey Salmond. However, the latter died only a month later and at that point ACM Edward Ellington was selected to assume the post.

65. *FRUS, 1933, I*, 265.

66. Hugh R. Wilson, *Disarmament and the Cold War in the Thirties* (New York: Vantage, 1963), 40. In fairness to the British Foreign Office, however, it should be noted that the official papers of this period reflect far more interest and concern over the domestic situation in Germany than with the technical details of disarmament. Woodward and Butler, *British Foreign Policy*, IV and V, *passim*.

67. Wilson, *Disarmament and the Cold War*, 52.

68. Edward L. Homze, *Arming the Luftwaffe: The Reich Air Ministry and the German Aircraft Industry, 1919–1939* (Lincoln: Nebraska University Press, 1976), 4–6.

69. For the significance of the glider experience in interwar Germany, see Peter Fritzsche, *A Nation of Fliers: German Aviation and the Popular Imagination* (Cambridge: Cambridge University Press, 1992).

70. Bennett, *German Rearmament*, 79–84; Homze, *Arming the Luftwaffe*, 8-15; James S. Corum, *The Roots of Blitzkrieg: Hans von Seeckt and German Military Reform* (Lawrence: University Press of Kansas, 1992), 159–64; Eden, *Facing the Dictators*, 28; Maj. B. T. Reynolds, 'Germany and Equality in Armaments', *RUSI Journal*, LXXVII (November 1932), 847; Woodward and Butler, *British Foreign Policy*, III, 487; Temperley, *Whispering Gallery*, 221.

71. In an unusual lapse into clarity during the Air Commission meetings, the New Zealand delegate stated blandly that 'from the European point of view, the internationalisation of civil aviation might or might not be workable, but from the world point of view, it was ridiculous'. *Records of the Conference, Minutes of the Air Commission*, 98.

72. John W. Wheeler-Bennett, *Disarmament and Security Since Locarno, 1925–1931* (London: George Allen & Unwin, 1932), 354.

73. *FRUS, 1932, I*, 123.

74. During one speech by Maxim Litvinov calling for total disarmament, worldwide, the audience broke into laughter on several occasions – to be joined by Litvinov himself! Temperley, *Whispering Gallery*, 188.

75. *Records of the Conference, Conference Documents*, 630–2. In fact, aircraft tended to grow in size over the next few years, and by World War II most fighter planes were heavier than three tons.

76. Temperley, *Whispering Gallery*, 271.

77. *FRUS, 1932, I*, 543.

7

Air Power and Joint Operations during World War II

One of the hot topics in contemporary military affairs is 'jointness' – the effective employment of forces from more than one service. Like so many other terms today, jointness has become politically correct. It is a rare officer who dares not to murmur its mantra. Those who speak out against jointness, regardless of the logic or illogic of their arguments, are automatically termed parochial and cast into the darkness. In truth, however, jointness is a good thing for the country and the services – as long as its true meaning is always borne in mind. Real jointness means choosing the right military force for the objectives sought. It is not little-league rules where everyone must play. The need for joint operations became apparent at the beginning of World War II. All of the belligerents were unprepared to conduct such operations, but they were forced to learn quickly. Fortunately, the Allies learned more quickly than did the Axis.

INTRODUCTION

In the military today there are a number of politically correct words and phrases. To cross them or to decry them is risky; a step taken, if at all, only after careful thought. One such minefield is the concept of jointness. We can no longer be parochial about a service; we must be purple. In truth, this is a very good thing. Jointness *is* highly desirable and even essential if we are truly to maximize military effectiveness. That does not mean every operation must consist of equal parts land, sea and air. Nor does it mean we must forget that we are, first and foremost, airmen, soldiers and sailors. I still believe that young officers must learn to be blue or green or brown or white, before they can be purple. But at some point, the broadening must occur.

It was not always the case that jointness was seen as necessary, and certainly not desirable. In centuries past, it was possible to fight wars, with sailors and admirals having virtually no contact with one another. Coordination was only necessary at the highest levels of government. The few times in war that armies and navies had to work together could be dealt with as the situation arose. There was certainly no need to practice bleeding. The words of Field Marshal Bernard Montgomery come to mind: 'A soldier should be sworn to the patient endurance of hardships, like the ancient knights; and it is not the least of these necessary hardships to have to serve with sailors'.

This attitude changed dramatically in World War II; it had to. Not because armies and navies were working together more closely than they had before, although that was part of it; rather, jointness was forced on the services because of air power. The airplane was essential to the conduct of operations on both land and sea – never mind that the airmen foresaw independent air operations occurring as well. Scarce air assets had to be apportioned between air, land and sea commanders. Aircraft could fly from bases on land and attack targets at sea – and vice-versa. The air, and airmen, could not be ignored. As a result, all the services were, by necessity, drawn more closely together. This would not occur overnight, and it would not happen without several missteps along the way.

A key thing to bear in mind regarding joint operations is not that soldiers, sailors and airmen are inherently parochial and self-serving. In fact, that is generally not the case at all, especially in war when the stakes are too high to permit such pettiness. Yet, disagreements and tensions occur nonetheless. The reason for this is that soldiers, sailors and airmen have different views on the nature of war, on battle, on strategy, and on doctrine. To cite one example: the term 'center of gravity' (COG) is used by all the services, but it does not always mean the same thing. To a soldier, a COG is generally the enemy's great strength that must be broken or overcome. Thus, in Clausewitzian terms, the object of an army is to find and destroy the enemy army.[1] To a sailor or airman, however, a COG is not generally seen as the enemy's great strength, but rather is often his great weakness or vulnerability. Thus, if a nation is dependent on its sea lines of communication or its railroad network, then those COGs would be more appropriate targets because they avoid the enemy's strength while instead striking at his point of greatest vulnerability. Obviously, the selection of the enemy's COG will have a profound effect on military strategy. Thus, it is easy to see how differing interpretations of the same term can lead to fundamental differences of opinion between the services. Other such diverse outlooks and perspectives permeate joint operations. My purpose in this chapter is to identify some of these differences and show how they affected the use of air power in joint operations during World War II. I will focus largely on the European theater, but believe the observations drawn also apply to a great extent for all theaters during the war. I will start with the Norwegian campaign in the spring of 1940.

THE NORWEGIAN CAMPAIGN

Britain and France declared war on Germany in September 1939 over Poland, but could do little to help the latter against the German and Soviet onslaught. They were simply unwilling and unable to take the offensive on the Western Front. Instead, they hoped to buy time, build up their forces, gain world public opinion, attract allies from among the neutrals, and use the economic weapons of embargo and blockade to soften the Germans. The Allies believed time was on their side. It soon became apparent, however, that the partnership between Germany and the Soviet Union made such a policy ineffective – neutrals remained cowed, world public opinion was irrelevant, the people in Britain and France were becoming bored by a war that saw no action and the blockade leaked. The French and British, therefore, began to think of other options. The British wanted to mine the River Rhine so as to impede German commerce, but the French feared this would invite retaliation upon their cities and industry, so they refused. Instead, they looked to the peripheries of German power. The Reich was dependent on oil from the Caucasus: perhaps an invasion by the Allies to capture this area would be useful. The major drawback, of course, was that such a plan involved war against the Soviet Union as well as Germany. This, nonetheless, was seriously considered, as was an attempt to assist Finland, which also would have entailed war against the Soviets.[2]

Another, less suicidal, action also looked north. Germany was heavily dependent on the high-quality iron ore of Sweden. This ore, which came largely from the northern area of the country, was then shipped by rail to either Luleå on the Gulf of Bothnia, or through Norway to the ice-free port of Narvik. From there it traveled by freighter south to Germany. In 1937 and 1938, over 40 per cent of all Germany's iron ore imports came from this source.[3] Although Sweden and Norway were declared neutrals, the Allies nonetheless began considering options to deny Germany this iron ore, while also ensuring its use for themselves. Within two weeks of the outbreak of war, the First Lord of the Admiralty, Winston Churchill, suggested mining Norwegian territorial waters – a clear violation of international law – to force German ore freighters into the open sea where they could be met and destroyed by the Royal Navy.[4] As the months passed, this option, and even the thought of occupying parts of Norway, were increasingly considered and then planned, especially because it was feared Germany might act first and simply invade Sweden and Norway to ensure access to the iron ore. On 8 April 1940, therefore, the Royal Navy began laying mines in Norwegian territorial waters.

The Germans were not idle during this period. Indeed, they *were* concerned about their access to Swedish ore and the safety of the Norwegian ports. In February 1940, for example, the Royal Navy had violated the territorial waters of Norway to intercept and capture the German transport *Altmark*. This, along with memories of the Allied starvation blockade of World War I, which killed hundreds of thousands of German civilians, warned Germany that its access to trade with neutrals could not be guaranteed. In addition, Norway would serve as a valuable submarine base for the Reichsmarine as it would outflank the Allied blockade of Germany proper. As a consequence, on 3 March 1940, Hitler ordered detailed plans to be developed to occupy both Denmark and Norway, to protect access to the

Baltic and to ensure the ore lines remained intact. He wanted the Wehrmacht
to move on Norway 'quickly and with force'.[5] After a series of delays, the
invasion of Denmark and Norway was set for 9 April 1940 – coincidentally,
the day following the Allies' mining operation.

Since Napoleonic times, Germany had enjoyed a reputation for meticulous
and effective military planning. The Great German General Staff was the
model for the military staffs of most major powers.[6] Germany was not yet
adept however – nor indeed was anyone else – in the planning of major joint
operations. Nonetheless, things started auspiciously. A small working group
headed by senior officers from the navy, army and air force began drawing
up plans. Almost immediately, however, problems arose over the issue of
command and control. The joint planning group posited a theater command
with one officer having control over all the forces in his theater. This joint
commander would be a soldier. Reichsmarschall Hermann Göring
immediately protested: he would not allow air units to come under the
operational control of any other service. The irony of this situation was that
whereas the navy had studiously ignored all attempts at joint training,
exercises or doctrine formulation during the interwar period, the army and
air force had developed a close and effective relationship.[7] Now, Göring
seemed to disavow such a relationship. During the campaign, the
commanders of air, land and sea forces would receive their orders separately
from Germany.

The German plan called for a series of quick, powerful and wide-ranging
attacks. Denmark would be seized and its two main airfields at Aalborg
would be immediately put to use by the Luftwaffe, ferrying troops and
supplies into Norway and serving as a base for long-range strike aircraft.
(Eventually, nearly 30,000 German troops would be airlifted into Norway by
the Luftwaffe – the first major airlift of the war.) The five major port cities
of Norway would be attacked simultaneously: Oslo, Bergen, Trondheim,
Kristiansand and Narvik, as well as the main airfield at Stavanger. These
attacks would employ most of the German surface fleet, six army divisions
and a paratroop battalion, and approximately 1,000 aircraft – virtually half
the entire airlift capacity of the Luftwaffe.

The plan went off well despite the usual 'unforeseen' problems with bad
weather and despite the unexpectedly determined resistance of some
Norwegian units. By the end of the first day, the situation was under control.
Denmark surrendered, and the five major Norwegian cities fell, as did the
main airfields near Oslo and Stavanger. (Of interest, the first major combat
paratroop drop in history secured the airfield at Stavanger.) German losses,
however, were unexpectedly heavy – two cruisers sunk and another heavily
damaged.[8] Moreover, the Norwegian government failed to surrender and
continued to fight. The next day, Allied help arrived but it would prove to
be too little and too late.

Allied joint planning was similarly in its infant stages. Although a joint
planning group was established in March 1940 to draw up a scheme for a
pre-emptive landing in Norway, it was not effective. For example, it was not

thought that air units would even be necessary for the initial stages of the operation – an incredible oversight. Indeed, one historian has stated that the joint planning staff 'displayed an amateurishness and feebleness which to this day can make the reader alternately blush and shiver'.[9] To make matters worse, relations were strained between the navy and air force over the issue of the Fleet Air Arm (FAA). When the Royal Air Force (RAF) was established in 1918 it was given control over the navy's aviation assets. For the next two decades the Admiralty protested bitterly about this arrangement. In 1937, the British Government returned the FAA to the navy but the matter still rankled.[10] Caught between the warring sides for 20 years, the FAA was an unlucky stepchild that suffered in the crossfire. In 1940, it was armed with obsolete aircraft such as the Swordfish, an open-cockpit biplane, and the Skua, which was totally outclassed by modern fighters.

Like the Germans, the Allies did not institute a joint theater command for Norway, although British doctrine called for such a headquarters. Instead, in the Narvik area Admiral Lord Cork commanded naval forces, and Major General P. J. Mackesy headed the ground troops. Both, however, received orders from London – sometimes contradictory. Moreover, the two men seldom saw eye to eye. Cork, for example, thought the army should assault Narvik forthwith, but Mackesy considered this 'sheer bloody murder' and refused. Instead, he landed 45 miles away on an undefended island and determined to approach Narvik by a systematic land operation, all the while Cork chafing at the 'delay'.[11] Such problems were aggravated when Mackesy established his headquarters on land, while Cork's remained afloat. Mackesy was eventually relieved in the hope joint relations would improve. However, his replacement, Lieutenant General Claude Auchinleck, arrived just in time to make plans for the evacuation of the Allied forces.

To sum up the Allied campaign launched to liberate Norway: the Allies (British, French, Free Poles and Norwegians) formed two task forces – independent of each other – to land and reoccupy Trondheim and Narvik. Trondheim, however, was well within range of Luftwaffe aircraft and Allied operations there were a disaster. Major-General Carton de Wiart signaled London the day following his landing: 'I see little chance of carrying out decisive, or indeed, any operations unless enemy air activity is considerably restricted'.[12] The following day he was even more emphatic: there was 'no alternative to evacuation' unless he could gain air superiority.[13] With its nearest airbase over 600 miles distant, the RAF could not intervene, and the FAA was simply outmatched. Moreover, a consequence of German air superiority was that the Allies were forced to operate in the blind regarding the location and disposition of the enemy. It also became apparent that even if the Allies had been able to recapture Trondheim, they could not have held it in the face of the Luftwaffe. Within a fortnight, the Allies evacuated their forces from central Norway, losing two destroyers to the Luftwaffe in the process.

The situation at Narvik was not quite so dismal for the Allies simply because it was so far north even the Luftwaffe had difficulty covering the area. The RAF, through Herculean efforts, managed to carve three airstrips out of the snow and ice, and deploy some Gladiators and Hurricanes – transported north by aircraft carrier. The German garrison had been re-supplied by sea plane and flying boat; these were driven off by the RAF. As a result, Allied ground forces were able to make some headway. Unfortunately, on 11 May 1940 the Battle of France began and Norway quickly became a sideshow. Before the Allies had even retaken Narvik they were already planning its evacuation. It finally fell on 25 May, but the Allies returned to their ships and departed two weeks later. The Germans quickly moved back in and the Norwegian campaign was over.

Unquestionably, the key observation of the entire campaign was the necessity for air superiority. The RAF's bases were too far distant for it to intervene effectively, and the FAA's outmoded aircraft were of limited utility. As a consequence, the Luftwaffe controlled the air and the Royal Navy could not maintain a presence in the face of that control. The sole exception was at Narvik. This Allied assault was ultimately successful, but only after the RAF had gained local air superiority. As planners phrased it: 'The crux of the Narvik operations would be our ability to establish the necessary anti-aircraft defences and to operate fighters from a shore aerodrome'.[14] This was indeed the case. The Allies hoped that a landing at Narvik would allow them to establish a foothold, build airbases and then use land-based air power to both interdict the ore rail line in Sweden and to gradually push their forces farther south to re-conquer Norway. Such were their long-range plans that went unfulfilled.

It had been a main tenet of naval theorists that one of sea power's great strengths as a strategic weapon was its ability to prevent an enemy from conducting a major amphibious operation. Or, if for various reasons such an operation was successfully initiated, the Royal Navy would be able to strangle it by preventing re-supply to the troops ashore. This Mahanian concept was a serious miscalculation that did not take into account the emerging importance of air power. The British Cabinet initially believed, for example, that sea power would allow them to dispose of the German landing forces 'in a week or two'.[15] Instead, the tone of the campaign was set on the first day when a portion of the British fleet was intercepted far out at sea by the Luftwaffe. Without air cover, one destroyer was sunk and the battleship *Rodney* was damaged. The fleet withdrew and moved north out of range of German aircraft.[16] The Allies hoped that sea superiority would allow them to land in Norway, after which they could seize or establish airbases for defense of the lodgment. This was impossible because the Luftwaffe had already achieved air superiority over the littoral. In short, control of the air determined who would control the surface beneath it.

I should also note here a false lesson regarding air power in this campaign. It did *not* prove that land-based air power was superior to sea-based air power. For two decades the RAF had maintained that for technical reasons of weight and performance, carrier-based aircraft were inherently inferior to land-based aircraft. Although the Luftwaffe did indeed make short work of the FAA's Swordfish and Skuas, the lesson here is simply that modern aircraft are superior to obsolete ones.

There were certainly other aspects of this campaign that bear remembering. For example, modern warfare would be joint warfare. The days when admirals and generals could blithely ignore each other while fighting their separate wars were over. The arrival of air power, necessary for both land and sea operations, helped make joint planning and command an absolute necessity. The lack of jointness – on both sides – manifested itself in numerous ways. There was no unity of command, and conflicting orders were sent to component commanders regarding the same operation. Intelligence was poorly shared, so numbers, quality and location of enemy aircraft, vessels and shore batteries were often unknown to the key parties.[17] Doctrines between the services were seldom compatible, and the lack of joint exercises during peacetime became painfully obvious. This was especially apparent in the poor results gained by naval gunfire in support of troops, and, on the Allied side, close air support of ground forces. In truth, Germany's joint planning, command and control and operations were more effective than those of the Allies. However, it was the Allies who took the lessons of Norway more to heart. They learned more quickly than the Germans. In the future, it would be they who excelled in the area of joint operations.

D-DAY AND THE NORMANDY CAMPAIGN

By 1944 things had changed. The USA and USSR were now British allies and the French had been conquered. Although in true Clausewitzian fashion the US Army Chief of Staff, General George C. Marshall, wanted to strike quickly and directly at the main German force in France, wiser counsel prevailed. Instead, the Allies attacked in North Africa, Sicily and then Italy, all the while gaining experience and confidence for their commanders, staff and troops. But now, the big invasion – Operation Overlord – was coming and it was time to nail down the details.

Although the focus of this chapter was initially intended to be on joint operations, it quickly became apparent that the issue of combined operations – those involving more than one country – was inextricably bound up with it. Allied commands had become combined: General Dwight D. Eisenhower's deputy was Air Chief Marshal Arthur Tedder; his staff was a mix of mainly American and British officers from all the services; and the units he commanded were similarly a mixture of nationalities and services, fighting and working side by side. If joint operations are often problematic, the introduction of the combined factor adds significant layers of complexity. As a result, I have found it necessary to broaden my scope to some extent. Given that future military operations will no doubt increasingly involve coalitions and/or alliances, I think this is a useful expansion.

As was proven over Norway, air superiority is the first priority, not just for an air force, but for the entire joint force. This was clearly recognized by Overlord planners. It is useful to note that Normandy was only one of three landing sites proposed for Overlord. The other two were in the Pas de Calais and Dieppe areas, but they were out of effective range for the aircraft based in England. The planners were not about to repeat the mistake of Norway. As a consequence, an operation was begun, termed Pointblank, the main purpose of which was to defeat the Luftwaffe and achieve air superiority over France. This was easier said than done. The Luftwaffe, well aware of the danger of getting into an attritional battle for command of the sky, simply refused to engage Allied fighters over France. The RAF attempted fighter sweeps to goad the Germans into action, but they were unsuccessful. It therefore became plain that in order to force a fight, Allied bombers would have to attack something that Germany was compelled to defend. In short, the bombers had to be the bait that would lure the Luftwaffe into battle. But that was not enough. The bombers could not protect themselves adequately, as was demonstrated in the fall of 1943.

The arrival of long-range escort fighters, the Thunderbolt and Mustang, along with their jettisonable fuel tanks, put the air battle on the favorable terms desired by the Allies. In February 1944, an unusual string of clear days allowed a maximum effort by RAF Bomber Command and the heavily escorted Eighth and Fifteenth Air Forces. Their main targets were aircraft and engine manufacturing plants, as well as ball-bearing factories. The Luftwaffe rose to the challenge and the results of 'Big Week' were dramatic. The bombers dropped more tonnage in six days than they had in the previous year. Although the Allies lost 426 aircraft – mostly heavy bombers – the Luftwaffe lost nearly 300 fighters in air combat. Moreover, the destruction of the aircraft factories was so great that hundreds more aircraft were damaged or destroyed.[18] Even at the time observers recognized this as a turning point in the air war. Air superiority was achieved, and this permitted not only a more effective strategic bombing campaign but also a landing in Normandy that would enjoy a far better chance of success.

As D-Day approached, the Allies had nearly 13,000 aircraft ready to strike, of which 5,400 were fighters; the Luftwaffe had 300 fighters to defend against them. On the day of the invasion, the Allies flew 10,585 sorties over the beachhead. The Luftwaffe, its back broken three months before, could manage a mere 100 – only two fighters were able to penetrate Allied air defenses to the beach area.[19] The importance of this to the success of the invasion cannot be exaggerated. Field Marshal Erwin Rommel, the German commander in France, said simply that his operations in Normandy were 'tremendously hampered, and in some places even rendered impossible' by the 'immensely powerful, at times overwhelming, superiority of the enemy air force'.[20] General Eisenhower later stated in emphatic terms how crucial air superiority was to Overlord:

> The Normandy Invasion was based on a deep-seated faith in the power of the air force in overwhelming numbers to intervene in the land

battle...Without that air force, without the aid of the enemy air force out of the sky, without its power to intervene in the land battle, that invasion would have been fantastic, it would have been more than fantastic, it would have been criminal.[21]

Air superiority is not, however, an end in itself. Once achieved, it must be exploited, and that speaks to Eisenhower's comment concerning the ability of air power to intervene in the land battle.

AIR INTERDICTION

One of the ways in which air superiority is exploited is through the use of tactical air power in cooperation with ground operations. Such cooperation can take the form of reconnaissance, airlift, artillery spotting, air interdiction or close air support. I will now focus on air interdiction (AI). A great deal has already been written on the subject, but I hope to provide some insight into what makes such joint operations successes or failures.

In a discussion of joint operations, which are inherently contentious, AI is a subject that inspires a special degree of inflammation. Although airmen and soldiers in World War II sought the same ends, they often disagreed over the methods of achieving them. Both wanted to win wars as quickly as possible with the least expenditure in human life. Soldiers, however, saw the ground battle as the decisive event that would achieve the goal of victory; thus, all actions and all weapons should be directed at facilitating victory in battle. Airmen hoped that a ground battle could be avoided. Ideally, strategic bombing would so soften the enemy's will and capability that a ground battle would be secondary. If that were an unrealizable goal, then the isolation of the battlefield via air interdiction would be the next best use of scarce and high-value air assets. If necessary, if the ground battle was already joined, then in certain circumstances aircraft could perform close air support (CAS). However, given the cost of aircraft and their crews, and given their vulnerability while performing CAS, airmen were reluctant to give priority to that mission if organic ground firepower such as field artillery could be used instead. The US Army's 1940 doctrine manual on tactical air operations stated the issue succinctly: 'Support aviation is not employed against objectives which can be effectively engaged by available ground weapons...[and] aviation is poorly suited for direct attacks against small detachments of troops which are well entrenched or disposed'.[22] In fact, CAS was termed a 'phase three operation', meaning that it was third in priority for tactical air assets, behind air superiority and interdiction. Soldiers were not impressed with this line of reasoning.

AI obviously requires close cooperation between air and ground forces. Performed extensively in the Great War, it became one of the fundamental roles of the US Air Service, later Air Corps, in the two decades following the war and was so codified in US Army doctrine. In Britain, then-Wing

Commander John C. Slessor wrote what I believe is the best book on air-power theory prior to World War II, *Air Power and Armies*. Bearing in mind the book is a collection of lectures Slessor gave while an instructor at the Army Staff College, we can see that he deliberately spoke to an audience of soldiers as well as airmen. As a consequence, Slessor posited that an expeditionary joint force had already been deployed to the Continent, as in the Great War, and thus the air and ground units involved must plan together and must fight together. *Air Power and Armies* is therefore a detailed and insightful work that examines how a joint force operates. Slessor discussed command and control, logistics, force structure, intelligence, and targeting. He concluded, as did his US counterparts, that AI is more effective and efficient than close air support, although the latter will be necessary under certain circumstances. He even stated that there were occasions when ground forces should support the air effort – a heretical belief among ground officers at the time.[23]

Prior to World War II, interdiction was a major mission of both the RAF and the Air Corps. Doctrine manuals in both services wrote about it in depth, and many fine airmen devoted their careers to its practice. It should be noted here, contrary to what some may say, that the tactical airmen in Britain and the United States did not suffer for their beliefs. Slessor, for example, went on to become the Chief of Air Staff with the rank of Marshal of the RAF, and Trafford Leigh-Mallory, a fighter pilot and commander of the Allied Expeditionary Air Force for Overlord, was an Air Chief Marshal at the time of his death in 1944. In the United States, George Kenney, later one of the most senior US airmen of World War II, was an attack aviation instructor at the Air Corps Tactical School from 1927 to 1930, and both Hoyt Vandenberg and Nathan Twining, later Air Force chiefs of staff, began their careers as attack pilots.

Unfortunately, US attack aircraft of the early 1930s, like contemporary pursuit aircraft, lagged in performance. In the leapfrog nature of technological development, bombardment aircraft were temporarily in the ascendancy. Aircraft like the B-10 clearly outclassed the P-26 and A-12. By the beginning of the war, however, two-engine light and medium bombers like the A-20, A-26 and B-25 had become standard. These designs proved useful and effective during World War II, but especially against interdiction targets behind the front. In addition, fighter-bombers like the P-47 Thunderbolt and Typhoon were also extremely successful, as subsequent combat would show.

The Allies conducted many AI campaigns during the war. The first was in North Africa. Although the British had been fighting the Germans and Italians there for over a year, it was the Torch invasion in November 1942 that propelled AI into the forefront. The conditions in North Africa were unique and made interdiction efforts there particularly effective. In essence, virtually everything the German forces needed had to come from Europe either by boat or by airplane. Supplies generally traveled by rail to southern Italy where they were ferried by boat across to Sicily. There they were put back on trains and shipped to the island's western ports. Re-embarking by boat, they traveled the 90 or so miles across the Mediterranean to North Africa. This route was heavily mined by the Italians to protect the convoys from the Royal Navy. This, however, made their routes predictable and more vulnerable to air attack. The Northwest African Air Force, under the command of General Carl Spaatz, bombed the African, Sicilian and Italian ports and rail lines incessantly, while also attacking German and Italian convoys en route. The intensity of the bombing in Sicily caused increased use of seaports on the Italian coast, which then shipped goods directly to Africa. This, however, drove the convoys out of mine-protected channels and into open water where the Royal Navy was waiting for them. This highly symbiotic interdiction effort meant that the amount of supplies getting through to the Afrika Korps was less than 50 per cent of that required. The German commander, General Hans von Arnim, stated he needed 69,000 tons of supplies each month to sustain his 350,000 personnel. By April 1943, he was getting less than 30,000 tons.[24] Attempts to re-supply the Afrika Korps by air were largely unsuccessful due to Allied air superiority. When supplies did make it through the Allied gauntlet to Africa, they were then shipped by truck to the front-line units. Given the terrain, these roads and their convoys were easy to detect and hit. In short, the Afrika Korps was seriously constrained by supply shortages caused by Allied air and sea interdiction efforts. On 10 April the Allies intercepted a message stating that a German armored division, out of fuel, had abandoned its equipment and was retreating on foot.[25]

Italy was a totally different story. The weather and terrain were significantly different from that in North Africa and most supplies moved by road and rail. Attempts to interdict traffic and supplies far from the front, with numerous work-arounds and bypasses available, rendered significantly less results than had similar AI efforts in North Africa. Statistics for this operation, regrettably called Strangle, tell an interesting story. Allied intelligence estimated that the Italian transportation network had the capacity to move 100,000 tons daily. Yet, the 19 German divisions in Italy required only 5,500 tons to operate – even less if combat operations were not in progress. Thus, even if Allied air power was able to stop 95 per cent of all traffic – an impressive feat – it still would have been insufficient to strangle the German forces.[26]

Let me also point out some qualifiers. First, the German army traditionally needed less supplies than its Allied counterparts. Therefore, Allied intelligence figures, based on Allied consumption, were too high when assigned to the Germans. Second, the Germans were able to derive supplies locally far more easily than their counterparts in the African desert. As a result, the Germans were not starved for supplies and were able to conduct a very effective defensive ground campaign against the Allied armies.

On the positive side, however, the Allied interdiction campaign placed an enormous additional burden on the German forces. The destruction of rail lines meant work crews to repair them, while also placing a greater burden on motor transport. This, in turn, meant that combat troops could not react as quickly as they would like – their transports and supply personnel were already busy. Offensive operations also suffered because the incessant air attacks meant that more troops and weapons had to be devoted to defending the rail and road lines and their work crews. This *disruption* of German supply lines had more important effects – even if unintended by planners – than the *destruction* of those forces by Allied aircraft, impressive though it was. This was evidenced in May when, after two months of Strangle operations, the Allies launched a ground offensive, Diadem. German forces, for the first time in the Italian campaign, broke quickly and fled north. Rome fell one month later.

In Normandy the problem was of a different nature. German defenses were so strong that the planning for the landings was long and complex. In a real sense, actions before D-Day would be crucial to the success of the landing itself. Air power, both strategic and tactical, would play a major role – all recognized that – but what precisely that role was to be was the subject of much debate between the services. One of these differences occurred over the issue of targeting: ultimately, the decision made was to use air power as a mighty interdiction force.

When General Dwight Eisenhower asked for ideas on how best to use his overwhelming air assets to further the chances of success for the invasion, two targets presented themselves, oil and rail lines. Both were important targets and were recognized as such by all concerned. But in war, a commander or planner must prioritize, and must do so for the good of the entire joint force. Given limited resources, which of these two target systems was *more* important and *more* likely to harm the Germans? The debate tended to split along national lines. US airmen pushed for attacks on oil, whereas British airmen preferred rail lines – or as they called them, 'transportation targets'. To the Americans, because all aircraft, tanks, trucks and ships ran on petroleum fuel, the destruction of German oil refineries would have a devastating effect on the entire German war machine. The British, on the other hand, pointed to the German and French rail network which supplied the entire Reich, not just the military, with the resources needed to sustain the total war effort. If this transportation network were disrupted, Germany's economy would grind to a halt. Because the airmen could not agree among themselves, they turned to the Supreme Commander, General Eisenhower, for a decision. Eisenhower's rationale was simple and direct. He realized the oil plan would have catastrophic effects on Germany, but he saw these effects as too long-range and time-consuming. The rail plan, on the other hand, would have more immediate results. Moreover, it would have a more direct impact on the invasion itself: if rail lines in France and Germany were cut, it would be difficult for the Wehrmacht to rush reinforcements to the lodgment area. Eisenhower therefore opted for the rail plan, and for the three months prior to the invasion, and indeed for nearly three months afterwards, the rapidly growing weight of Allied air power was directed primarily at the German transport network to ensure the success of the invasion.[27]

The results of the air interdiction campaign were dramatic. By D-Day every bridge across the Seine had been dropped. Over 50 rail centers in France were destroyed, resulting in rail traffic in France declining by 60 per cent between 1 March and D-Day. In the crucial northern region it dropped by 75 per cent. Nearly 3,000 locomotive engines were destroyed, 33 per cent of the total, with a further 2,300 damaged and out of use because the facilities needed to repair them had also been destroyed by air. To make matters worse, Germany did not have the motor transport in France to compensate for the loss of so many trains and rail centers.[28] This disruption translated into severe reinforcement and supply problems for the German defenders. There are several epic tales of German divisions being decimated and delayed en route to the lodgment area, notably Panzer Lehr, 3rd Parachute and 77th Infantry. In fact, plans called for 17 divisions to be moved in to reinforce the defenders in the beachhead area by 18 June; instead, only five made it. Those that did arrive were severely constrained by fuel and ammunition supplies. One of the few bright spots for the Germans, if it can be called that, is that the bridges over the Loire had been deliberately spared. It was feared that attacks on these targets would give away the location of the invasion – the Germans believed, almost until July, that the Normandy landings were a feint and the real attack would fall in the Calais area.[29] These arteries were some of the few that still functioned relatively well in the period around D-Day. Overall, British inspection teams estimated that air attacks destroyed approximately 10,000 vehicles and guns during the campaign in France.[30]

What are the lessons to be learned from these three air interdiction campaigns? First, planners must have realistic objectives. It is virtually impossible to isolate totally a battlefield – something will always get through. As Strangle showed, even if 95 per cent of all supplies are stopped, interdiction is unsuccessful if the remaining 5 per cent is sufficient for enemy needs. At times, destruction may not even be feasible. In such cases the disruption of enemy logistics, causing inefficiency and forcing redundancy, may be the end result of AI. It is then necessary to re-evaluate the interdiction campaign to ensure the disruption caused to the enemy exceeds the effort expended in creating that disruption.

Intelligence on enemy dispositions, supplies, stockpiles, intentions, defensive capabilities and activities is crucial. There were numerous occasions in North Africa, for example, when Ultra intercepts provided the exact sailing time, routes and even specific cargoes of Axis re-supply convoys. On the other hand, not knowing the exact requirements of the German forces in Italy caused planners to underestimate the level of destruction necessary to truly 'strangle' them. Adequate intelligence for AI also includes information not generally thought important for other operations: the weak points of specific route segments or networks, engineering designs of various types of bridges, aqueducts and viaducts, and the volume of traffic along certain rail lines. If the intelligence function is not geared to collect such information, the AI effort will suffer.

Terrain and weather can determine the focus, tactics and results of an AI campaign. In North Africa they favored Allied efforts; in Italy they did not. The narrow channel between Sicily and Cape Bon in Tunisia was an ideal venue for interdiction. All convoys having to traverse that short distance across open water were easy prey to aircraft based in Algeria and Malta; if they ventured outside their mine-protected channels to avoid air attack, they came under the guns of the Royal Navy. On the other hand, the weather in Italy cancelled nearly 50 per cent of the sorties scheduled for Strangle. It is important to note, in this regard, that such weather problems are disproportionately severe to the interdictor. During such periods when aircraft are grounded, the enemy can exert great efforts to move supplies, replenish stockpiles, re-position forces and improve defenses. When the weather breaks, the air interdictors face a far more powerful and rejuvenated enemy. Perhaps even more importantly, it became clear that the inability to conduct AI effectively at night was a serious shortcoming. Until overcome, the enemy would have the 'privileged sanctuary' of the night and could use it to undo much of the damage aircraft had done during the day.

It must be remembered that the enemy is not a static, two-dimensional wire diagram: he is a living organism that responds to various stimuli in a variety of often unpredictable ways. He will react to our moves by defending himself, hiding, camouflaging, building decoys, redoubling his efforts, building workarounds, using substitute materials, possibly panicking, but more likely being devilishly ingenious. It was discovered, for example, that German work crews quickly repaired the rail damage caused by aircraft in as little as four hours.[31] Thus, AI cannot be an event, it must be a process. Persistence is essential. We must continually adjust, just as the enemy is adjusting to us.

Related to intelligence requirements, but important enough to be listed separately, is the need for effective analysis. How do we know if our efforts are successful? Destroying bridges is irrelevant if their destruction does not result in an appreciable reduction in the flow of supplies. As noted, dropping the bridges over the Seine was useful, but the maximum benefits would have been gained by destroying those over the Loire as well.

Air, ground and sea forces must understand each other's strengths, weaknesses and methods. Soldiers, sailors and airmen often have differing views on the nature of strategy and of battle. They often disagree regarding issues of timing and mass. Their intelligence requirements are generally different. Their command and control networks are usually incompatible. These differences are not insurmountable. Joint education, joint training, joint planning and joint staff can resolve most of these issues. The Allies were learning their trade in North Africa: by Normandy they knew their business very well.

Air and ground operations must be made symbiotic. Initially, airmen chafed at being considered a 'support' service for the ground; later, soldiers would rebel at the thought that their operations should assist an air effort. Both needed to get over it. There are times when each of the two arms can support or be supported by the other. AI is far more effective, for example, when ground action forces the enemy to move or expend supplies. Strangle was only moderately successful until Diadem was launched. At that point the German supply lines, already stretched thin, broke under the strain. Similarly, the numbers of tanks, trucks and other vehicles destroyed went up dramatically after the landings at Normandy when the Germans attempted to move reinforcements and supplies. This type of cooperation can only be achieved by close working relations. Ideally, the air and ground staff should be collocated, liaisons should be numerous and commanders should attend each other's staff meetings.

Last but not least, air superiority is crucial. The AI mission is an inherently dangerous one. This was especially true for the fighter-bombers that flew 'armed reconnaissance' missions over Europe looking for targets of opportunity. Heavy enemy air activity adds tremendously to this hazard. Moreover, exposure to ground-based air defenses is best minimized. This means that a target should be destroyed on the first attack. If enemy defenses are heavy, they may not only induce losses but they may cause inaccuracy in the attackers. This could necessitate a re-strike, which, in turn, would further increase the risk.

Overall, AI was a success story in North Africa and Europe, but this was only through the dint of thorough planning and hard work. As with many things, lessons learned are perishable. They would need to be relearned in the wars that followed.

Let me make another point on the tactical air power issue. It is commonplace for historians to decry the 'unbalanced nature' of the Air Corps and RAF during the interwar years and to accuse the airmen of slighting the needs of tactical air power in favor of strategic bombing. The argument generally continues that as a result of this distorted emphasis, the United States entered World War II with inadequate tactical aircraft – in both numbers and performance – and inadequate tactical air doctrine. In one account, for example, authors state that in 1935 there were 45 squadrons in the Air Corps and 'the army field headquarters had direct control of only 10 observation squadrons'. They go on to state that 'only 7 [squadrons] were committed to the ground attack mission'. They therefore conclude that the rest of the Army Air Corps had missions related to 'bombing enemy industrial sites or invading fleets or protecting airbases and cities from enemy bombers'.[32]

As Mark Twain once said, there are lies, there are damned lies, and there are statistics. The authors provide no source for their statistics, but the most authoritative reference provides some significant differences. For example, in 1939 there were 57 squadrons in the Air Corps and of those, 29 reported to GHQ Headquarters, 17 more belonged to the overseas commands – Hawaii, Philippines and Panama Canal – 8 were assigned to the various army corps within the United States and 3 more were attached directly to the War Department.[33] In short, because there was no separate air force, *all* of the squadrons in the Air Corps reported directly to army ground commanders. Moreover, to state that the bulk of the Air Corps had missions that directly related to strategic bombing is simply untrue. The army commanders in charge could direct that *none* of these units be used for strategic bombing. Reconnaissance and pursuit, similarly, could and often did perform missions totally unrelated to the strategic offensive. Gaining air superiority was recognized by the army as the first priority of the air arm. This air superiority was necessary to conduct ground operations successfully – not just to protect cities or airbases.

In a related matter, the authors go on to note that the Air Corps budget 'jumped' to 15 per cent of the US army budget in 1935.[34] Once again, there is no source given, but the chief authority for this period notes that this increase occurred in 1937, not 1935 (and it dropped back to 14.1 per cent the following year). More importantly, however, the fact is the Air Corps received only 11.2 per cent, on average, of the army budget during the entire interwar period. Note, this is not one-ninth of the US defense budget, just one-ninth of the army budget, or perhaps 5 per cent of the annual defense budget.[35] This is hardly a flood of money being directed towards army air power. More to the point, what were those meager funds being used for? Certainly not strategic bombers. On 1 September 1939, the Air Corps had a grand total of 26 heavy bombers in their possession. Over the next two years they procured a total of 20,914 aircraft; of these, a mere 374 – or 1.7 per cent – were heavy bombers.[36] At the Air Corps Tactical School (ACTS), the alleged hotbed of radicalism where the air zealots supposedly spun their theories of strategic bombardment to the exclusion of all else, it is important to note that, in 1935, only around half of the curriculum even covered air matters. Fully 47 per cent of the subjects taught at ACTS dealt with sea power, ground operations, intelligence, logistics, administration and the like. Only 18 per cent of the School's curriculum concerned strategic air power.[37]

Unquestionably, airmen placed too great a faith in air power's unique ability to operate at the strategic level of war. The technology of the day was simply unable to fulfill all the promises of the air advocates. But what was the alternative? World War I had been a fearful slugging match – a tactical bloodbath which killed millions. Was it not the duty of planners, of all officers, to seek ways to avoid such carnage in the future? Was it not their duty – is it not still our duty – to find a better answer than simply doing what we did previously?

OBSERVATIONS

What are the overall conclusions from this brief overview of air power in joint operations?

Air Superiority

Air superiority is essential to the success of any major air, land or sea operation. To quote Rommel again: 'Anyone who has to fight, even with the most modern weapons, against an enemy in complete command of the air, fights like a savage against modern European troops, under the same handicaps and with the same chances of success'.[38] This conclusion is so obvious, to all the services, that it scarcely seems necessary to mention it. However, three points need to be raised here. First, although everyone might agree that air superiority is necessary, they may disagree over how it should be achieved. Early in the war, surface officers wanted friendly aircraft overhead, in combat patrols, protecting them from enemy air attacks.[39] This defensive mindset was disputed by most airmen. They believed in taking the war to the enemy – in achieving air superiority over Berlin rather than over London, and over Japan rather than over the Marianas. The ultimate goal – air superiority – was the same for all, but the method of its achievement was significantly different.

Second, air superiority must be continually won, almost on a daily basis. It will be extremely difficult to destroy totally an enemy air force or its defensive capability. There will generally be ebbs and flows. Planners must therefore be ever mindful of the need to continue counter air operations so as to prevent a resurgence in enemy air activity.

Third, and this is an observation that transcends World War II, air superiority has been an accepted condition for the West, especially the United States, for so long, it is tempting to take it for granted. This would be dangerous. Air superiority was won in World War II the old-fashioned way: it was earned. It was earned at great cost in blood and treasure over a period of years. It has been maintained at a similarly high cost. It is not luck or fate that have made our air forces superior to our potential adversaries, it has been the billions of dollars and countless hours of training and preparation that we have expended over many decades.

Intelligence

The intelligence function grew dramatically in size and significance during World War II. Prior to the war, for example, the US Army did not even have a career path formally established for intelligence officers. It was usually considered an additional duty.[40] That all changed, partly due to the enormous use of wireless communication in war. This, in turn, generated the establishment of an organization whose function was to intercept, decipher and analyze the huge volume of traffic transiting the airwaves at all hours of the day and night. The contribution of Ultra – the breaking of the German enigma codes – is well known. Another reason for the growth of intelligence organizations had to do with the nature of the information needed. The connection between targeting and intelligence was crucial. Air planners had to know the exact locations, functions, weak points and alternate uses of entire networks – electrical power, railroad, communications, munitions, etc. – which had not been required previously. It took time to establish this new infrastructure, but it was time and effort well spent. Air commanders relied heavily on Ultra, as well as other intelligence sources, to plan their operations at all levels.[41] It is no surprise that intelligence organizations have exploded in size and complexity since World War II. Air power and intelligence will continue to enjoy a close and essential relationship.

Personalities

It may not be scientific or measurable, but personalities nonetheless can have an enormous impact on joint operations. Despite logic, sincerity, common cause and even necessity, it is remarkable how often success or failure in an operation can hinge on the personal relationships established between commanders of different components or units. When individuals trust one another and can 'get along together', the results achieved are usually greater than when commanders, regardless of how competent or intelligent, do not trust, like or respect one another.

Lieutenant General Lewis Brereton was commander of the US Ninth Air Force in the spring of 1944. A Naval Academy graduate, he had piloted fighter, bomber and observation aircraft during his career and had served as an instructor at both ACTS and the Army's Command and General Staff College at Fort Leavenworth. During the war, Brereton had commanded large air units in the Pacific, India, North Africa and Europe. Unquestionably, he knew his job and had the rank, experience and intellectual credentials to prove it.

Unfortunately, he was not popular with his colleagues in Europe. General Omar Bradley, whose 12th Army Group worked closely with the tactical aircraft of the Ninth Air Force on a daily basis, did not think Brereton was sincere, energetic or cooperative. General Edward Almond thought Brereton was 'taciturn almost to the point of rudeness and inclined to be too stubbornly an airman in matters pertaining to the air and ground'.[42] Even airmen, both British and American, had difficulty getting on with him. Eisenhower, therefore, made the decision to move Brereton out. The Ninth was too important to the success of the Normandy campaign to have an air commander in charge who could not work effectively with his colleagues. Brereton was transferred and his place was taken by Major General Hoyt Vandenberg, also a highly capable commander, staff officer and tactical pilot. 'Van' was, however, also universally liked and trusted by everyone – soldiers and airmen, Brits and Americans. It is debatable whether Vandenberg was more technically qualified than Brereton to be commander of the Ninth Air Force, but his ability to work well and effectively in a joint environment made him the superior choice.

Other conflicts involved the tension that existed between Montgomery and the commander of the Second Tactical Air Force, Air Marshal 'Mary' Coningham. Although the two had gotten along famously in North Africa, things had soured and by D-Day the two men were barely speaking to each other. Instead, Montgomery would routinely bypass Coningham by going over his head, or, worse, going under him to deal directly with Air Vice Marshal Harry Broadhurst, one of Coningham's group commanders. This was not conducive to smooth joint operations. There were other such negative examples throughout the war, including the celebrated hostility between Generals Joe Stilwell and Claire Chennault in China. There were, fortunately, positive examples of commanders who worked together extremely well, such as Generals Douglas MacArthur and George Kenney, Eisenhower and Tedder, and Generals George Patton and 'Opie' Weyland, commander of the XIX Tactical Air Command.[43] A wise theater commander selects commanders who are committed to working together effectively. One of Eisenhower's great strengths was his ability to forge a successful team from a group that included strong personalities from various services and countries. It would appear this issue was just as important in the Gulf War and Yugoslavia at it was in World War II.

Command and Control

'Centralized control of air assets' has been a catchphrase for airmen since World War I. For reasons doctrinal, theoretical, administrative, bureaucratic and even parochial, this idea has been a frequent source of argument between airmen and surface officers. Army doctrine going into World War II tended away from centralized control; instead, ground officers were assigned air assets for their own use. In North Africa, airmen and soldiers both found this system wanting. As a result, the British and the Americans rewrote their doctrine manuals to reflect more closely the airmen's views. The fact that noted soldiers like Bernard Montgomery supported this trend was certainly welcome. In 1943 he wrote:

> Nothing could be more fatal to successful results than to dissipate the air resources into small packets placed under command of army formation commanders, with each packet working on its own plan. The soldier must not expect, or wish, to exercise direct command over air striking forces.[44]

This belief was echoed in the AAF. To illustrate how much things had changed, the words of Army Chief of Staff General Malin Craig in 1938 are significant: 'It alone [infantry] can win a decision. Each of the other arms is but an auxiliary – its utility measured by the aid that it can bring to the Infantry'.[45] In contrast, a new doctrine manual, FM 100-20, was released in mid-1943 soon after the lessons learned in Torch. It proclaimed in bold type that land power and air power were co-equal and interdependent, neither being the auxiliary of the other. It went on to state that a theater air commander should be appointed by the supreme commander to exercise command over all air units in the theater.[46] In reality, this doctrine was not always followed. In northwest Europe, for example, Eisenhower had an air deputy, ACM Leigh-Mallory, who controlled *tactical* air forces, but who had little control over the *strategic* air forces. To help solve this problem, Eisenhower appointed as his chief deputy ACM Arthur Tedder, a highly respected officer who was better able to coordinate the efforts of the tactical and strategic air forces than was Leigh-Mallory. Even so, there were problems. The Ninth Air Force reported to the Eighth Air Force for administrative matters, and the Ninth's commander, though nominally equal to the 12th Army Group commander, was of lower rank.

In his after-action report in 1946, the Ninth's commander, Lieutenant General Hoyt Vandenberg, argued forcefully against a decentralized control of air assets which would cause waste, inefficiency and sub-optimum combat results:

> It is recommended that the equality and interdependence of air and ground forces be maintained as inviolable military policy, that direct control of all available air power be centralized under the air force commander and that the air force commander be responsible for operations directly to the Supreme Commander.[47]

I would note here that this sounds remarkably like the modern Joint Force Air Component Commander (JFACC) concept. However, it took 40 years and two major wars for the USA to adopt the JFACC model in its joint doctrine.

One aspect of the command and control issue was the need for joint planning. Once again, the Ninth Air Force's experience was important – and note that the Ninth, responsible for providing air assets to the entire 12th Army Group, was the largest tactical air unit in history with nearly 180,000 personnel and over 4,000 aircraft. So it speaks with authority on the subject of tactical air power in joint operations. The Ninth insisted that air and ground headquarters be collocated and that all planning had to be conducted jointly, 'on a hourly or minute-by-minute basis if necessary'.[48] Failure to maintain such close coordination could be disastrous. At Cherbourg on 22 June 1944, for example, 25 of the Ninth's fighter-bombers were lost due to inadequate planning and a lack of understanding between the air and ground forces involved regarding the correct procedures to be followed.[49]

An interesting facet to the issue of joint planning regarded staff composition. Airmen advocated separate but equal staffs working in close proximity and maintaining close liaison. Ground officers, on the other hand, argued for a single, joint staff to ease planning difficulties and smooth coordination. The airmen believed that so-called joint staffs were often really ground staffs with a few token airmen thrown in for show; whereas ground officers saw a separate air staff as duplicative and inefficient. This debate is still with us.

Air Interdiction

AI is one of the most effective uses of air power in a joint environment. There are many factors that will spell success or failure for AI: good intelligence, sustained pressure, symbiotic ground and air operations, high consumption, weather, terrain, etc. In addition, planners must think through whether it is more advantageous to limit an enemy's mobility, his reinforcements or his supplies. Which of these is chosen will, to a large extent, determine the targets, tactics and timing of air strikes. If, for example, the goal is to limit mobility, then bridges or other choke points close to the battlefield should be struck just prior to suspected enemy movement in order to reduce the enemy's options and flexibility. If, on the other hand, the goal is reduction of supplies, then a fuel depot farther back from the front would have a greater effect, even if taking longer to achieve. The goal is to always keep the adversary off balance and to continually fail to meet his expectations.

Let me close by reiterating my opening comments regarding the importance of jointness: joint thinking, joint planning and joint understanding. Certainly, as an airman I believe strongly in the utility of our chosen weapon. At the same time, however, I recognize that every form of power, every service, has strengths and weaknesses. We must understand each other in order to plan and fight our wars effectively, before they occur. The Allies had to learn the complexities of joint operations during war. We no longer can afford that luxury.

NOTES

In 1999 I was asked to give a paper on air power in joint operations at a conference in Canberra sponsored by the Royal Australian Air Force. This chapter was the result. It was published in the proceedings of the conference, edited by Keith Brent under the title, *Air Power and Joint Forces* (Canberra: Aerospace Centre, 2000).

1. 'To sum up: of all the possible aims in war, the destruction of the enemy's armed forces always appears as the highest'. Carl von Clausewitz, *On War*, trans. Peter Paret and Michael Howard (Princeton: Princeton University Press, 1976), 99. I counted 19 more instances in *On War* where Clausewitz stated this principle in similar, unequivocal terms.
2. J. R. M. Butler, *History of the Second World War: Grand Strategy, Vol. II: September 1939–June 1941* (London: HMSO, 1957), 119–21.
3. Butler, *Grand Strategy*, 188–9; Klaus A. Maier, *et al.* (eds), *Germany and the Second World War, Vol. II: Germany's Initial Conquests in Europe* (Oxford: Clarendon Press, 1991), 184–5.
4. Butler, *Grand Strategy*, 93.
5. Maier, *Germany and the Second World War*, 192.
6. For an excellent account, see Walter Goerlitz, *The German General Staff, 1657–1945* (New York: Praeger, 1966).
7. James S. Corum, *The Luftwaffe: Creating the Operational Air War, 1918–1940* (Lawrence: University Press of Kansas, 1997), *passim*, but especially chapters 4, 5 and 7.
8. For the entire campaign, naval losses on both sides were heavy: the Allies lost 1 carrier, 2 cruisers, 9 destroyers and 6 submarines. The Germans lost 3 cruisers, 10 destroyers and 4 submarines. Although roughly comparable, Germany could ill afford such losses. In addition, both sides suffered around 5,000 casualties among their personnel. Maier, *Germany and the Second World War*, 218.

9. John Terraine, *A Time for Courage: The Royal Air Force in the European War, 1939–1945* (New York: Macmillan, 1985), 115; Denis Richards, *Royal Air Force 1939–1945, Vol. I: The Fight at Odds* (London: HMSO, 1974), 78.

10. Phillip S. Meilinger, 'Between the Devil and the Deep Blue Sea: The Fleet Air Arm Before World War II', *Royal United Services Institute Journal*, 144 (October 1999), 73–8.

11. Butler, *Grand Strategy*, 132–4, 141, 149.

12. Richards, *Royal Air Force*, 86.

13. Ibid.

14. Butler, *Grand Strategy*, 142.

15. Ibid., 128.

16. Geoffrey Till, *Air Power and the Royal Navy, 1914–1945* (London: Jane's, 1979), 15.

17. Although the British had broken the German enigma codes, they were totally unprepared for the volume and complexity of the signals generated by the Germans during the Norwegian campaign. As a consequence, the intelligence collected was late, incomplete and inadequately disseminated to the commanders who needed it. F. H. Hinsley, *et al. British Intelligence in the Second World War*, 5 vols (London: HMSO, 1979–90), I, 136–43.

18. Stephen L. McFarland and Wesley Phillips Newton, *To Command the Sky: The Battle for Air Superiority over Germany, 1942–1945* (Washington, DC: Smithsonian Institution, 1991), 190–1.

19. Richard J. Overy, *The Air War, 1939–1945* (London: Europa, 1980), 77; McFarland and Newton, *To Command the Sky*, 241.

20. Basil H. Liddell Hart (ed.), *The Rommel Papers* (London: Collins, 1953), 476.

21. Quoted in Richard Hallion, 'Airpower from the Grand Up', *Air Force Magazine*, November (2000), 40.

22. Daniel R. Mortensen, *A Pattern for Joint Operations: World War II Close Air Support in North Africa* (Washington, DC: Office of Air Force History and US Army Center of Military History, 1987), 12–13.

23. Wing Commander John C. Slessor, *Air Power and Armies* (London: Oxford University Press, 1936), 82.

24. Eduard Mark, *Aerial Interdiction in Three Wars* (Washington, DC: Center for Air Force History, 1994), 36, 45.

25. Ibid., 46.

26. In reality, the Allies overestimated German requirements considerably. Mark, *Aerial Interdiction*, page 165, notes that in April 1944 the German forces consumed less than 3,000 tons of supplies daily.

27. For the best accounts by participants, see, for oil, W. W. Rostow, *Pre-Invasion Bombing Strategy: General Eisenhower's Decision of March 25, 1944* (Austin, TX: University of Texas Press, 1981); and for the transportation argument see Solly Zuckerman, *From Apes to Warlords* (New York: Harper & Row, 1978). For a balanced account see Alan J. Levine, *The Strategic Bombing of Germany, 1940–1945* (Westport, CT: Praeger, 1992).

28. Mark, *Aerial Interdiction*, 238–41.

29. Ibid., 246–9, 257. For an excellent account of the deception campaign for Overlord, see Michael Howard, *British Intelligence in the Second World War, Vol. 5: Strategic Deception* (London: HMSO, 1990), ch. 6.

30. Ian Gooderson, 'Allied Fighter-Bombers Versus German Armour in North-West Europe 1944–1945: Myths and Realities', *Journal of Strategic Studies*, 14 (June 1991), 225.

31. Robert E. Schmaltz, 'The Uncertainty of Predicting Results of an Interdiction Campaign', Saber Measure (Alpha) Report, December 1969, 9.

32. Williamson Murray and Allan R. Millett, *A War to be Won: Fighting the Second World War* (Cambridge, MA: Harvard University Press, 2000), 32–3.
33. Maurer Maurer, *Aviation in the US Army, 1919–1939* (Washington, DC: Office of Air Force History, 1987), 472–4.
34. Murray and Millett, *A War to be Won*, 33.
35. Maurer, *Aviation in the US Army*, 475–6. Similarly, the RAF received, on average, only around 15 per cent of the British defence budget during the interwar period. Robin Higham, *Armed Forces in Peacetime* (Hamden: Archon, 1962), 326–7.
36. Irving B. Holley, Jr, *Buying Aircraft: Material Procurement for the Army Air Forces* (Washington: Government Printing Office, 1964), 550.
37. Peter R. Faber, 'Interwar US Army Aviation and the Air Corps Tactical School: Incubators of American Air power', in School of Advanced Airpower Studies, *The Paths of Heaven: The Evolution of Airpower Theory* (Maxwell AFB: Air University Press, 1997), 212.
38. Liddell Hart, *Rommel Papers*, 285.
39. In early 1943 in North Africa, Lt. Gen. Kenneth Anderson demanded that an RAF fighter group be put directly under his command to fly combat patrols overhead to keep the Luftwaffe at bay. Mark, *Aerial Interdiction*, 30.
40. Carl Kaysen, *Notes on Strategic Air Intelligence in World War II (ETO)* (Santa Monica, CA: RAND, 1953), 30.
41. See SRH-013, 'Ultra: History of US Strategic Air Force Europe vs. German Air Forces', June 1945.
42. Phillip S. Meilinger, *Hoyt S. Vandenberg: The Life of a General* (Bloomington, IN: Indiana University Press, 1989), 49. Bradley's aide, Major 'Chip' Hansen, confided in his diary that he could barely stand to be in the same room with Brereton.
43. For two excellent books exploring this subject, see Dominick Graham and Shelford Bidwell, *Coalitions, Politicians and Generals: Some Aspects of Command in Two World Wars* (London: Brassey's, 1993), and D. Clayton James, *A Time for Giants: Politics of the American High Command in World War II* (New York: Franklin Watts, 1987).
44. General Bernard Montgomery, 'Some Notes on High Command in War', September 1943.
45. John F. Kreis (ed.), *Piercing the Fog: Intelligence and the Army Air Forces Operations in World War II* (Washington, DC: Air Force History and Museums Program, 1996), 37.
46. War Department FM 100-20, 'Command and Employment of Air Power', 21 July 1943, 1–2.
47. *Condensed Analysis of the Ninth Air Force in the European Theater of Operations*, 1946 (Reprinted by the Office of Air Force History in 1984), 94.
48. Ibid., 105.
49. Ibid., 24.

8

The B-29 Air Campaign against Japan

It has always surprised me how energetic and emotional debates can be regarding past events. This seems especially true when discussing events in war. As our World War II veterans grew into and beyond middle age they had a great desire to re-examine the events that occurred during their youth. They tended, not unnaturally, to color their memories and memoirs with a nostalgia and nobility not always justified. At the same time, a later generation that had lived through the experience of the Vietnam era sought the roots of their frustration by looking backwards. It was not uncommon for that new generation to see far more duplicity and hypocrisy in World War II than was actually there. This clash of generations and viewpoints was epitomized by the uproar over the Enola Gay exhibit at the Smithsonian Institution in the mid-1990s. As an airman and a historian, I was intellectually caught up in this debate to the extent that I forced myself to go back and examine the strategic bombing campaign against Japan. I confess that little changed in the interpretation I had come to two decades earlier, but it is always useful and important to undergo such retrospection.

The 50th anniversary of the end of World War II brought the usual spate of books re-examining the events that have been examined so many times before. Regarding the end of the war against Japan, the spotlight often fell on the cataclysmic events that shattered the will and the capability of the Japanese to continue the war – specifically, the strategic air campaign. Movies, film clips, histories and novels tend to highlight the horror of that air campaign, and horrible it certainly was. But when remembering that perhaps as many as 400,000 Japanese civilians died by air attack, it is useful to remember the more than six million innocents in China, Indochina, Korea, the Philippines, Malaysia, Burma, the Indies, the Pacific islands and elsewhere who died in the more traditional way: via starvation, artillery barrage, small arms fire, disease and simple maltreatment by Japanese occupation forces. Air power, for all its clumsiness more akin to the bludgeon than to the rapier, did in fact do what it had been promising for the previous 25 years; it ended the war more quickly and with less overall loss of life than would otherwise have been the case.

My intent is to provide an overview of the strategic air campaign against

Japan during the last year of the war and its results, noting also, briefly, the issue of the scheduled invasion of Japan and the number of casualties it might have incurred. I will argue that the air campaign, including the atomic strikes, was far less deadly, for both sides, than the other military alternatives advanced for ending the war.

US war plans prior to World War II anticipated a number of contingencies against several possible opponents, one of whom was Japan.[1] As a result, as early as 1939 air planners suggested the bombing of Japan from the Asian mainland in the event of war. Almost immediately after Pearl Harbor, Army Air Force (AAF) leaders sought the use of Soviet bases in Siberia for that purpose. Although a precedent seemed established when three airbases were actually established in the Ukraine for bombing Germany, and despite supplies being stockpiled in the Soviet maritime provinces at anticipated US bases for eventual use, Siberian airfields were never made available for US operations against Japan.[2] The alternative, therefore, was a requirement for a 'very long-range' bomber that could reach Japan from islands in the Pacific or from bases in western China. Specifically, due to greater ranges in the Pacific, an aircraft with twice the range of the B-17, or at least 3,000 miles, was necessary. This was to be the Boeing B-29 *Superfortress*. Significantly, although the United States adhered to the Europe-first strategy in the war, the B-29 was to be an exception because of the enormous distances involved; all of the heavy bombers would be deployed to the Pacific.

The Boeing B-29 was first sketched out in 1940 and was a technological gamble, despite the experience the company had had with building large aircraft. Eventually, the B-29 became one of the most expensive weapons programs of the war, costing around $3 billion, or about $639,000 per copy. In comparison, a B-17 cost $238,000. This high cost was partly due to innovations such as a pressurized cabin for the crew positions which allowed high-altitude operations above antiaircraft fire and some interceptors; a fire control system that included remote-controlled gun turrets (twelve .50 caliber guns; early versions also had a 20mm cannon in the tail); and new engines, the Wright R-3350 that promised 2,200 horsepower. To illustrate the need for the plane and the risks the AAF was willing to take, the B-29 was put into production even before its first flight. In fact, 1,664 were already on order at the time of its maiden flight on 21 September 1942. Eventually, about 4,000 B-29s would be built, with another 5,000 on order that were canceled at the end of the war. The plane's normal combat range was 3,500 miles, carrying four tons of bombs. It had an 11-man crew and its cruising speed was around 300 mph.[3] Ironically, the technology that made the B-29 so problematic and so expensive was ultimately not required against Japan.

Twentieth Air Force Command Issues

When the B-29s began coming off the assembly line, General 'Hap' Arnold, commanding general of the Army Air Forces, decided to command them personally from Washington and under the strategic guidance of the Joint Chiefs of Staff (JCS) – not the Combined Chiefs of Staff (CCS). This was an unprecedented arrangement. (Imagine General George Marshall, the Army Chief of Staff in Washington, concurrently commanding the American Third Army during its drive across France.) The official history explains that Arnold always wanted to command a combat unit in war; he had spent World War I in Washington and greatly regretted never having reached the front.[4] This is not an adequate explanation. There were other, more practical, reasons for Arnold's unusual decision.

First, he did not want the CCS involved – namely, the British – as in Europe, where Air Chief Marshal 'Peter' Portal gave orders to the US strategic bombers. Nor did Arnold want theater commanders involved (Admiral Louis Mountbatten in Southeast Asia; Admiral Chester Nimitz in the Central Pacific; General Douglas MacArthur in the Southwest Pacific; General Joseph Stilwell in China; and of course, Chiang Kai-Shek himself) due to the fear that these men would divert air power as had happened in Europe at Normandy, the campaigns against the submarine pens, the V-weapon sites, etc. Not surprisingly, none of these individuals liked the proposed arrangement. In fact, Chiang expressed irritation because as a head of state he thought he should have priority over the theater commanders, especially since some of the B-29s would be staged out of bases in China. President Roosevelt himself finally intervened by stating that *he* would be commanding the B-29s personally; this mollified Chiang and allowed him to save face. Finally, Arnold did not want 'tainted' airmen involved, like General George Kenney, MacArthur's airman, Major General Claire Chennault, commander of the Fourteenth Air Force in China, or Lieutenant General 'Miff' Harmon, Nimitz's airman, who were seen as tied too closely to the army and navy, or in Chennault's case, was simply not trusted by anyone in the Air Force hierarchy. Arnold's problem was convincing everyone else that his proposed command arrangement was a good idea.

Arnold's chief staff officer, Brigadier General Haywood Hansell, later stated that the Army Chief of Staff, General George Marshall, was easily sold, but the navy chief, Admiral Ernie King, was another matter. One argument used was to push for 'unity of command' in the target area, not the basing area. By this it was meant that if the target was Japan and the B-29s were deployed to India, China and later the Marianas, the planes should not be divided between three different theater commanders; rather, their control should be centralized to achieve decisive results over Japan. There was a precedent for this concept in Europe where the Eighth Air Force in the European theater and the Fifteenth Air Force in the Mediterranean theater were combined to form the US Strategic Air Forces under the command of General Carl Spaatz to better focus the airwar against Germany. In addition, Hansell told King this proposed setup was similar to navy practice; King was, after all, both chief of naval operations and Commander of the US Fleet.[5] Surprisingly, King agreed with the command arrangements.

As a consequence, Arnold commanded the Twentieth and double-hatted his staff; Hansell, his Chief of Staff, thus also became Chief of Staff of Twentieth Air Force. In practice, due to Arnold's onerous duties and poor health (he suffered several heart attacks during the war), Hansell became the de facto commander of the Twentieth from Washington. Of import, there was a provision in the JCS directive to the Twentieth that, in the event of 'strategic or tactical emergencies', the theater commanders could assume control of the B-29s. This later occurred as we shall see.

XX BOMBER COMMAND OPERATIONS − CHINA AND INDIA

The first B-29s of the XX Bomber Command, a sub-unit of the Twentieth Air Force, were 'secretly' deployed to India in April 1944, while at the same time a single B-29 was openly sent to England as a feint to confuse Japanese intelligence. It did not. The XX was under the command of Brigadier General Ken Wolfe, who had been responsible for seeing the aircraft through its development stage. Immediately, however, extreme logistical problems began to develop. First, the B-29s had to share supplies with the Tenth Air Force and the Fourteenth Air Force; in this regard, the army and air commanders that Arnold had hoped to avoid had a significant impact after all. Second, all supplies had to come over the Himalayas; flying the massive amounts of supplies necessary to sustain the war effort over the Hump was one of the greatest aerial feats in history. Nonetheless, this requirement added to the difficulties of the XX.[6]

To speed things up, Wolfe decided to have his B-29s double as tankers and haul fuel. In fact, about 85 per cent of the XX's flying was done on logistics missions. Although this helped solve one problem, it also put a heavy strain on the already overstretched maintenance system, thus causing other problems. At the same time, base construction was slow, partly due to the low priority of the theater. The plan, however, was to base the B-29s in India and stage them out of bases near Chengtu in China. Finally, the B-29s, which as noted had been rushed into production prematurely, suffered severe teething problems with their engines, which had a distressing tendency to suck valves and for the magnesium crankcases to catch fire and burn violently.[7]

As a consequence, XX combat operations proceeded very slowly. Arnold, ever impatient, relieved Ken Wolfe in August 1944 and replaced him with Major General Curtis LeMay. It is important to say a few words about this remarkable officer.

LeMay was recognized as one of the best pilots and navigators in the AAF before the war. In August 1937, he found and simulated bombing the US battleship *Utah* in maneuvers off California in poor weather, despite having been given the wrong coordinates by the navy. He was the lead navigator on the flight of B-17s to South America in 1937–38 − not a commonplace occurrence then as it would be today − and in 1938, he found and then intercepted the Italian liner *Rex* while it was still 600 miles out to sea from New York. In 1942, he was sent to Europe as a lieutenant colonel and bomb group commander, and two years later he was a major general and a bomb division commander in the Eighth Air Force. LeMay had unquestioned physical courage and flew many missions personally, including the bloody Regensburg–Schweinfurt mission of August 1943 when 60 bombers went down. He was an excellent tactician, developing formations and bombing techniques adopted by all of Eighth Air Force. LeMay was hard and uncompromising, and once made the comment: 'I don't mind being called a tough guy, because in this business I've found it's the tough guys who lead the survivors'. LeMay was a survivor. He was also a firm believer in rigorous and realistic training, which was one of his hallmarks.[8] Later, he would become, at age 44, the second-youngest full general in US history as the Commander of Strategic Air Command, and eventually went on to serve as Air Force Chief of Staff from 1960 to 1964.[9]

Because of the small numbers of B-29s available to the XX – generally less than 100 per mission – Wolfe decided to concentrate on closer and more lightly defended targets in Manchuria, Korea and Indochina. The first mission was flown on 5 June 1944 against Bangkok. Combat missions were also flown against Kyushu, and the first was launched on 15 June against an iron and steel works. Overall, the 49 combat missions of the XX over the five months of its combat life achieved limited results to say the least; only 11,000 tons were dropped before operations from China were discontinued (compared to 156,000 tons dropped by XXI Bomber Command in the Marianas). But on the positive side, some of the bugs were worked out of the new aircraft. Its use bolstered Chinese morale, a somewhat unquantifiable but nonetheless significant factor, and it gave LeMay Pacific and B-29 experience.[10] Clearly, however, the Marianas bases were essential for the strategic air campaign against Japan.

XXI BOMBER COMMAND OPERATIONS IN THE MARIANAS

In October 1944, the XXI Bomber Command, another sub-unit of the Twentieth Air Force, began moving into the Marianas after the islands were captured. Hansell came from Washington to take command, and Brigadier General Lauris Norstad took his place as Chief of Staff of the Twentieth Air Force – still commanded by Arnold from Washington. Let me say a few words about these two men. Hansell was a leading bombardment theorist at the Air Corps Tactical School in the mid-1930s, where he acquired the nickname 'possum' – because he looked like one. He helped write AWPD-1, the initial air plan used against Germany, as well as AWPD-42 (the updated plan of the following year) and the Combined Bomber Offensive plan. He was the only American to be intimately involved in all three key bombing campaign plans. He was a bomb wing and then a bomb division commander in Eighth Air Force in combat. He was also one of Arnold's trusted subordinates. On the face of it, he was the obvious and the best choice for such an important command. Hansell was an excellent strategist, planner, staff officer and proven combat commander.

'Larry' Norstad was a brilliant staff officer. He had been director of operations for the Twelfth Air Force during the North African invasion, and then occupied the same position in the Mediterranean Allied Air Forces. He spent much time on Arnold's staff in Washington and consequently he held no combat command during the war. Significantly, he also had the reputation as Arnold's 'hatchet man'; when Norstad arrived in a theater as Arnold's emissary, he seldom brought good news. Later, Norstad would become the *third*-youngest full general in US history – four months behind LeMay – and the first airman to command NATO.

The first XXI combat mission was flown on 24 November 1944 – 111 B-29s hit aircraft factories and docks near Tokyo. Only one aircraft was lost but the damage inflicted was negligible. As in India there were severe problems which surfaced immediately. The B-29's engines were still a problem, as were supply shortages. Due to maintenance and logistics shortages, the sortie rate was only three sorties per aircraft per month. Incidentally, Hansell relates in his memoirs that when he passed through Hawaii en route to his headquarters in Guam and met with Admiral Chester Nimitz – in whose theater the B-29 bases were located – Nimitz warned him:

> You are probably in for a rough time. You are going out to the Forward Area where my commander, Vice Admiral John Hoover, breaks my admirals and throws them overboard without the slightest compunction. God knows what he is going to do to you'.[11]

With those words of encouragement, Hansell continued on to the Marianas.

Another problem was weather, specifically the jet stream, which was up to 200 mph at 33,000 feet and played havoc with the B-29s. In addition, typhoons were a concern; a particularly bad storm swept through in November, for example, damaging a number of planes and delaying operations for two weeks. Overall, the weather and jet stream caused serious navigation as well as accuracy problems. The famed Norden bombsight – never as accurate as legend would have it – simply could not cope.[12] For example, the Mushashi aircraft engine plant was attacked eight different times with almost no success.

Supplies continued to be a problem. The B-29s were still at the end of the food chain, although General Harmon, the senior airman under Nimitz in the Central Pacific, did perform great deeds. These logistics problems were exacerbated by the decision to give resource priority to operations functions, rather than infrastructure. Consequently, the XXI had no organic service command, ordnance squadron, depot maintenance, etc., unlike other units of comparable size. This decision, in the long run, would further hamper the logistics effort of the B-29s.

Targeting has always been a key component of strategic air warfare, so even before the B-29s were deployed there was a major effort under way to study the Japanese economy so as to select the most appropriate targets. Unfortunately, the intelligence apparatus required to conduct such a study and thereby provide competent targeting advice was faulty. To explain the problem, let me digress briefly. The type of intelligence needed for airwar was a new phenomenon in warfare. Although armies had had spies for centuries, the information they required was of a decidedly tactical and operational nature: the location and size of the enemy army and its route of march, the status of its supplies, its command structure, the capabilities of its weapons, etc. Airwar, on the other hand, required economic and industrial intelligence, information never really required before in war, because a ground commander could not do much with that intelligence even if he had it. The AAF entered the war seriously deficient in this area. Indeed, a separate air intelligence division was not even established until shortly before the war broke out in Europe. Moreover, Japan was an especially difficult intelligence challenge due to the closed nature of its society, especially since the early 1930s when their invasion of Manchuria caused considerable strain in relations with the United States. In many cases, the air planners had to rely on old maps, an occasional tourist report and prewar insurance data.[13]

Nonetheless, building upon the lessons and experiences of Europe, air planners identified several key systems in Japan that needed to be targeted. Coke ovens, essential for the production of steel, was one of the key systems singled out for attack. Other target systems included merchant shipping, oil refineries, the transportation network and munitions factories. Again, following the lead of the airwar against Germany, the munitions factories that most concerned airmen were the aircraft and engine complexes.[14] Unless and until air superiority was achieved, it was feared that a bombing campaign would be a long and bloody war of attrition. As events would prove, achieving air superiority was far easier than expected, but carrying out a precision bombing campaign against specific industries would be far more difficult.

Another important aspect of the B-29 operations out of the Marianas that needs to be mentioned concerns the issue of doctrine versus dogma. Hansell, as noted, was one of the true experts in strategic bombing theory. He had arrived in theater fresh from experience in fighting the Luftwaffe, understood the need for air superiority before effective operations were possible, and had debated – successfully – the Royal Air Force over the relative merits of daylight versus night bombing. Thus, he had learned from bitter experience in combat and was the obvious choice to command the XXI. Unfortunately, this was a different enemy, in a different theater, employing a different airplane, under different conditions, and he was unable to adjust. The somewhat unreasonable impatience of Arnold back in Washington certainly did not help matters. Hansell resisted pressure from Arnold to hurry the XXI into combat against what were expected to be strong defenses. Hansell did not want the B-29 offensive to begin with a disastrous Schweinfurt-type attack. The first three months of the XXI's operations were not impressive: by January 1945 the XXI had dropped a mere 1,500 tons of bombs on Japan, and only 1 out of 50 hit within 1,000 feet of the target.[15] Once again, Arnold ran out of patience.

LEMAY AND THE XXI BOMBER COMMAND

Ironically, the XXI's most successful mission to date was on 19 January 1945 when 62 B-29s – note that small number even after three months of operations – struck the Akashi aircraft plant near Kobe. Flying at 25,000–27,000 feet to escape the worst effects of the jet stream, the results were excellent. But it was too late for Hansell. Two weeks before, Norstad had flown out from Washington to Hansell's headquarters on Guam and told LeMay to travel from India and meet him there. On Arnold's orders, Norstad relieved Hansell, telling him LeMay would officially take over on 20 January, after he wrapped up matters with the XX. Norstad, in an attempt to explain the change to Hansell said simply: 'You and I are planners; Curt is an operator'.[16] Of note, Hansell was the oldest of the three generals; he was 41. As an aside, Hansell's biographer points out that he was firmly grounded in theory, whereas his successor, LeMay, was merely a pragmatist who had only attended the Air Corps Tactical School's short course of 1939 and therefore did not 'truly understand' air-power theory. Thus, LeMay was interested in results unencumbered by official thought.[17] Here we have a clear example of a biographer who unwittingly falls into the same trap as his subject – he was unable to determine the difference between doctrine and dogma.

As usual, LeMay began by emphasizing training and efficiency. By April, the sortie rate had more than doubled, from 3.3 to 7.1 sorties per aircraft per month. The capture of Iwo Jima in February gave the XXI a fighter escort base for P-51 Mustangs, while also denying the Japanese an interceptor base. In addition, it served as an emergency landing field for over 2,400 B-29s – an enormous psychological boost to the crewmembers of damaged or incapacitated aircraft otherwise condemned to the long flight of 1,500 miles over water back to Saipan.

LeMay, taking his cue from Hansell's experiments, also began to lower bombing altitude by several thousand feet to improve range and decrease the effects of the jet stream. (Note: as opposed to a jet engine, reciprocating engines operate more efficiently at low altitudes, not high. Thus, operations at lower altitudes would both save gasoline and reduce wear and tear on the still temperamental engines.) More significantly, LeMay moved to night incendiary attacks.

It should be noted that incendiaries were not developed until after the war broke out, although there was a realization somewhat earlier that Japanese cities would be particularly susceptible to fire. The Japanese, surprisingly, were absolutely unprepared for fire bombing.[18] Tests on Japanese-style buildings and industrial areas constructed at Eglin Field, Florida, indicated significant vulnerabilities: the wood and paper construction burned quickly and completely; due to congestion within the cities there were insufficient firebreaks established; automatic sprinkler systems, fire walls, fire doors and air-raid shelters were scarce or inadequate; and fire departments were poorly equipped and trained. Moreover, even the fire-resistant buildings contained highly flammable interiors. As one observer phrased it, they were 'concrete ovens filled with kindling'.[19] Incendiary attacks had been suggested by Norstad the previous November, but Hansell had resisted. LeMay, however, was more amenable to the idea, and also suspected that the Japanese had negligible night defenses. He was soon proved right. Intelligence, as noted, was still an imprecise science at this stage, but it had determined that the Japanese economy was organized into 'cottage industries', unlike the large factory complexes prevalent in Europe; indeed, half of all Japanese workers were employed in factories of fewer than 100 people.[20] Significantly, throughout the war Allied intelligence tended to overrate Japanese industrial production, perhaps as a reaction to having underestimated German production to an embarrassing degree.

As a result of these various factors, in March 1945 LeMay decided to make a radical change. LeMay lowered the bombing altitude to between 5,000 and 9,000 feet. Because he suspected weak night defenses, he stripped the B-29s of guns, ammunition and the gunners, except for the tail gun. The combination of lower altitude and reduced armament approximately doubled the plane's bomb load to about six tons. His decision was resisted by some of his subordinate commanders who did not share the belief that Japanese night fighters would not be a problem, but they obeyed. Significantly, LeMay did not inform Arnold of his changed tactics prior to their first use against Tokyo, although Arnold was certainly aware a night incendiary attack was scheduled.

On the night of 9/10 March 1945, 334 aircraft struck Tokyo. It was the most destructive air attack in history: 15.8 square miles were destroyed (compare that to 1 square mile in London during the entire war); 83,000 were killed (although 1.7 million civilians had already left the city); and 22 major industrial targets were destroyed.[21] Fourteen B-29s were lost, all due to flak. LeMay had been right about the weak night defenses.

Between March and August 1945, LeMay continued to mix area and precision attacks (including experimental radar strikes which gave excellent results), but the bulk of the missions were area incendiary attacks. It should be noted that there was obvious confusion over objectives to be achieved and thus the targeting to achieve those objectives. If, as the airmen offered, the intent was to win the war before the scheduled ground invasion, then why strike barracks, depots and munitions factories? If, on the other hand, the intent was to prepare for invasion – which was the JCS (Joint Chiefs of Staff) plan – then why launch the urban area attacks designed to destroy industry and lower morale? It would appear the airmen, like the Allied leaders in general, could not decide precisely which strategy to follow, so they hedged their bets and followed several.

Partly as a result of the new P-51 escorts based on Iwo Jima, bomber losses dropped from 5.7 per cent in January to 1 per cent by the end of the war (1.4 per cent overall – about half due to enemy fighters and 40 per cent due to flak). A total of 485 B-29s and 3,041 crewmen were lost. It should be noted that Arnold recognized that B-29 losses should not be compared to B-17 losses. Because the B-29 cost three times as much as a B-17 and was also so much more expensive to operate, even a small loss of aircraft was a serious reverse. As Arnold phrased it: 'We must consider the B-29 more in terms of a naval vessel, and we do not lose naval vessels in threes and fours without a very thorough analysis of the causes'.[22]

In July 1945, the Eighth Air Force, newly outfitted with B-29s, arrived in theater under the command of Jimmy Doolittle. Also arriving that month was General Carl Spaatz, who then became commander of the combined Eighth and Twentieth Air Forces in a command organization termed the US Army Strategic Air Forces. Arnold finally dropped out of the command picture. (It is an interesting insight into internal AAF politics that although George Kenney was senior to Spaatz in date of rank and had been in the theater for the previous three years, he was still not totally trusted by Arnold, so he was bypassed.)

The Eighth was just getting geared up when the war ended, but as a sign of what was about to happen, the strategic air forces carried out a 1,000-plane strike on 14 August. It is important to note that 96 per cent of all bombs dropped on Japan fell after 10 March (about 140,000 tons). This remarkable total was achieved despite the fact that the B-29s were diverted to support the Okinawa invasion for four weeks in April–May 1945. For that assault, 75 per cent of the B-29 effort was directed to hit airfields and fuel reserves on Okinawa in an effort to stop the kamikaze attacks that were taking a heavy toll on Allied warships. These operations, in addition to the extensive mining campaign of Japan's inland waters that began at the end of March, were the types of 'diversions' airmen had feared – although in these instances they certainly seemed justified. Once again, to give an idea of the crescendo of bombing that occurred, the B-29s had dropped 14,000 tons in March (with 385 aircraft available), and 43,000 tons in July (with nearly 900 aircraft on hand). It was expected that this figure would rise to an astonishing 115,000 tons in September with the combination of the Eighth and Twentieth Air Forces in full operation. In short, once the bombing began in earnest, the results were both immediate and massive.

SURRENDER AND CASUALTY ISSUES

Others with far greater authority than I will discuss the diplomatic efforts and tentative peace overtures occurring during the last few months of the war, but in my view, quite simply, these efforts were not serious. At least, they were not serious in that they were not supported by those really in power in Tokyo. Certainly, some men like Foreign Minister Shigenori Togo and Ambassador Naotake Sato in Moscow were desirous of peace, but the military leaders in Tokyo, and they were actually in charge, did not support peace initiatives. For example, in mid-July 1945, Foreign Minister Togo was still telling Ambassador Sato that he should be working on renewing the Soviet–Japanese non-aggression pact, not working on peace. Sato was specifically instructed 'to avoid giving the impression that our plan is to make use of the Russians in ending our war'. On 13 July, Togo wrote, 'the Japanese Empire has no alternative but to fight on with all its strength for the honor and existence of the Motherland'. Ominously, Magic intercepts indicate there was no slackening of Japanese resolve; they were intending to fight to the death. On 20 July, Togo wrote that the Japanese government was convinced 'that our war strength can still deliver considerable blows to the enemy . . . the Japanese are unanimous in their resolve to wage a thoroughgoing war'. On 24 July, the Allies again called for surrender; this call was rejected on 26 July. It is important to note that the Allies' Potsdam Declaration, although calling for unconditional surrender, also stated that the Japanese could pick their future form of government; no mention was made of the emperor – a significant omission. As late as the first week of August, Togo was still mulling over the possibility of the Soviets as a constructive influence; Sato quashed this optimism by bluntly responding that the government was deluding itself if it thought the Soviets were interested in facilitating a peace; they wanted back the Kuriles, Sakhalin and a free hand in Manchuria.[23]

The atomic bomb was dropped on Hiroshima on 6 August; there was no response from Tokyo. The Soviets invaded Manchuria on 8 August. On 9 August a second atomic bomb was dropped, on Nagasaki; nonetheless, at a cabinet meeting on 14 August, the emperor had to break a 3-3 tie. (General Korechika Anami, War Minister, General Yoshijiro Umezu, the Chief of the General Staff Headquarters, and Admiral Soemu Toyoda, Chief of the Naval General Staff, were still opposed to peace.) After the emperor's surrender announcement, some senior generals attempted a coup so as to continue the fighting, but this quickly fizzled out. What had finally pushed the emperor into suing for peace? The Chief Cabinet Secretary, Hisatsune Sakomizu, later stated: 'The chance had come to end the war. It was not necessary to blame the military side, the manufacturing people, or anyone else – just the atomic bomb. It was a good excuse'.[24] Baron Kantaro Suzuki, the premier, confirmed this (he was selected as premier in April, after the fall of Okinawa), but stated he needed the right circumstances to overcome the intransigence of the military leaders, and the atomic strikes gave him that opportunity. (Note: at the time of the surrender there was enough material for a third bomb; it was never shipped but could have been available by 17 August. One source states that perhaps ten bombs would have been available by the date of the scheduled invasion on 1 November.[25])

There were two main reasons for dropping the atomic bombs: the desire to save American lives and the desire to end the war quickly. The argument that the bombs were dropped to deter the Soviets in the postwar era has never reasonably been demonstrated. If anyone in authority even thought of such things, it was a distant third choice behind the rationale of shortening the war and thus saving lives.

Regarding the casualty figures resulting from an invasion of the Japanese home islands, there are a whole range of numbers floating around, but to my mind the issue is fairly clear-cut. There were over two million soldiers under arms in the Japanese home islands, over three million more throughout Asia and several million more being formed into a home guard. On Kyushu, there had been a flood of reinforcements throughout June and July; in fact, estimates of defenders there grew to 600,000 by the first week of August, two-thirds of them in the south where the landings were to take place.[26] In addition, there were 10,000 aircraft left in the islands, and half of them had been converted to kamikazes. Recall that 2,500 kamikazes had already sunk 45 Allied ships. Besides this, there were hundreds of suicide bombs, boats, torpedoes and mini-submarines. Ultra intelligence also revealed vigorous activity to build bunkers, caves and tunnels for tenacious defense in depth throughout the islands.[27] Based upon the operations on Iwo Jima and Okinawa, preparations for a death stand were obviously not a charade. It should be noted that Japanese defenders tended not to surrender: 95 per cent fought to the death during the war, with 97 per cent dying at Saipan and 99 per cent at Iwo Jima. Indeed, 150,000 Japanese died at Iwo Jima and Okinawa, including thousands of civilians, many of whom committed mass suicide. US losses at Iwo Jima were 7,000 killed and 18,000 wounded. At Okinawa, the United States suffered 50,000 casualties, including over 12,000 killed; this was its most deadly battle of the war.

Throughout the Pacific war there had been a high, but acceptable, ratio between Allied and Japanese casualties, but it had jumped to 1:5 in the Philippine liberation, and jumped again to 1:2 at Okinawa. In a memo to President Roosevelt in July 1945, the JCS stated that thus far, Allied losses had averaged over 30 per cent of the attacking force; thus, if the 1 November invasion called for a landing involving 750,000 Allied troops, they could expect nearly 250,000 casualties – and that was just for Kyushu; 1,000,000 troops were scheduled to land on Honshu a few months later.[28] (Of interest, Edward Drea implies that the army *understated* casualty figures so as not to discourage the JCS and President Truman from approving the invasion plans.[29]) The Strategic Bombing Survey even suggests that the Japanese war leaders welcomed such an invasion, believing it would be so costly to the attackers they would opt for a negotiated peace.[30] In short, an invasion would have been extremely bloody for both sides, and for both civilians and soldiers alike.[31]

It must be noted here that the famous statement in the Strategic Bombing Survey that Japan would have surrendered by 1 November even without atomic bombs, and without an invasion, and without Russia entering the war, was based on the assumption of the crescendo of bombing noted earlier: with the arrival of the Eighth Air Force on Okinawa, the tonnage of conventional bombs dropped on Japan was scheduled to triple beginning in September.[32] This hardly seems a preferred strategy.

What if there had been no bombing at all and no invasion as has been suggested by some? Would the starvation naval blockade have been more humane? Rationing started in 1941, and by 1945 the food situation was 'critical'. How long would a starvation blockade have lasted and how many civilians would have died before the military leaders gave in? Recall that the starvation blockade of Germany in World War I had killed over 700,000 civilians. Moreover, what of the Chinese, Koreans, Indochinese and other Asians who would have continued to suffer under Japanese occupation for perhaps years; and finally, of course, what of the 145,000 Allied prisoners of war (POWs) held in Japanese prison camps (mostly from the Commonwealth)? The liberation of the Philippine POW camps showed clearly how awful conditions were in those camps; half of all Allied POWs died while in Japanese captivity.

RESULTS AND CONCLUSIONS

The XX Bomber Command operations out of China, as noted, were of very limited use; but XXI operations were far more successful. The Twentieth Air Force dropped 91 per cent of all bombs on Japan – 146,000 tons. (The remainder were evenly divided between Kenney's Far East Air Forces and the navy – the latter were mostly airfield raids.) These attacks destroyed approximately 600 factories and thousands of 'feeder shops'. Of interest, the Japanese attempted to disperse into underground factories and caves to avert the air attacks, but this effort was totally ineffective and only further dissipated scarce resources. Overall, Japanese production dropped by 53 per cent between November 1944 and July 1945. In cities that had *not* been bombed, production in July 1945 was at 94 per cent of its wartime peak, but in cities that had been bombed, production had plummeted to 27 per cent of its wartime peak.[33] By July 1945, aluminum production was 9 per cent, while oil refining and ingot steel production were at 15 per cent of their wartime peaks. The B-29s also sowed some 12,000 mines, which sank 12 per cent of all enemy ships during the last year of the war.[34] The Strategic Bombing Survey concluded:

> By July 1945 Japan's economic system had been shattered. Production of civilian goods was below the level of subsistence. Munitions output had been curtailed to less than half the wartime peak, a level that could not support sustained military operations against our opposing forces. The economic basis of Japanese resistance had been destroyed'.[35]

It should be noted that 8.5 million people evacuated the Japanese cities. This was one-quarter of the entire urban population of Japan, although in big cities like Osaka and Kobe over half fled. One-third of the 8.5 million evacuees were factory workers, and this was evidenced by an absentee rate in the factories of 49 per cent by the end of war.[36] This trend towards flight was spurred by LeMay, who in July began dropping leaflets on Japanese cities telling them they would be bombed; 12 cities were warned and then four were actually struck. One Japanese official noted that these leaflet drops caused absolute panic and contributed heavily to the evacuation of the cities. Hundreds of thousands of people were pressed into service to fight fires, restore utilities and clear rubble after bombing missions, further hindering production and attempts at the dispersion of industry. Morale and hope plummeted. Polls taken in Japan after the war indicated that in June 1944, only 2 per cent thought Japan would lose the war; by December it was 10 per cent; in March 19 per cent; in June 46 per cent; and by August it had climbed to 68 per cent.[37] In addition, navy and army intelligence personnel interviewed over 3,150 Japanese civilians after the war – a cross-section of Japanese society. The reasons these individuals gave for the surrender were as follows: 50 per cent said it was the air strikes; 25 per cent said food shortages; and 20 per cent blamed it on other military losses.[38]

Overall, perhaps 400,000 Japanese civilians were killed by the air attacks, about the same total as in Germany, although the losses had occurred in much less time and with only one-tenth the tonnage. In addition, about 2.5 million homes were destroyed in the air attacks, as well as over 600,000 more that were pulled down by the government to build firebreaks.[39]

It should be pointed out that there was an incredible synergy between air, land and sea power. For example, airbases for the B-29s were won by the combined efforts of the army, navy and AAF. The bombers based there then struck Japanese aircraft factories, but these factories were already low on aluminum supplies because of the blockade. However, even if aircraft had been built, there were no engines to power them because bombing had destroyed the power plant factories. Yet, even if engines had been available, there was no petroleum to fuel them because of the blockade. If indeed there had been petroleum, there would have been no gasoline, because the oil refineries had been destroyed from the air. In short, the Japanese were presented with multiple catastrophic failures they could not handle; one or two of the above might have been worked around, but not all of them.

Similarly, the Japanese food situation was always precarious. As the war progressed, more and more farmers had to leave the land to fight or to work in the factories, thus causing food shortages. The cutting of sea lines by submarines and aerial mines lowered imports, and the bombing of the factories cut fertilizer production; this in turn cut the yield per acre. The need to rebuild the bombed factories pulled more farmers off the land, and by the end of the war over one million acres of arable land had been abandoned. However, due to a consequent lack of food, the productivity of all workers was lowered drastically.[40] It was a vicious and ever tightening downward spiral from which Japan could not recover.

The air campaign was not, however, an unmitigated success. The biggest strategic errors made by the airmen according to the Strategic Bombing Survey were that the B-29s should have struck railroads and inland waterways, as well as laying mines, much sooner.[41] This would have thoroughly disrupted internal transportation, as well as significantly curtailing the influx of reinforcements to Kyushu that so concerned army planners. As in Europe, such a transportation plan would have made beachhead defense much more difficult. Again, we can see here a disconnection between the mating of objectives with the appropriate targets.

In conclusion, it is my judgment that the B-29s played a decisive role in the defeat of Japan. This was the case partly because it reinforced the naval blockade that so disrupted the economy of the country as a whole, but primarily because it made ultimate victory seem so utterly hopeless to the Japanese people and their leaders. Could the country have gone on fighting – enduring really – for months and perhaps years if the only threats had been the starvation blockade and the slow but inexorable march of Allied armies towards the home islands? Certainly, but it was the psychological effect of the nightly air strikes that broke the will of the Japanese. As Premier Kantaro Suzuki phrased it: 'merely on the basis of the B-29s alone I was convinced that Japan should sue for peace'. Prince Konoye echoed that statement: 'Fundamentally, the thing that brought about the determination to make peace was the prolonged bombing of the B-29s'.[42] More specifically, I would add that it was the psychological effect of the atomic bombs which created a climate within the Japanese leadership allowing the emperor to overrule his chief military advisers and sue for peace. In this regard, it is my contention that over the past 2,000 years man has not been able to increase his capacity for destruction by one iota. The Romans destroyed Carthage every bit as totally as atomic air power destroyed Hiroshima. The difference, however, was that it took 20 Roman legions 20 years to accomplish their task; it took one B-29 only two seconds. It was this instantaneous destruction, the conquest of time not of matter, that so stunned the Japanese mind and led to peace.

Partially as a consequence of this psychological paralysis – and I do not mean this to sound callous – it allowed the Allies to achieve one of their foremost objectives in the war against both Germany and Japan: to utterly root out the militaristic spirit of those countries that had been so aggressive over the previous century and caused such bloodshed. The Allies wanted to implant in those countries a loathing for war and a determined commitment to peace – to not again disturb the tranquillity of their neighbors. To that end, air power was instrumental, and has continued to play a major role in that quest as the past 50 years have demonstrated. Wars truly are about ideas. In the words of perhaps the leading historian of air operations in World War II, Richard Overy:

> The Allies were united by nothing so much as a fundamental desire to smash Hitlerism and Japanese militarism and to use any weapon to achieve it. This primal drive for victory at all costs nourished Allied fighting power and assuaged the thirst for vengeance. They fought not only because the sum of their resources added up to victory, but because they wanted to win and were certain that their cause was just.[43]

NOTES

This chapter was given as a paper in Canberra at a conference sponsored by the Australian War Memorial in 1995. The proceedings of that conference were edited by Peter Denis and published under the title, *1945: War and Peace in the Pacific* (Canberra: Australian War Memorial, 1999).

1. The best discussion of American war plans can be found in Steven T. Ross, *American War Plans, 1941–1945* (London: Frank Cass, 1997).
2. For an excellent discussion of the 'shuttle bombing' operations from the Ukraine, see Mark J. Conversino, *Fighting with the Soviets: The Failure of Operation FRANTIC, 1944–1945* (Lawrence, KS: University Press of Kansas, 1997).
3. For an overview of the B-29's development see Kenneth P. Werrell, *Blankets of Fire: US Bombers over Japan during World War II* (Washington, DC: Smithsonian Institution, 1996), ch. 3.
4. Wesley Frank Craven and James Lea Cate, *The Army Air Forces in World War II*, 7 vols (Chicago, IL: University of Chicago Press, 1948–58), V, 35–6.
5. Maj. Gen. Haywood S. Hansell, Jr., *The Strategic Air War against Germany and Japan* (Washington, DC: Government Printing Office, 1986), 137–8, 153–8.
6. The best account of this operation is provided by its architect: Lt. Gen. William H. Tunner, *Over the Hump* (New York: Duell, Sloan, 1964).
7. For a good discussion of the B-29's mechanical problems see Werrell, *Blankets of Fire*, ch. 3.
8. LeMay's autobiography was written with MacKinlay Kantor and is titled *Mission With LeMay* (Garden City, NJ: Doubleday, 1965). The only biography of him to date is by Thomas M. Coffey, *Iron Eagle: The Turbulent Life of General Curtis LeMay* (New York: Crown, 1986).
9. The youngest full general in US history has been U. S. Grant, who was several months younger than LeMay when he pinned on his fourth star in 1866.
10. For the operational account of the XX Bomber Command, see Craven and Cate, *Army Air Forces*, V, ch. 4.
11. Hansell, *Strategic Air War*, 173.
12. For a fascinating and informative account of the Norden's development – and its limitations – see Stephen L. McFarland, *America's Pursuit of Precision Bombing, 1910–1945* (Washington, DC: Smithsonian Institution, 1995), ch. 4.
13. For an outstanding discussion of the problems with air intelligence before and during the war, see John F. Kreis (ed.), *Piercing the Fog: Intelligence and Army Air Forces Intelligence Operations in World War II* (Washington, DC: Government Printing Office, 1996), ch. 1, 2, 6 and 7.
14. Craven and Cate, *Army Air Forces*, V, 27, 93.
15. Werrell, *Blankets of Fire*, 135.
16. Ibid., 138.
17. Charles R. Griffith, 'The Quest: Haywood Hansell and American Strategic Bombing in World War II' (PhD dissertation, University of Tennessee, 1994).
18. The exception was Nagoya. Although hit by nearly the same amount of bomb tonnage as Tokyo throughout the war, it suffered only one-tenth the casualties due to more effective and efficient fire department and civil defense system. United States Strategic Bombing Survey (USSBS), 'Effects of Incendiary Bomb Attacks on Japan', no. 90, April 1947, ch. 8. The Strategic Bombing Survey was a team of several hundred civilian economists, industrialists and labor specialists, who were chartered by President Roosevelt to study the effects of strategic bombing in both Europe and the Pacific. They produced a prodigious amount of

work over a period of two years: 212 reports covering the war against Germany, and a further 108 reports documenting the air war against Japan. These reports are unprecedented in the depth and breadth of their research and analysis, which included extensive on-site inspections, thousands of interviews and the review of countless documents. There were, however, shortcomings: because of their focus on strategic bombing, the researchers tended to ignore the vital role of tactical air power, as well as the effect of strategic bombing on tactical operations. In addition, because of the large number of authors involved in these hundreds of reports, it is not uncommon to find discrepancies and contradictions between studies. Nonetheless, USSBS is the definitive starting point for any study of strategic bombing in World War II. For an excellent overview, see David MacIsaac, *Strategic Bombing in World War II: The Story of the United States Strategic Bombing Survey* (NY: Garland, 1976).

19. USSBS, 'A Report on Physical Damage in Japan', no. 96, June 1947, 82. See also Horatio Bond, *Fire and the Air War* (Philadelphia, PA: National Fire Protection Association, 1946), 244–5.
20. USSBS, 'Effects of Air Attacks on Urban Complex Tokyo-Kawasaki-Yokohama', no. 56, June 1947, 1.
21. USSBS, 'Incendiary Attacks' study, 67.
22. Craven and Cate, *Army Air Forces*, V, 601.
23. Bruce Lee, *Marching Orders: The Untold Story of World War II* (New York: Crown, 1995), see chapters 18–20 for a thorough examination of the various Ultra/Magic messages that discussed the issue.
24. USSBS, 'The Effects of Strategic Bombing on Japanese Morale', no. 14, June 1947, 99.
25. Maj. Gen. K. D. Nichols, *The Road to Trinity* (New York: Morrow, 1987), 215, 224.
26. Edward J. Drea, *MacArthur's Ultra: Codebreaking and the War against Japan, 1942–1945* (Lawrence: University Press of Kansas, 1992), 222. Indeed, Drea states it was later determined that in actuality, there were 900,000 defenders on Kyushu.
27. Ibid., 213.
28. Lee, *Marching Orders*, 491.
29. Drea, *MacArthur's Ultra*, 210.
30. USSBS, 'Japan's Struggle to End the War', no. 2, July 1946, 12.
31. The most detailed and analytical examination of the casualty issue is D. M. Giangreco, 'Casualty Projections for the US Invasions of Japan, 1945–1946: Planning and Policy Implications', *Journal of Military History*, 61 (July 1997), 521–81.
32. USSBS 'Japan's Struggle' study, 13.
33. USSBS, 'The Effects of Air Attack on Japanese Urban Economy', no. 55, March 1947, 11.
34. USSBS, 'The Effects of Strategic Bombing on Japan's War Economy', no. 53, December 1946, 43; USSBS, 'Summary Report (Pacific War)', no. 1, July 1946, 88.
35. USSBS, 'War Economy' study, 2.
36. USSBS 'Morale' study, 13; USSBS 'Urban Economy' study, 25.
37. USSBS 'Morale' study, 19.
38. Ibid., 11.
39. USSBS gives a total of 330,000 civilians killed, about 1 per cent of the total population, but other estimates run higher. Approximately 45 per cent of those killed were part of the Japanese labor force. USSBS 'Summary' study, 92.

40. USSBS 'War Economy' study, 53–4; USSBS, 'The Japanese Wartime Standard of Living and Utilization of Manpower', no. 42, January 1947, 3–11.
41. USSBS 'War Economy' study, 61–5; USSBS 'Summary' study, 91.
42. Craven and Cate, *Army Air Forces*, V, 756.
43. Richard Overy, *Why the Allies Won* (London: Jonathan Cape, 1995), 325.

9

Air Strategy: Targeting for Effect

I have long felt that a history of air strategy is really a history of targeting. From the beginnings of flight it was realized that aircraft could strike an enemy's centers of gravity and do so directly, opening new vistas in war. As a consequence, the various air theorists tended to become distinguished from one another based on their belief as to what was the main center of gravity that should be the focus of a strategic bombing campaign. They did, however, tend to assume that air warfare was an inherently economic weapon – similar to the blockades and disruption of sea lanes characteristic of sea power. Modern air theorists have begun to move away from this economic/industrial focus and turned instead towards a more leadership or cultural-centered model. Regardless, however, the process of thinking through precisely how one plans an air campaign is complicated. My intention with this chapter was to identify some factors as well as pitfalls that air campaign planners should take into consideration when going about their task. It is certainly not an exhaustive look, but perhaps can serve as an introduction to this important subject.

Airmen have always believed that the airplane is an inherently strategic weapon. Air power, operating in the third dimension, can bypass the tactical surface battle and operate directly against the centers of gravity (COGs) of an enemy nation: the industrial, political, economic and population loci that allow a country to function. However, air-power theorists have differed significantly over which specific targets should be struck or neutralized so as to achieve the greatest results. We must understand the various air targeting strategies because they collectively define the boundaries of strategic air-power thought, and they clarify the connection between the air weapon and its role in war. Moreover, understanding these concepts leads to a more balanced and flexible grasp of air strategy and the factors that go into its determination.

Psychologists tell us that the most traumatic event of a person's life is birth. If so, the birth of air power was doubly traumatic, because it occurred in concert with World War I. That war smashed empires, spawned dictatorships, caused the deaths of at least ten million people, and had a profound effect on the conduct of war. The loss of a generation of European men, as well as over 100,000 Americans, convinced military leaders that tactics and strategy had to be altered. Radical solutions were therefore given greater consideration than would ordinarily have been the case. Air power was one of those radical solutions.

When a country wishes to influence another it has several instruments at its disposal: the military, economic, political and psychological 'levers of power'. Depending on a country's objectives, it can employ these levers against another country. For example, if the objective is to express displeasure over a dictator in country A who oppresses his people, then country B may impose sanctions – the economic lever of power – in an attempt to modify his noxious behavior. Country B may also petition the United Nations to condemn the dictator and turn world opinion against him – the use of the political and psychological levers of power. Obviously, as things become increasingly serious, the military lever becomes most prominent.

These levers of power are directed against an enemy's centers of gravity. These COGs can be the strengths of a country – perhaps the army or the industrial infrastructure – but they can also be a vulnerability. This is important to recognize. In attempting to bend an enemy to our will it is not always necessary or desirable to attack him at the strongest point; rather, we should hit him at his weakest point, if by doing so it causes collapse. Thus, a country's strength may be its navy, but its weakness may, at the same time, be dependence on sea lanes that provide food and raw materials. In such an instance a strategist may wish to avoid the enemy's strength while simultaneously attacking his weakness. This is analogous to the situation in World War I when the German surface fleet remained in port in fear of the Royal Navy, while German submarines carried out a highly effective campaign against British merchant shipping. The generic COGs of a country can loosely be grouped into the categories of military forces, the economy and the popular will. In sum, strategy consists of employing levers of power against the enemy's COGs.

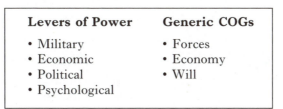

Levers of Power	Generic COGs
• Military	• Forces
• Economic	• Economy
• Political	• Will
• Psychological	

Figure 9.1: Levers of Power and Generic Centers of Gravity

Traditionally, armies have used the military lever of power to operate against an enemy's military forces. This was due, quite reasonably, to the fact that the other COGs within a country were protected and shielded by those military forces. As a consequence, war became a contest between armed forces; the losers in battle exposed their country's COGs to the victor. Usually, actual destruction or occupation was unnecessary: with the interior of the country exposed and vulnerable, the government sued for peace. Small wonder that military theorists over time equated the enemy army with the main COG, because when the army fell, so did resistance.[1] As noted, however, World War I demonstrated that such attritional contests had become far too bloody – for both sides – to serve as a rational instrument of policy.

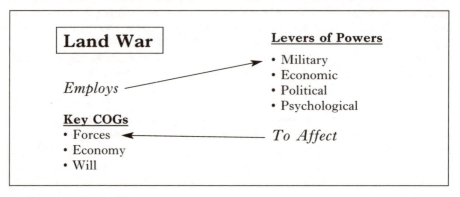

Figure 9.2: Land Warfare

Sea warfare is fundamentally different from war on land. It is difficult for navies to impact armies or events on the ground directly, so navies have traditionally relied on a form of economic warfare, exemplified by blockades, embargoes and commerce raiding, to achieve their war aims. Thus, although navies do indeed fight other navies, for the most part they use the economic and psychological levers of power against an enemy's economy and his will. Blockade and commerce raiding strangles a country of the food and raw materials it needs to carry on the war effort. Over time, the people begin to suffer the effects of prolonged starvation, and their will to continue the war dissipates.

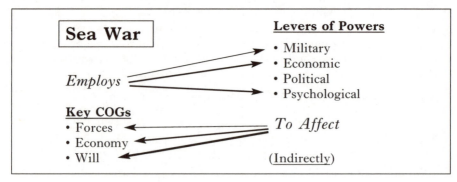

Figure 9.3: Sea Warfare

Airwar is, in turn, fundamentally different from both land and sea warfare. Airmen have always recognized that because the airplane operates in the third dimension, it has the unique ability to strike all of an enemy's COGs. Moreover, although air power operates against the enemy's economy and will – as do navies – it does so *directly*. Navies block or sink ships at sea that carry raw materials to a smelting plant that turns those materials into steel, which is then transported to a factory that turns it into weapons. Aircraft can strike those factories and weapons directly. Indeed, an enemy's entire country becomes open to attack.

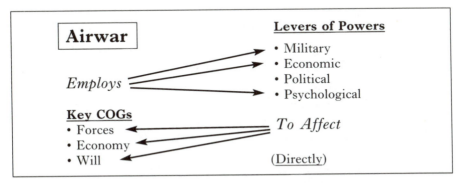

Figure 9.4: Airwar

This, however, tends to complicate things for the air strategist. Obviously, it is essential for airmen to become intimately familiar with the inner workings of an enemy nation. Knowing that a country depends on its railroads, canal system, political leaders, steel mills, electrical power grid, arable land, telephone system, chemical factories, etc. is of limited practical value because not all of these targets can be attacked. Which COGs are the *most* important? Selecting the correct targets is the essence of air strategy. Remember, however, simply because something can be targeted does not mean it is valuable, and a thing that is valuable is not necessarily targetable. Perceptive air planners realize that destruction of target sets does not automatically equate to victory, and there are intangible factors such as religion, nationalism and culture which are no less important in holding a country together during war than are its physical attributes. Moreover, the situation has become even more complex with the introduction of a host of 'new targets' critical to the functioning of a modern state: fiber-optic networks, communication satellites, nuclear power plants and their distribution systems, and the new electronic medium, often referred to as 'cyberspace', which plays an increasingly important role in all aspects of personal and professional life. How is a modern airman to sort it all out? A schematic representation of a modern country illustrates the problem and may also point to a solution.

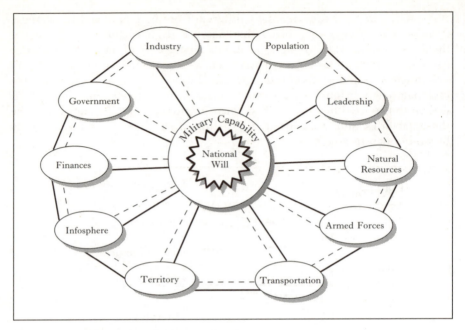

Figure 9.5: The Notional Nation-State

The key to all war is the amorphous and largely unquantifiable factor known as the 'national will'. It occupies the central place in the schematic because it is most crucial to a country at war. At its base, war is psychological. Thus, in the broadest sense, national will is always the key center of gravity – when 'the country' decides the war is lost, then, and only then, is it truly lost. However, saying that really says very little. The obvious challenge for the strategist is to determine how to shatter or at least crack that collective will. Because it is an aggregate of so many different factors, and because it has no physical form, attacking national will directly is seldom possible. Rather, the manifestations of that will are the things that must be targeted. In a general sense those manifestations can be termed 'military capability'.

Military capability is the sum of the physical attributes of power: land, natural resources, population, money, industry, government, armed forces, transportation networks, etc. When these things have been dissipated or destroyed – when there is no capability left with which to fight – then the national will either expires or becomes unimportant. Thus, in the schematic at Figure 9.5, military capability is closely tied to national will. By the same token, because military capability is at the center of a nation's being and is the sum of a country's total physical power, it is extremely difficult to destroy entirely. The key is selectively to pierce this hard shell of military capability in one or several places, thereby exposing the soft core. Through these openings the national will can be punctured, prodded, shaped and influenced. In most cases, will collapses under such pressure before capability has been exhausted.[2]

The nodes surrounding the central core are the de facto COGs that can be targeted. As noted above, in the past it was generally the armed forces and the territory of the enemy that were the foci of operations, because they were the most accessible. It was often true that if the army was defeated, or if a strategically located province was overrun, a negotiated settlement would follow. New capabilities offered new opportunities. The history of air strategy is a history of targeting – trying to discover which COG is the most important in a given place, time and situation. Although air theorists might agree that air power is intrinsically strategic, they have generally disagreed, vigorously, over which targets are most appropriate to achieve strategic objectives. What follows is a summary of the various strains of air-power targeting theory.

General Giulio Douhet believed that the population was the prime target for an air attack and that the average citizen, especially the urban dweller, would panic in the face of air assault.[3] Limited experience from World War I seemed to support that contention. Douhet was therefore convinced that dropping a mixture of incendiary, chemical and high explosive bombs on a country's major cities would cause such disruption and devastation that revolt and subsequent surrender were inevitable. Although his predictions regarding the fragility of a country's vital centers and the weakness of a population's resolve were to prove grossly in error during World War II, his basic premise has had an enduring appeal.

Fortunately, Douhet's US and British counterparts saw in air power the hope of targeting things rather than people. Air doctrine in the United States and Britain during the interwar years focused on the enemy's industrial infrastructure, not his population. In this view, the modern state was dependent on mass production of military goods – ships, aircraft, trucks, artillery, ammunition, uniforms, etc. Moreover, essentials such as electrical power, steel, chemicals and oil were also military targets and of great importance because they were the essential building blocks for other manufactured military goods needed to sustain a war effort.

In the United States, the ideas of Billy Mitchell heavily influenced the Air Corps Tactical School, where a doctrine was refined that sought industrial bottlenecks – those factories or functions that were integral to the effective operation of the entire system.[4] This 'industrial web' concept envisioned an enemy country as an integrated and mutually supporting system, but one which, like a house of cards, was susceptible to sudden destruction. If the right bottleneck was attacked or neutralized, the entire industrial edifice could come crashing down.[5] It was this doctrine that the Army Air Forces carried into World War II.

The Royal Air Force, led by Air Marshal Hugh Trenchard, took a slightly different approach. Trenchard himself had witnessed the extreme reaction by the population and their political leaders to the German air attacks on Britain in 1917 and 1918 – it was, after all, these attacks that led to the creation of the RAF. He argued, as did Douhet, that psychological effects of bombing outweighed physical effects. Unlike the Italian, Trenchard did not believe that attacking the people directly was the correct strategy to produce that psychological trauma.[6] Such a policy was morally and militarily questionable. Instead, he advocated something similar to the Tactical School: a country's industrial infrastructure was the appropriate target. He reasoned that the disruption of the normal life of the people – the loss of jobs, wages, services, transportation and goods – would be so profound the people would demand peace. In short, whereas the United States wished to bomb industry to destroy capability, Trenchard and the RAF sought to bomb industry so as to destroy the national will.

Another RAF officer who grappled with the complexities of air theory between the wars was Wing Commander John C. Slessor.[7] He argued that the enemy army's lines of supply and communication were the key COG and that if the transportation system of the enemy was disrupted and neutralized, not only would the enemy army be unable to offer effective resistance but the entire country would be paralyzed and vulnerable. This paralyzation would, in turn, have a decisive effect, not only on the enemy nation's capability but also on its will. In essence, Slessor was advocating strategic and operational-level air interdiction. Significantly, during World War II the RAF pushed strongly for just such an air campaign against Germany in 1944. The 'transportation plan', as it was called, assured the success of the Normandy landings by severely restricting the flow of German reinforcements to the lodgment area. In addition, the wholesale destruction of the German rail system in western Europe had devastating effects on their entire war effort, as Slessor had predicted.

It is significant that most of the individuals and theorists mentioned thus far are from the pre-World War II era. In truth, the massive and decisive use of air power in that war should have spawned an outburst of new thinking in the years that followed. Surprisingly and unfortunately, this was not the case. The atomic strikes on Japan had both a catalyzing and numbing effect on military leaders worldwide. The new weapon appeared to revolutionize warfare in ways that made all prior experience obsolete. As a consequence, a different group of theorists arose in an attempt to explain the use of military force in this new age. These theorists were not, however, from the military. Rather, a new breed of civilian academics, with little or no experience of war, emerged to define and articulate theories of nuclear war. Since there was virtually no experience with this type of war, civilian academics were seemingly as capable of devising a theory of nuclear air warfare as were uniformed professionals. The ideas they proposed – balance of terror, mutual assured destruction, strategic sufficiency and the like – were elegant, reasoned, and served the West well throughout the Cold War era. Regrettably, however, military airmen all too easily and quickly abandoned the intellectual field to the civilians. At the same time, the military accepted the premise that future wars would involve nuclear weapons. The result: few airmen gave serious thought to the use of conventional air power, especially at the strategic level.

The Vietnam War had many negative effects on both the United States and the military services. One positive aspect, however, was the growing realization that nuclear war between the two superpowers was an interesting intellectual exercise, but hardly likely to occur – if only because they were so well prepared to wage it. At the same time, tactical air power seemed not to be a war-winning weapon as Vietnam amply demonstrated. Thus, while air power had become polarized between those who thought only of nuclear holocaust and those who prepared to fight the tactical air battle, world conditions seemed to indicate that neither extreme offered useful and decisive results. The vast middle ground between these two poles had to be recaptured. The revitalization of strategic conventional thought began with a Fighter Weapons School instructor at Nellis AFB, Nevada, by the name of Colonel John Boyd.

John Boyd was intrigued by the astounding success of the F-86 in air combat with the MiG-15 (a ten-to-one superiority) during the Korean War.[8] Upon reflection, he decided that the F-86's advantage was due largely to its hydraulically operated flight controls and all-flying horizontal stabilizer, which allowed it to transition from one aerial maneuver to another more rapidly than the MiG. After further thought, Boyd saw broader implications of this theory. The key to victory was to act more quickly, both mentally and physically, than your opponent. He expressed this concept in a cyclical process he called the OODA Loop (observe-orient-decide-act). As soon as one side acted, it observed the consequences and the loop began anew. The most important portion of the loop was the 'orient' phase. Boyd speculated that the increasing complexities of the modern world necessitated an ability to take seemingly isolated facts and ideas from different disciplines and events, deconstruct them to their essential components, and then put them back together in new and unusual ways. He termed this process 'destruction and creation'. It was this process that dominated the 'orient' phase of his OODA Loop.

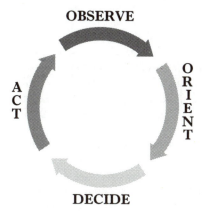

Figure 9.6: John Boyd's 'OODA Loop'

The significance of Boyd's tactical air theories is that he later hypothesized that this continuously operating cycle was at play not only in an aerial dogfight but at the higher levels of war as well. In tracing the history of war, Boyd saw victory consistently going to the side that could think the most creatively – orienting itself – and then act quickly on that insight. Although military historians tend to blanch at such a selective use of history, the thesis is an interesting one. Significantly, because of the emphasis on the orientation phase of the loop, in practical terms Boyd was calling for a strategy directed against the mind of the enemy leadership. Although posited by an airman, these theories encompassed far more than a blueprint for air operations. Warfare in general was governed by this process. Nonetheless, because of the OODA Loop's emphasis on speed and the disorienting surprise it inflicts on the enemy, Boyd's theories seem especially applicable to air power, which embodies these two qualities most fully.

Another airman who has thought deeply on strategic air power, and who also focused on enemy leadership as the key COG, is Colonel John Warden. Like Boyd, a fighter pilot and combat veteran, Warden began a serious and sustained study of air warfare while a student at the National War College in 1986. The thesis he wrote that year was soon published and is still a standard text at Air University.[9] His subsequent assignment in the Pentagon put him in an ideal location when Saddam Hussein invaded Kuwait in August 1990. Putting his theories into practice, Warden designed an air campaign that called for strategic attacks against Iraq's centers of gravity.[10] The device he used to illustrate his plan was a target bull's-eye consisting of five concentric rings, with leadership at the center, the most important COG while also the most fragile – and armed forces as the outermost ring – the least important but also the most hardened. Warden posited that the enemy leader was the key to resistance. If he could be killed or captured, then the entire country would be incapacitated. It is apparent that both Boyd and Warden have turned away from the economic emphasis of previous air-power theorists. Instead, they focus on the enemy's leadership. However, whereas Boyd seeks to disrupt the *process* of the enemy's leadership, Warden wishes instead to disrupt its *form*. The epitome of such an air strategy was the Gulf War. Air strikes against the Iraqi communications network, road and rail system, and electrical power grid made it extremely difficult, physically, for Saddam to control his military forces, but it also induced enormous confusion and uncertainty into his decision-making process. His OODA Loop was expanded dramatically, and its cycle time was slowed accordingly.

Information warfare has become a growth industry. Seemingly, everyone in the world has, or soon will have, a fax machine, cellular telephone, powerful microcomputer and access to the Internet. As a result, the accelerating pace of information exchange has become both a strength and a vulnerability for a modern country. Knowledge, presumably, is power. Whoever controls information flow has a tremendous advantage: 'perfect information' for oneself and imposed ignorance, through either denial or corruption, for an enemy. To be sure, information, when broadly defined as intelligence, reconnaissance and communications, is not new. However, the explosion in the volume and dissemination of such information, made possible by technology such as the microchip, fiber optics and satellites, has given new intensity to an old concept. The ability to dominate information is often referred to as 'infowar', and almost presumes a physical entity, sometimes called an infosphere, in which information resides or through which it is channeled. This infosphere is thus a potentially very important COG and one which has interesting implications for how future air warfare might be conducted.

Another 'new' wrinkle in military theory stresses the cultural aspects of conflict. Although physical manifestations of power are the most discernible – the easiest to target and the easiest to quantify – the cultural and social aspects of a society are also crucial. John Keegan, for example, has argued that the Clausewitzian model of war is flawed because it presumes conflict occurs between nation states that are what we would call 'rational actors' – they make decisions regarding peace and war based on a logical calculus grounded in policy. Keegan maintains that such factors explain only some motives for war; other societies are far more culturally based. He cites examples of Zulus in Africa, Siberian Cossacks and Japanese Samurai to demonstrate that some groups make war because it is traditional, a rite of passage to manhood, or a safety valve to release excess energy.[11] In such cultures, what Westerners would term the traditional causes of war and peace are largely irrelevant. The significance of this argument is not that small groups of isolated natives have, in times past, gone to war for reasons we would consider quaint. Rather, if these factors are present in some peoples, they are present in all peoples. In more modern societies, however, these cultural factors are subsumed or overshadowed by the more traditional political imperatives; they are not replaced by them. Thus, all people and countries do things, or do not do things, based on a collection of reasons, some physical and some cultural or psychological. The military strategist must be aware that he is dealing with an enemy who is part rational and part irrational, and who is motivated by reasons of both policy and passion. When a modern country is dominated by a world-view that is seemingly completely alien from a Clausewitzian perspective, the problem for the air strategist becomes extremely complex.

One could argue, for example, that it is the passionate faith of Islamic fundamentalism that effectively holds modern Iran together, not oil resources or the traditional political bonds of a Western country. Rather than the notion that the Iranian state uses religion as a tool of its policy, it would seem that radical Islam uses the state as a tool to achieve its religious goals. Air strategists have a difficult enough time attempting to predict effects and responses when dealing with a 'similar enemy'; when dealing with a dissimilar enemy the problem is greatly magnified. Nevertheless, realizing the importance of such intangible factors as the enemy culture is crucial to military planners. Because something may not have a physical form does not mean it is not important – nor does it mean it is impervious to attack. In such instances the need for psychological warfare operations – the use of propaganda, ruse, deception, disinformation, perhaps even the truth – can be decisive. In my schematic (see Figure 9.5) these intangible but vital connections are represented by the dotted lines linking the physical COGs to each other and the national core.

It is useful at this point to introduce some new terms that are used to describe air strategy. It is usually stated that the object of war is to impose your will on the enemy by destroying his will or capability to resist. There has always been a debate as to whether it is more desirable and feasible to focus on the enemy's will or on his capability, so military strategists and thinkers are often put into two categories. The first includes those who focus on seeking methods of confusing, deceiving, frightening or otherwise influencing the mind of the enemy in the hope of shattering his *will* and thus causing surrender. The other school is more physical and direct; it believes that if one attacks the enemy's military forces or industrial infrastructure, thus removing their *capability* to resist, then surrender must follow. Some, especially those trained in the social sciences, have put new terms on these old concepts and now refer to *coercion* and *denial* strategies. There has been ongoing and vigorous debate over the past decade between the proponents of these two camps. In truth, it is virtually impossible to separate these two types of strategy in practice. If the point of attacking, say, an enemy's forces is to deny them the ability to fight, then it is highly likely that such an inability will also have a strong coercive effect on the enemy's will. Conversely, if an attack on the enemy's oil refineries is intended to break an enemy's will because it destroys something they value, then, at the same time, the value of the oil revenue lost will decrease their ability to fight. The issue therefore becomes one of emphasis.

To a great extent, the choice of strategy will be driven by objectives and by the nature of the war. In a total war, with surrender and subjugation of the enemy as the goal, it is likely that the destruction of the enemy's will *and* their capability will be necessary. Thus, in World War II the Allies conducted a war directed against both Germany's will and its capability – coercion and denial. In the case of Iraq, it was similarly a question of both strategies being employed, albeit for different reasons: the coalition wanted to coerce Saddam to leave Kuwait, but it also wanted to deny him the capability of remaining an offensive threat in the region thereafter. Other conflicts, such as that in Kosovo, are more problematic regarding the type of strategy employed. It was NATO's goal to coerce Serbia into stopping its ethnic cleansing in Kosovo. *Coercion* would ordinarily entail the attack of high-value targets in Serbia itself, but planners also employed a *denial* strategy: they targeted Serbian military forces and infrastructure in Kosovo. Milosevic surrendered, but was it the coercion or the denial targeting that brought him to that decision? We may never know. Realize, however, that the choice of strategy will have a significant effect on the targets selected for air attack – power lines versus munitions factories versus rail yards versus artillery pieces. Our policy goals and the nature of the war will determine the most effective air strategy to be employed.[12]

The task of the air strategist is to understand these various targeting theories and select one, or a combination of several, to make into a workable plan. This is done by first asking three fundamental questions: what is the goal; how much is it worth to achieve that goal; and what is it worth to the enemy to prevent you from achieving it? The air strategist must then devise a plan that involves transforming broad goals into specific military objectives, identifying the target sets that need to be affected (not necessarily destroyed) to attain those objectives, and then converting the whole into an operations order that can be implemented.[13] What cannot be overemphasized is that there must be a clear linkage between the targets chosen and the objectives sought. What specifically do you expect the enemy to do if you, say, bomb the power grid? If your overall objective is to force the enemy to halt an invasion, then how will striking the power grid – or munitions factory or armored divisions or intelligence headquarters – contribute towards achieving that goal? In other words, just because a target is destroyed or neutralized does not mean that you are any closer to gaining your goals. The intellectual process of linking ends and means is a crucial, yet too often overlooked, requirement for the air strategist.

Perhaps one of the most important factors to remember in this entire discussion of COGs is that society is a living organism that reacts to a myriad of internal and external stimuli. Indeed, all the COGs are connected to each other in the schematic (Figure 9.5) to illustrate that an attack on one will usually have an impact on all the rest. Hence, if one strikes industry, it will affect the overall military capability of a country, which will be transmitted to the national will. In turn, the will may crack, or, more likely, a signal will be sent by the leaders to direct more people and resources to rebuild the damaged industries. The organism will react to counter the threat. In short, and this is crucial to note, this schematic depicts a living entity – precisely what a country is – that can act and react to various stimuli, and it can do so in ways that are not necessarily predictable: they move, shift, alter their appearance, defend themselves, panic and/or steel themselves. Indeed, organisms develop scar tissue after they have been injured, sometimes making subsequent injury less severe. As a result, the second attack is, to some extent, hitting a different organism to the first. Correspondingly, the results may also be different. Thus, the tendency to view an enemy country as an inanimate, two-dimensional model is extremely dangerous, because it assumes a static laboratory condition that is far from the case. It is foolhardy to attempt to impose rationality on an enemy society via computer simulations and models. War can never be completely rational, any more than the people who wage it.

Also understand that the COGs of one country are not necessarily those of another. In the case of World War II Japan, for example, sea lanes were vital because so many required raw materials came from the Asian mainland or the East Indies. However, sea lanes were not vital to Nazi Germany.

Because Hitler controlled most of Europe, he was largely self-sufficient in raw materials and was barely affected by the Allied blockade. Similarly, an autocratic country like Nazi Germany may be more dependent on the personality and power of the leader than is a democracy with a clearly established line of succession in the event of the leader's death.

Moreover, not only are COGs often different between countries, they may change over time within the same country. During the Battle of Britain, for example, the Royal Air Force was perilously short of pilots and aircraft. Had the Luftwaffe continued to attack the RAF airfields in the fall of 1940, this key British COG might have cracked. The following year, however, the RAF was no longer in such dire straits because planes and pilots were far more plentiful. By that point, however, the key British COG had moved into the Atlantic. German U-boats were sinking British shipping at an alarming rate, and there was serious concern as to whether or not Britain could endure this for long. Significantly, this key COG also changed when the United States entered the war and the massive infusion of shipping capacity alleviated Britain's plight.

If one agrees that an enemy country is a living organism composed of multiple centers of gravity that act and react with one another and the outside world, then several conclusions follow. First, air power is an especially effective weapon against those COGs. Most of the vital centers noted above are physical and thus can be directly targeted. Indeed, because they are for the most part immobile and thus vulnerable, they are often especially susceptible to the effects of air power – a power grid, railroad network or factory complex, for example. Other types of military force generally cannot act against such targets directly and are limited to operations against fielded forces.[14] Of course, air power can attack those forces as well and can do so quite effectively. What is important to note is that the reasons for turning to air power in the post-World War I era when anticipating war against an industrial opponent – the desire to avoid bloodshed, the interdependence of modern economies, the perceived vulnerability of strategic COGs and air power's ability to affect them at relatively low risk – have tended to increase over the decades. To be sure, the intangible aspects of a country – its culture, religion and tradition – will be difficult to influence, but that is the case when using all military forces, not just air power.

Determining the key target or group of targets within a country requires careful and accurate measurement of the effects of strategic air attacks. This analysis is essential to ensure the results are what were expected, so that adjustment can be made for future operations. This is not a minor consideration. Air intelligence is a relatively new phenomenon. Although information-gathering agencies have existed for centuries, the types of intelligence they sought ran to two extremes. On the one hand, diplomatic insights were sought to determine potential adversaries' foreign policy, the strength of the government, alliance commitments, or the soundness of the economy. On the other hand, it was also necessary to ascertain military information such as the size of the enemy army and navy, the route of march, adequacy of supplies and rate of fire of the artillery. Although tactical information is also necessary for the air battle – the strength, disposition and capability of the enemy air force and air defense network – strategic air warfare demanded a totally new type of intelligence. Detailed economic and industrial information is also now required. Because aircraft can strike military, economic and governmental centers deep within enemy territory, it is necessary to know the precise location and function of such targets. Air warfare required a detailed understanding of the electrical power grid, rail and road networks, iron and steel industry, communications network and a host of other such items. This was a fundamentally different type of military intelligence to that of previous eras. As a result, new bureaucracies arose during World War II, composed of economists, industrialists and engineers, whose main function was to study the make-up and vulnerabilities of an enemy state.[15] Today, these intelligence agencies form a major part of the military and their products are vital to the formulation of a viable air campaign plan.

At the same time, air leaders quickly realized in World War II that understanding how an economic or industrial system *failed* was just as important as how it operated. A way was needed to measure the effects of air attacks on a complex, interconnected and multi-layered system. This is an extremely difficult task because it requires analyses of complicated networks. For example, it is relatively easy to determine the amount of physical damage an air attack causes to a railroad marshaling yard – the number of buildings or rail cars destroyed, tracks torn up, etc. It is more difficult to measure the effect such damage will have on an entire rail network, given the redundancy of such systems, the availability of repair teams and the ability to route traffic through other yards. It is more difficult still to judge what effect the shortage of materials *not* moved by the destroyed trains will have on the economy as a whole. An illustration of this problem and its complexity is given by one historian who has examined the records of the German railroad bureau in World War II. His analysis revealed that the destruction and disruption of German rail traffic severely curtailed the movement of coal throughout the Reich. Coal was the primary fuel for most industrial production and power generation. Therefore, the shortage of coal caused by the disruption of the rail system had a major effect on the production of steel, and this resulted in the decreased output of tanks, ships and heavy artillery.[16] Thus, the overall military capability of the German armed forces was reduced by air strikes against seemingly unrelated targets deep in Germany. Clearly, such analysis requires intimate familiarity with the enemy's economy, as well as keen analytical skills. These are not the only problems.

If John Keegan is correct, that social and cultural factors play a far greater role in war than has hitherto been acknowledged, then the problem of analysis becomes even greater. This difficulty becomes compounded if it is considered that a country may strike a particular target not because of the effect it expects to produce on the enemy, but rather for the effect on its own domestic population. The Doolittle Raid of April 1942, by 16 bombers against targets in Tokyo, was carried out at least as much to bolster US morale after a series of defeats as it was to influence the Japanese leaders or the Japanese economy. Similarly, attacks may be carried out so as to influence a third country. There are those who would argue, for example, that the atomic bombs were dropped on Hiroshima and Nagasaki not to compel Japanese surrender, but to send a political message to the Soviet Union – the bombs were an act of deterrence for the future.[17] Similarly, did the air strike on Libya in 1986, in response to the terrorist bombing in Berlin, have an equally deterring effect on Syria as it did on Libya? In short, remember that warfare consists of living organisms fighting other living organisms while still other living organisms look on and are affected. If such complex and layered motives are indeed at play, the problems of analysis are enormous. It thus becomes necessary for intelligence organizations to focus on making a second leap – from an understanding of industrial and economic processes, to cultural and psychological ones. This will not be easy.

Until it becomes possible accurately and predictably to measure and quantify such macro-level effects, airmen will always be at a disadvantage relative to their surface counterparts. It has been traditional for centuries to measure victory or defeat on land in terms of armies destroyed, soldiers slain and territory captured. Such standards are both quantifiable and widely recognized. It must be remembered, however, that just as the absence of hard statistics does not necessarily mean a theory is wrong, their presence does not confirm that a theory or policy is correct. Americans seem to have a cultural penchant for measuring things, especially in war – bomb tonnage, sortie rates, body counts, tank kills – and this can beguile one into thinking that the mere presence of numbers infers either accuracy or success. If one is measuring the wrong things, however, the statistics are worse than meaningless.

In summary, it has become apparent over the past six decades that air power is playing an increasingly important role in warfare. Surface force commanders have realized that their operations are extremely difficult, if not impossible, without the extensive employment of air power. Indeed, the US Navy has built most of its force structure around air power – the carrier battle groups. The Marines have organized their air–ground task forces around air power, and the Army's 5,000 helicopters constitute one of the largest air arms in the world. Few question the ability of air power to be decisive at the tactical and operational levels of war. The issue of its effectiveness at the strategic level of war is, however, a different matter. Airmen have claimed, since the first decade of flight, that warfare has been changed forever because of their new weapon. Without denying the dominance of air power on the battlefield, they argue for its pre-eminence at the strategic level as well. Their arguments for this contention have relied upon their various targeting philosophies. The question as to which strategic targets should have priority in an air campaign is surprisingly complex and the answer is not at all self-evident. As a result, a whole variety of air theories have sprung up, each with its own logic and evidence.

It has become an aphorism that flexibility is the key to air power. This is just as true in the theoretical sense as in the operational. What are needed now are airmen conversant and well-grounded in all aspects of warfare, including the theoretical. Only then will they be able to select the employment concept best suited to the situation at hand. Flexibility is also the key to air strategy. Ultimately, air targeting strategy is an art not a science. Unfortunately, it is an incredibly complex art. The purpose of this discussion has been to better arm air strategists with an appropriate array of questions so that they can make better decisions in peace and war.

NOTES

This chapter originally appeared under the same title in *Aerospace Power Journal*, Winter 1999.

1. Hence, Clausewitz's dictum: 'Destruction of the enemy forces is the overriding principle of war, and, so far as a positive object is concerned, the principal way to achieve our objective'. Carl von Clausewitz, *On War* trans. Howard and Paret (Princeton, NJ: Princeton University Press, 1976), 258.

2. An exception was Nazi Germany. It was not until the German air force, army and navy were largely destroyed, the economy in shambles, and Soviet troops had actually entered Berlin, that Hitler's successor sued for peace. Given the state of the Reich at that point his official surrender was almost irrelevant.

3. Douhet's primary work was titled 'Command of the Air' and was first published in 1921, with a revised edition appearing in 1927. In 1942, this essay was combined with three other of his major works, translated by Dino Ferrari, and published as *Command of the Air* (New York: Coward-McCann). This translation was reprinted with a new introduction by the Air Force History Office in 1983. For analyses of Douhet's theories, see Bernard Brodie, *Strategy in the Missile Age* (Princeton, NJ: Princeton University Press, 1959); and 'Giulio Douhet and the Origins of Airpower Theory', in School of Advanced Airpower Studies (SAAS), *The Paths of Heaven: The Evolution of Airpower Theory* (Maxwell AFB: Air University Press, 1997).

4. Lt. Col. Peter R. Faber, 'Interwar US Army Aviation and the Air Corps Tactical School: Incubators of American Air power', in SAAS, *Paths of Heaven*.

5. The origins of the industrial web theory can be found as early as the mid-1920s. Maj. William Sherman, an instructor at the Tactical School, wrote: 'in the majority of industries, it is necessary to destroy certain elements of the industry only, in order to cripple the whole. These elements may be called key plants'. Maj. William Sherman, *Air Warfare* (New York: Ronald, 1926), 218. For the developments of the 1930s, see the account by one of the participants, Maj. Gen. Don Wilson, 'Origins of a Theory of Air Strategy', *Aerospace Historian*, 18 (Spring 1971), 19–25.

6. For an analysis of Trenchard's theories see 'Trenchard, Slessor and Royal Air Force Doctrine Before World War II', in SAAS, *Paths of Heaven*.

7. Slessor's ideas have not yet been adequately explored. For his excellent memoirs, see *The Central Blue: Recollections and Reflections* (London: Cassell, 1956). His

most impressive theoretical work is *Air Power and Armies* (Oxford: Oxford University Press, 1936).

8. John Boyd never published his theories, but the best description and evaluation of them is by Lt. Col. David S. Fadok, 'John Boyd and John Warden: Air Power's Quest for Strategic Paralysis', in SAAS, *Paths of Heaven.*

9. Col. John A. Warden III, *The Air Campaign: Planning for Combat* (Washington, DC: Pergamon, 1989) has had a major impact on US Air Force thinking, even though relatively modest in its calls for strategic air power. Indeed, it is illuminating that Warden's book today elicits little controversy; the ideas he proposed then have become accepted wisdom. Warden's ideas took a sizable leap with the experience of the Gulf War.

10. For a readable and illuminating account of air campaign planning in Desert Storm, see Col. Richard T. Reynolds, *Heart of the Storm: The Genesis of the Air Campaign Against Iraq* (Maxwell AFB: Air University Press, 1995).

11. John Keegan, *A History of Warfare* (New York: Knopf, 1993). For an excellent analysis of how cultural factors apply to air warfare, see Lt. Col. Pat Pentland, 'Center of Gravity Analysis and Chaos Theory: Or How Societies Form, Function and Fail', thesis (Air War College, Maxwell AFB, 1993), and Paul M. Belbutowski, 'Strategic Implications of Cultures in Conflict', *Parameters* XXVI (Spring 1996), 32–42.

12. For good discussions, see Robert A. Pape, *Bombing to Win: Air Power and Coercion in War* (Ithaca, NY: Cornell University Press, 1996), and Michael Clarke, 'Air Power, Force and Coercion', in Andrew Lambert (ed.), *The Dynamics of Air Power* (Bracknell: RAF Staff College, 1996).

13. For excellent discussions of this process see Lt. Col. Maris McCrabb, 'Air Campaign Planning', *Airpower Journal* 7 (Summer 1993), 11–22; and David E. Thaler and David A. Shlapak, *Perspectives on Theater Air Campaign Planning* (Santa Monica, CA: RAND, 1995).

14. Actually, airmen do believe in the decisiveness of the counterforce battle – the one for air superiority. Without air superiority, gained by neutralizing the enemy's air force and ground defenses, all other military operations on land, sea and in the air will be extremely difficult.

15. A study of these economic warriors has yet to be written, but for the views of two participants see, for the Americans, W.W. Rostow, *Pre-Invasion Bombing Strategy* (Austin, TX: University of Texas Press, 1981), and for the British, Solly Zuckerman, *From Apes to Warlords* (New York: Harper & Row, 1978).

16. Alfred C. Mierzejewski, *The Collapse of the German War Economy, 1944–1945* (Chapel Hill, NC: University of North Carolina Press, 1988).

17. For an excellent discussion of these ideas see Maj. Thomas P. Ehrhard, 'Expanding the SAAS Airpower Analysis Framework', Master's thesis, School of Advanced Airpower Studies, 1995.

10

Precision Aerospace Power, Discrimination and the Future of War

The issue of casualties in war has always interested me. It is truly astonishing how ready man has been to slaughter his neighbors, a readiness that has not decreased as he has become more 'civilized'. The twentieth century was the bloodiest in history, and events in its last decade, Rwanda and Kosovo come to mind, were just as mindless and vicious as those in the beginning of the century. Somewhat paradoxically, despite modern technology, the old methods of killing people are still preferred – small arms and starvation have been the great killers of the past century. Fortunately, as air power has become increasingly dominant and decisive in war, this murderous trend has begun to reverse. In truth, air advocates have always claimed that air warfare would bring a measure of humanity and discrimination to battle, but that promise's fulfillment had to await the development of precision weapons and the intelligence necessary for their effective targeting. The last decade of the twentieth century offered a compelling vision of how warfare can indeed be waged in a manner that limits its horror for non-combatants.

During Operation Allied Force over Kosovo, there were some observers who questioned the tactics of NATO airmen. No less a worthy than Senator John McCain, a fighter pilot himself during Vietnam, wondered aloud as to the morality of flying and bombing above 15,000 feet. McCain and others were concerned that bombing from that altitude, where it was 'safe', was inherently less accurate and therefore less humane than if the aircraft had gone lower.[1] These critics were wrong. In the vast majority of cases, NATO airmen flew at the optimum altitude for achieving accuracy, while also fulfilling NATO political demands to avoid risk.

It is the thesis of this chapter that air warfare over the past decade has significantly humanized war – if such a phenomenon is possible. Tremendous technological strides in the use of precision weapons, as well as developments in air and space intelligence-gathering tools, have made it far easier to discriminate between military and civilian targets, and then effectively to strike those military targets. Moreover, such effectiveness has been accomplished with a marked reduction in risk to the attackers. In short, modern air warfare has reduced casualties among both the attackers and the attacked, thus making it an increasingly efficient, effective and humane tool of US foreign policy.

It is true that General Wesley Clark, the NATO commander, directed the airmen to take all precautions to limit 'friendly' losses. Clark realized that the fragility of the NATO alliance during Allied Force necessitated such risk avoidance. Enemy missiles, antiaircraft artillery and small arms fire can be extremely deadly at low altitude. As a consequence, strike aircraft were directed to stay above 15,000 feet when deploying their weapons. An important question is whether or not this significantly and adversely impacted accuracy. In the vast majority of cases it did not. A brief discussion of new air weapons and their characteristics is necessary.

Precision-guided munitions (PGMs) are air-launched weapons that have improved accuracy by orders of magnitude. These weapons are equipped with adjustable fins that allow them to alter course in flight and home in on their targets. PGMs have several different types of guidance systems – laser-homing, inertial, optical or infrared imaging, or the use of GPS (global positioning system) satellite signals. These various guidance systems have strengths and weaknesses: for example, laser-guided bombs are highly accurate but, as lasers cannot penetrate clouds, they are unusable when bad weather obscures the target. The most successful new PGMs employed over Kosovo were those using GPS guidance. These are relatively inexpensive but highly accurate weapons that, in some cases, allow a standoff capability. They can be launched several miles from the target – thereby lowering the risk to the delivery aircraft and crew. Perfect accuracy is not guaranteed – failure of the guidance system, aircraft equipment or aircrew error means that accidents still happen – but current PGMs have an accuracy that is usually measured in feet.

Although used in Vietnam, PGMs truly came into their own during the Gulf War of 1991. The cockpit videos detailing the accuracy of these weapons were shown continually on television and have become one of the defining images of that war: bombs were seen going down chimneys, through doors and into specific windows. 'Airshaft accuracy' had become so seemingly routine it was now expected. When US aircraft struck Serbian targets in Bosnia in 1995 and Serbia/Kosovo in 1999, PGMs were used almost exclusively in populated areas. Once again, the accuracy of these weapons was extraordinary. Visitors to Serbia were amazed to see radio towers neatly separated from their concrete bases and toppled, while civilian buildings not more than 50 feet away were untouched. In another instance, a Serbian defense facility was razed, while buildings on either side were largely unscathed.

There were mistakes, but the relatively small number of such errors was remarkable. Human Rights Watch states that there were 90 instances during Allied Force when attacking NATO aircraft caused civilian casualties and collateral damage.[2] Most of these occurred in well-reported accidents where bombs went astray or targets were misidentified. For example, in one instance, aircrews were given the wrong target, which they nevertheless hit precisely – the Chinese embassy. In another case, the guidance system of a PGM dropped on an airfield failed, and the bomb landed in a residential area several hundred yards away. On another occasion, an aircraft attacked a bridge just as a passenger train unexpectedly passed over it. It is important to remember that these accidents were relatively infrequent given the number of strikes flown (14,000) and munitions dropped (28,000). It was essential for NATO solidarity that such precision was possible. Moreover, given that several NATO countries had already stated their opposition to a ground assault, it is probable that without a precision air campaign, there would have been no NATO military response whatsoever to Serb ethnic cleansing operations. Even the Serbs themselves realized the extreme accuracy and carefulness of the air campaign. Hence, Belgrade citizens wore shirts with targets painted on them and held rallies on bridges over the Danube, secure in the knowledge that the NATO air strikes were so precise and so discriminate that they would never have to pay for such foolishness. The charge that dropping these weapons from 15,000 feet was somehow inappropriate simply does not stand up under scrutiny.

For a PGM, maximum accuracy is achieved if it is dropped in the mid-altitude range – from 15,000 to 23,000 feet. This allows enough time for the weapon to correct itself in flight and hit its designated target as close to a bull's eye as possible. If dropped from a lower altitude, the weapon's steering fins will have less opportunity to correct the aim and the weapon will be less accurate. From the pilot's perspective, this altitude range is also the most desirable if attacking a fixed or pre-planned target. The middle altitudes allow time to identify the target at sufficient distance, 'designate it' (if laser-guided), and launch the weapon. In short, for PGMs against a fixed target whose position is already established – which was the case in most of the targets struck in Serbia – the optimum altitude to ensure accuracy is at or above 15,000 feet.

Non-guided munitions – 'dumb bombs' – are inherently less precise than their more intelligent brothers, so their optimum drop altitude is lower than that of a PGM. Even so, acquisition remains a limiting factor – coming in too low makes it nearly impossible to acquire the target, line up and put the bomb on target. One can imagine how difficult such target acquisition is for a pilot roaring in at 500 feet and 500 knots. At that speed and altitude the pilot generally has his hands full just trying to avoid impacting the ground. As a result, the compromise altitude for the delivery of unguided bombs is around 5,000 feet. This, however, puts the delivery aircraft right in the thick of fire from ground defenses. Allied Force air commanders resolved this dilemma by keeping aircraft at medium altitudes, but restricting the use of non-PGMs to areas where there was little or no chance there would be civilian casualties or collateral damage.

The difficulty arises when attacking mobile or transitory targets. In such cases, the key factor becomes target identification. Is the column below comprised of military or civilian vehicles? If both, which is which? At medium altitudes it is difficult to make such a determination. In this situation, to protect against misidentification, it is best to have someone closer to the target. This can be done by a FAC (forward air controller), an aircraft that generally operates at lower altitudes, a UAV (unmanned air vehicle), which is also at a lower altitude and can relay the video it takes of the suspected target to an analyst, who can rapidly determine its identity and relay that information to the airborne aircraft or spotters on the ground. Once the determination is made by one of these sources, strike aircraft can attack from the optimal altitude.

Problems arose when aircraft at 15,000 feet saw what appeared to be military forces below, but with no FAC, UAV or ground spotters available. In such instances, given the strictures against both civilian casualties and taking casualties themselves, aircrews were in a quandary: they could not positively identify the target and were restrained from going lower to do so. Usually, the pilots elected not to drop their bombs.

There were exceptions. On 14 April 1999, near Djakovica, Kosovo, NATO pilots attacked what intelligence sources had identified as a military column. It is now known the column also contained refugees: as many as 73 civilians were killed in the airstrikes.[3] This is the only known instance in the 78-day air campaign where NATO intelligence sources and aircraft at medium altitude combined to misidentify a target, thereby causing civilian casualties.

Could this accident have been avoided if the aircraft had been flying lower? Probably. Indeed, NATO changed the rules after this, allowing aircraft in certain circumstances to fly lower to ensure target identification. There is a tradeoff in such instances. Flying lower increases the risk to aircrews due to enemy ground fire, so at what point does the risk of misidentifying a target override the risk of losing a plane and its crew? The Law of Armed Conflict states that an attacker does 'everything feasible' to avoid harming civilians or non-military targets. 'Feasible' is a highly subjective term. Were friendly losses feasible if it meant the shattering of the Alliance, which would have allowed Milosevic to continue his atrocities unchecked?

What has tied together these new weapons to make them so effective is an intelligence, communications and geo-locating network that relies on assets positioned in space, the air and on the ground. Satellites collect imaging data, relay communications and provide precise geographic updates; airborne sensors do much the same tasks from closer in, while also providing more flexibility for short-notice operations. Personnel on the ground and in the air receive, analyze and disseminate the information gathered, while commanders at all levels use it to lead their forces. Over Kosovo, for example, a U-2 flying over a suspected target took video and relayed that video via satellite back to the United States. There, analysts determined that the objects captured on film were Serb military vehicles. This information was then fused with three-dimensional terrain data and satellite imagery taken earlier to generate precise geographic coordinates. These coordinates were relayed via satellite to orbiting command and control aircraft, which directed an airborne F-15E strike aircraft to attack. The F-15, using PGMs employing GPS, then knocked out the targets. All of this took place in minutes. As little as one decade ago, such an operation would have been considered a pipe dream.

The employment of these new technologies and tactics came together over the Balkans. Allied Force was a unique event because of its almost total reliance on aerospace power. Although the use of ground troops – or even the threat of their use – would have been very helpful in bringing pressure to bear on Serb leaders, NATO ruled out their use early in the crisis. The American public has become 'casualty averse' over the past two decades. Mercifully, few Americans died in Grenada, Panama and the Persian Gulf War, and such low losses have now become expected. Casualties, even few in number, are unacceptable. In October 1993, 18 American soldiers were killed and their bodies dragged through the streets of Mogadishu, Somalia. The revulsion felt by the American people caused the government to withdraw US forces from Somalia.

Partly as a result of this concern over casualties, air forces bore the brunt of the NATO campaign. After 78 days of airstrikes, Milosevic yielded and withdrew his military forces from Kosovo. More surprisingly perhaps, NATO suffered no casualties, while Serb losses were minimized through the rigid procedures that governed the use of weapons, tactics and the selection of targets. Today, what is often called 'the CNN factor' complicates the issue further and places even greater pressure on the commander.

In a sense, every bomb, missile or bullet fired by a US airman, soldier or sailor is a political act. When a bomb goes astray and hits a residential area, a Tomahawk missile crashes into a hotel lobby, or a sniper's bullet kills a pregnant woman getting water at a well, US *foreign* policy – not just military policy – suffers a setback. We can no longer afford to miss. More than that, even when we hit the target, we have to do so almost softly and with minimal impact.[4] One is reminded of the Western programs on television many years back: the good guy – the one in the white hat – never killed the bad guy; he shot the gun out of his hand and arrested him. That is our new standard.

There is, however, another issue that airmen have not adequately addressed but which is germane to the subject of discrimination in war. Cluster bombs, which can be air-delivered, are weapons that deploy a large number of baseball-sized bomblets over a fairly wide area. Some cluster bombs dispense landmines, while others dispense anti-armor, anti-personnel or simple fragmentation bomblets for use against structures, radar sites or runways. Some cluster bombs are precision weapons in their own right – the 'sensor fused weapon' consists of 40 individually targeted bomblets that home in on the infrared signature of a vehicle. Others are deployed by a 'wind corrected munitions dispenser' that makes the cluster bomb canister accurate to within 30 feet. Still other cluster bombs have no precision guidance at all.

The problem: an estimated 5 per cent of cluster bomblets fail to explode on impact, thus making them, essentially, anti-personnel landmines. International agencies are already jumping on this issue, and airmen should expect these groups to push for a ban on the use of cluster bombs.[5] Although a total prohibition would seem extreme, airmen must address this issue head on. How many cluster bombs have been employed over the past decade and by whom? How effective have they been against their intended targets? What is their accuracy in actual operations? What per centage are duds? How easy are these duds to defuse after the conflict has ended? How many noncombatants have been killed or injured by unexploded bomblets? These are all questions that airmen must answer. The use of cluster bombs could be seen by some as an anomaly in the continual drive towards the precision employment of air weapons. A strong case can probably be made for the military efficacy and legality of cluster bombs, but that case has not yet been made, and it will have to be made soon.

Similarly, there has been a growing concern over the use of depleted uranium (DU) munitions. DU is an extremely hard substance that is ideal for the warheads on artillery shells or bullets that must penetrate the heavy steel used in armored vehicles. During the Gulf War, the US Army and Air Force expended nearly one million such munitions. In the aftermath of the war there was a concern that those rounds exposed military personnel and civilians to dangerous levels of radiation. The shell fragments left behind could cause further problems for the indigenous populace. The situation was repeated in Allied Force when the US Air Force's A-10 fighter-bomber expended thousands of rounds of DU-tipped 30mm cannon shells. It is not clear how much damage these shells present to the Serbian/Kosovar populations.[6] Nonetheless, this is another area that airmen must examine to determine if there is a better way to perform the mission of killing enemy armored vehicles. If the price for killing enemy tanks is to poison the battlefield, then that price is too high.

Despite these two exceptions, it is clear that airmen have made great efforts to limit civilian casualties and collateral damage over the past decade. Yet, concerns are still raised regarding the humanity of air warfare. In one sense, the drive to limit the suffering of noncombatants and structures is highly commendable. In another sense, however, the calls for greater accuracy, greater discrimination and greater restraint in air operations are puzzling when it is realized that traditional forms of war are far more deadly, especially to noncombatants, than is modern airwar. Yet, there is little debate on how best to control these other forms of war.

Wars have always been harmful to noncombatants. Over the centuries, however, various attempts have been made to shield them from harm through the promulgation of various laws, treaties, conventions and protocols. On paper, these attempts look satisfying and noble; reality is another matter. Paradoxically, as legal activities to soften war's effects have accelerated, the numbers of civilian noncombatants killed have increased dramatically.

Well over 100 million people died in wars during the twentieth century –
the bloodiest in history. One source claims that 110 million people died in
just the first seven decades of the century: 62 million perished as a result of
genocide or starvation caused by blockade and siege; 24 million were killed
by small arms; 17 million by artillery and naval gunfire; and 2 million due
to air attack.[7] These statistics, horrible as they are, do not include several
million more deaths in Cambodia, Afghanistan, the Iran–Iraq War, Angola,
Rwanda, Chechnya and the Balkans. The vast majority of all those killed
were noncombatants. These statistics indicate that the principle of
noncombatant immunity is at best a goal we have striven unsuccessfully to
achieve, but at worst is a myth that hides the truth. Innocent people have
always suffered the most in war, especially in the traditional forms of land
and sea warfare. On the Eastern Front in World War II, it is estimated that
10 million Soviet civilians were killed through starvation, artillery barrage
and gunfire; air attack was a negligible factor in piling up that horrendous
death count. In fact, in all the wars of the twentieth century and all the tens
of millions of noncombatants who have been killed, a tiny percentage,
perhaps 2 per cent, have died as a result of air attack.

Sieges, artillery bombardments and ground campaigns have always been
deadly. One of the more celebrated sieges of the past century was that of
Leningrad during World War II. Over a period of nearly three years,
German forces surrounded the city, attempted to starve it out and
pummeled it with artillery fire. In one of the more startling incidents of the
siege, the Soviet garrison commander attempted to allow the civilians
trapped within the fortress city to escape. He called upon the German
commander, Field Marshal Wilhelm von Leeb, to cease firing while the
civilians departed. Von Leeb refused and ordered his troops to fire on the
defenseless civilians if they tried to escape. Many did try to flee and were
consequently slaughtered. At Nuremburg, von Leeb was tried as a war
criminal for this incident, but he claimed his actions were permissible under
the laws of war. He was acquitted.[8] Over one million Russian civilians –
allegedly protected by their noncombatant immunity – died during the siege
of Leningrad.[9] The sieges of the past decade at Sarajevo and Grozny in
Chechnya have shown once again the devastation and deadliness of such
operations. Recent instances of ground operations that have resulted in
hundreds of civilian deaths are the invasion of Panama and the failed effort
in Somalia.

Another pervasive and indiscriminate killer is the landmine. In 1993,
experts estimated that as many as 100 million unexploded landmines were
scattered throughout 62 countries. The US State Department estimated that
landmines killed or wounded more than 150 people per week worldwide. The
US Red Cross thought this estimate was low, and that 200 people were killed
each week and another 100 or so were wounded.[10] Both agreed that the
majority of those killed and wounded were civilians.

Virtually all belligerents use landmines. In the Gulf War, for example, the
United States and its allies laid approximately one million mines along the

Iraq–Kuwait border.[11] Millions more have been sown in South Korea along the border with the North. Although the purpose of these mines is defensive, these 'eternal sentinels' are unable to distinguish friend from foe. Once a war is over, the mines often remain, posing a huge danger to the local populace. Worse, removing mines is not an easy task: besides the risk, it costs nearly $1,000 to remove a mine that cost a fraction of that amount to plant.[12] Traditional war by sea has also been deadly to innocents.

Clausewitz was wrong. War does not necessarily have to be 'an act of violence'. For centuries, the weapons of war have included the seemingly benign operations of naval blockades and sanctions. Their purpose is to induce suffering in a target country or region. Cutting off trade, food and raw materials is expected to correspondingly lower the standard of living among the populace, thus causing unrest. When unrest grows to a certain level, the populace will, hopefully, move against its government and leaders to force a change of policy which will convince those imposing the blockade or sanctions to lift them. As Vice President Al Gore stated succinctly in the presidential debate of 3 October 2000: 'the people of Serbia know that they can escape all these sanctions if this guy [Milosevic] is turned out of power'. Unfortunately, this can be a slow, laborious and very deadly process. For example, according to the British official history, over 750,000 German civilians died as a result of the Allied starvation blockade of World War I. The Germans contend the figure was much higher, but, in any event, it does not include those civilians who died in Austria–Hungry, Bulgaria and Turkey – German allies also under blockade.[13]

More recently, the Organization of American States (OAS) in 1991, and then the United Nations (UN) in 1993, imposed sanctions on Haiti in the aftermath of a military coup that drove President Jean-Bertrand Aristide from office. It was believed that the use of military force to restore Aristide was too extreme an option, because it would cause excessive bloodshed and suffering. The goals of the OAS and the UN in imposing sanctions instead were eminently noble: to induce the military junta to step down and restore democracy to Haiti. However, even supporters of the sanctions admit that the junta and its inner circle 'not only survived but prospered' during the embargo. As a consequence, the price for this supposedly humane action was paid for by the Haitian population. Unemployment soared to 70 per cent, the Gross Domestic Product plummeted and the inflation rate climbed to 50 per cent. A 1993 study conducted by the Harvard Center for Population and Development Studies found that the sanctions were killing 1,000 children per month.[14]

An even worse example of how seemingly non-violent weapons of war can be incredibly deadly is currently taking place in Iraq. Since the end of the Gulf War, several reports have detailed the severe suffering of the Iraqi populace as a result of the UN embargo. Although the Geneva Conventions specifically prohibit the use of food deprivation as a weapon, the UN nonetheless imposed just such restrictions. Agriculture seed to grow crops, farm machinery and over 4½ million tons of food ordered by Iraq were turned back by the naval fleet enforcing the embargo. Between 6 August 1990 and mid-March 1991, no food was allowed into Iraq. As a consequence, the Harvard Study Group, which visited Iraq in 1991, estimated that as many as 50,000 children with leukemia, diabetes, asthma, heart disease and other ailments died.[15] The outrage in the world community over this situation was so great that the UN lifted the embargo on food and medicine, and instituted the 'oil for food' program which allows Iraq to sell some of its oil and use the proceeds to buy food, medicine and other necessities.[16] The results of this easing of the embargo have not been overly successful.

In March 1996, the World Health Organization published a report on conditions in Iraq. Comparing the levels of infant mortality rates in 1996 with those before the war, it found that the rates had doubled and the rate for children under the age of five had increased sixfold.[17] It concluded that the shortage of food and medicine was directly attributable to '*financial constraints* as a result of the sanctions [which] have prevented the necessary import of food and medicine'.[18] These findings were confirmed three years later when UNICEF (UN International Children's Emergency Fund) visited Iraq and noted that statistics showed a steady and continual decline in mortality rates between 1960 and 1990 – despite the oppressive dictatorship of Saddam Hussein, the Iraqi people were getting healthier as the economy grew. The war and subsequent UN embargo changed everything. The under-5-year-old mortality rate jumped from 50 per thousand live births in 1980 to 117 per thousand by 1995. By 1999, it had climbed further to 125 deaths per thousand. UNICEF concluded that if the mortality rates of the 1980s had been continued through the 1990s, 'there would have been half a million fewer deaths of children under five in the country as a whole during the eight-year period 1991 to 1998'.[19]

This is a staggering statistic. The UN has admitted that half a million infants have died as a direct result of their own embargo on Iraq. When this statistic is compared to the total of 2,300 civilians that Iraq claims were killed during the six-week air campaign in 1991, the disconnection between perceptions of what constitutes humanity and discrimination in war becomes glaring. When we conduct military operations that cause such enormous death and suffering, we have lost the moral high ground.

A great deal of ink has been spilled on the subject of whether or not sanctions and embargoes have succeeded in their purpose of forcing a change in behavior of the target leadership. The results are contradictory.[20] In truth, however, the question of whether or not sanctions and embargoes 'work' misses the point. A more relevant question would be: 'do the ends justify the means?' Sanctions, embargoes and blockades are not a 'clean' option, and they do indeed cause very real levels of human suffering to the weakest members of a target society. That suffering must be factored into the costs when evaluating different courses of action.

There is a wealth of empirical data over the past several centuries to show that blockades, embargoes, sanctions and sieges almost always have a percolating effect: they start killing at the bottom levels of society and slowly work their way upwards. The three-quarters of a million German civilians who died as a result of the starvation blockade in World War I were not the soldiers, politicians or factory workers – the productive members of the war society. Instead, the first to die were the old, the young and the sick. Eventually, and only very slowly, did the effects begin reaching the upper levels of society. This has certainly been the case in Iraq and Haiti. It is not Saddam and his generals who are going to bed without their supper. It is essential that we remember this fact, because it refutes the argument that a blockade, embargo or sanction is imposed as a bloodless and humane way of coercing the leaders of a target country.

Many have argued that such suffering is actually the fault of the country's leaders, who refuse to give in to the demands of the imposer or who hoard food and medicine for themselves.[21] History demonstrates, however, that dictators who are the subject of an embargo generally react by attempting to win the war or conflict in which they are engaged. They will accept casualties to achieve their objectives, and when attacked they will attempt to protect those things most valuable to their society that allows them to continue the fight. They will sacrifice – reluctantly perhaps, but they will nonetheless sacrifice – their weakest segments of society so that the strong can fight on. Nations at war for their survival (or the survival of their leader) don't generally take a 'women and children to the lifeboats first' mentality. They cannot afford to do so. We must understand this. Thus, if we know from dozens of cases over several centuries what the result of our actions will probably be when we embargo Iraq or Serbia or Haiti, then we cannot say afterwards that we didn't know the gun was loaded.

There is an alternative. During the past decade the world has seen air war conducted with humanity, precision and low risk, to both sides. It has been instrumental in achieving the political objectives of our leaders. Military force is not a pleasant option or one that should be employed lightly, but if it is necessary, we should do more than simply follow the letter of the law, we should limit as much as possible the harm to civilian noncombatants. Aerospace power should therefore be our weapon of first resort, because it is the most discriminate, prudent and risk-free weapon in our arsenal.

NOTES

A much-truncated version of this chapter appeared as 'A Matter of Precision' in *Foreign Policy*, March/April 2001. A longer version appeared in *Aerospace Power Journal*, Fall 2001 and in *Air Power Review*, Autumn 2001.

1. Over 700 surface-to-air missiles were launched at NATO aircraft, as well as tens of thousands of antiaircraft artillery shells. Two NATO aircraft were shot down but the pilots were recovered.
2. Human Rights Watch, 'Civilian Deaths in the NATO Air Campaign', 7 February 2000, 5. HRW investigators actually visited only 42 of the 90 sites of the alleged civilian casualties.

3. Ibid., 12–13.

4. During Operation Northern Watch over Iraq, US aircraft sometimes dropped bombs with concrete warheads to further limit the amount of damage caused in sensitive areas.

5. International Committee of the Red Cross, '2001 Review Conference of the United Nations Convention on Certain Conventional Weapons', 14 December 2000, 1–2.

6. Bill Mesler, 'Pentagon Poison: The Great Radioactive Ammo Cover-Up', *The Nation*, 5 May 1997; Scott Peterson, 'Aftershocks from Anti-Tank Shells', *Christian Science Monitor*, 9 January 2001, 1.

7. Gil Elliot, *Twentieth Century Book of the Dead* (New York: Scribner's, 1972), 125, 132–6, 232–4. In another such estimate, William Eckhardt, *Civilizations, Empires and War: A Quantitative History of War* (Jefferson, NC: McFarland, 1992), 273, states that between 1900 and 1989 there were approximately 111 million deaths due to war; he does not break down cause of death as does Elliot. *The Black Book of Communism: Crimes, Terror, Repression*, by Stéphane Courtois *et al.* (Cambridge, MA: Harvard University Press, 2000) states that 95 million people died at the hands of communist regimes in China, the Soviet Union, Vietnam, North Korea, etc. during the past century. This statistic *excludes* those killed in these countries during inter-state wars.

8. Michael Walzer, *Just and Unjust Wars* (New York: Basic Books, 1977), 166–7. The judgment of the court can be found in Volume XI of *Trials of War Criminals before the Nuernberg Military Tribunals* (Washington, DC: Government Printing Office, 1950), 563. Of note, the current US Army field manual on the law of war confirms the legality of this practice: 'Thus, if a commander of a besieged place expels the noncombatants in order to lessen the logistical burden he has to bear, it is lawful, though an extreme measure, to drive them back, so as to hasten the surrender'. US Army, FM 27-10, *The Law of Land Warfare*, July 1956 (Change 1, July 1976), 20.

9. Harrison Salisbury, *The 900 Days: The Siege of Leningrad* (New York: Harper & Row, 1969), 514–16.

10. Human Rights Watch, *Landmines: A Deadly Legacy* (New York: Human Rights Watch, 1993), 3–4.

11. UNICEF, *The State of the World's Children* (New York: Oxford University Press, 1996), 26.

12. Since the Mine Ban Treaty was signed in 1997, things have improved, but thousands of casualties still occur worldwide each year. Human Rights Watch, *Landmine Monitor Report* (New York: HRW, September 2000). Of note, the three largest producers of landmines – Russia, China and the United States – have not ratified the treaty.

13. A. C. Bell, *A History of the Blockade of Germany, 1914–1918* (London: His Majesty's Stationery Office, 1937), 672. The eminent British naval historian, Admiral Sir Herbert Richmond, was unequivocally blunt regarding the purpose of the blockade: 'what we have to do is to starve & cripple Germany, to destroy Germany. That is our prime object'. (Arthur J. Marder (ed.), *Portrait of an Admiral: The Life and Papers of Sir Herbert Richmond* (Cambridge, MA: Harvard University Press, 1952), 219–20).

14. David Weekman, 'Sanctions: The Invisible Hand of Statecraft', *Strategic Review*, 26 (Winter 1998), 40.

15. Eric Hoskins, 'Pity the Children of Iraq', *Middle East International*, 24 January 1992, 16–17. Dr Hoskins was the medical coordinator of the Harvard Study Group that visited Iraq in 1991. See also Alberto Ascherio, 'Effect of the Gulf

War on Infant and Child Mortality in Iraq', *New England Journal of Medicine*, 327 (24 September 1992), 931–6.

16. Even with the easing of the sanctions there were some bizarre aspects: syringes were initially prohibited, as were plastic bags for transfusions, chlorine for water treatment and even chemical fertilizer, because they *could* be used for military purposes. John Mueller and Karl Mueller, 'Sanctions of Mass Destruction', *Foreign Affairs*, 78 (May/June 1999), 43–50.

17. World Health Organization, 'The Health Conditions of the Population in Iraq since the Gulf Crisis', March 1996, 6.

18. Ibid., 16. Emphasis in original.

19. UNICEF, 'Child Mortality: Iraq, the Current Situation', 27 August 1999, www.unicef.org/reseval/cmrirq.html.

20. For a good overview of when and how sanctions do or do not work, which includes a review of the literature on the subject, see T. Clifton Morgan and Valerie L. Schwebach, 'Fools Suffer Gladly: The Use of Economic Sanctions in International Crises', *International Studies Quarterly*, 41 (March 1997), 27–50. This article notes that, in some cases, sanctions are imposed for domestic political reasons: the need to show a restive populace that *something* is being done.

21. Claudette Antoine Werleigh, 'Haiti and the Halfhearted', *Bulletin of the Atomic Scientists*, November 1993, 20–3; Jesse Helms, 'What Sanctions Epidemic?' *Foreign Affairs*, 78 (January/February 1999), 2–8.

11

Gradual Escalation: A Return to the Future?

There are few terms that cause more of a visceral reaction to military personnel than that of 'gradual escalation'. This was the hated non-strategy of Vietnam that was devised by civilian 'whiz kids' and foisted on the US military. Of course, the truth was not that simple, and the military commanders did as they were told with barely a whisper of disagreement. It was only after the war that a string of memoirs came out claiming 'I told you so'. Despite its despised lineage, however, gradual escalation made a comeback in Operation Allied Force over Kosovo. It may not have been planned or intended, but gradual escalation worked. Our military does not want to hear that, and will continue to argue that such a strategy is a dreadful idea and should never be attempted again. However, it is civilian leaders who call the shots, and the success of gradual escalation over Kosovo may be too tempting for policy-makers to resist in the future. Is the military ready to fight such a war? Do we have a doctrine in place that will accommodate the unique requirements in logistics, intelligence, command and control, and targeting?

Pundits and military analysts were vocally opposed to NATO's military strategy in Kosovo from the outset. Daily they intoned that air power alone could never be sufficient; ground troops were essential. Airmen, on the other hand, remained cautiously optimistic throughout Allied Force, believing that although a joint campaign with supporting ground forces was certainly desirable, it was not politically feasible. In such circumstances, they believed that air power could achieve the political objectives set, but they nonetheless deplored the *way* air power was being employed to achieve those objectives. The policy adopted by NATO of gradual escalation – the hated term that harked back to the Vietnam debacle – was seen as the worst possible way to employ air power.

Gradual escalation as a concept of employing military force was first proposed in the mid-1960s by Harvard economist Thomas Schelling. In theory, his idea of steady and inexorably increasing military pressure against an enemy until he breaks is a good one. The mind immediately conjures metaphors: a ratchet that tightens a noose with each turn of the wrench, while the neck it is squeezing correspondingly constricts and is unable to breathe. The 'beauty' of such a strategy is that it seems so rational. The individual applying the ratchet is in total control: he can tighten, stabilize or release as necessary, while the enemy with the noose around his neck is largely helpless; physical and psychological collapse – surrender – is seemingly inevitable. The theory was popular among the policy-makers managing the Vietnam War, who decided that air power employed against a recalcitrant Hanoi government would be their chosen tool.

The reality proved different. In the skies over North Vietnam, the ratchet proved defective: no matter how tightly the air campaign squeezed North Vietnam, it could not choke off the flow of supplies to the South, much less could it break the will of the North's leaders to continue the flow of those supplies. Worse, the air campaign – termed 'Rolling Thunder' – was enormously costly for the United States. Nearly 1,000 aircraft were shot down and over 800 aviators were either killed or captured. Moreover, it is estimated that the damage done to North Vietnam was $600 million, whereas the cost of the US aircraft lost was over $6 billion. The North Vietnamese believed, correctly as it turned out, that they could endure the punishment longer and more stoically than the United States could endure the losses it incurred in dealing out that punishment.

In contrast, air planners in the 1991 Gulf War, many of whom had been junior officers during the Vietnam War, reacted strongly to their earlier failure. Thus, in a direct reaction to the experience of Vietnam, they termed their air campaign against Iraq operation '*Instant* Thunder'. It entailed a violent, massive and effective air assault against Saddam's regime and military forces that began the first night of the war and continued unabated for the next six weeks. It appeared, however, that history was quickly forgotten.

The air campaign against Serbia resembled more the failure of Vietnam than it did the success of the Gulf War. On average, fewer that 50 strike sorties were flown each day over Serbia during the first two weeks of the air campaign, compared to the 1,200 strike sorties flown in the first 24 hours of Desert Storm. The number and types of targets struck were restricted and subject to rigid rules regarding weapon size, type and tactics employed. Although the intensity of the air strikes built steadily to over 500 sorties per day, airmen privately termed the Serbian airwar 'Rolling Blunder'. And yet, it proved to be successful. Although the choice of a gradual escalation strategy seemed to be more serendipitous than it was planned, perhaps it is time to re-evaluate it as a strategy.

The airwar for Kosovo introduced a new and unique twist to the concept of gradualism. The combination of stealth and electronic warfare, but especially precision-guided weapons – NATO claims a 99.6 per cent accuracy rate – allowed NATO to fight a one-sided war of attrition against the Milosevic regime. This is unique because wars of attrition, like that in Vietnam, are generally two-sided. Both adversaries attack and both sides suffer, but each believes it is stronger and more able to endure than the other. This belief in their own moral strength and superiority allows adversaries to continue to fight on while suffering heavy losses. But over Kosovo, only one side suffered. For 78 days, NATO aircraft precisely, methodically and effectively pummeled the Serbian army and its infrastructure. Although the figures are still debated, it appears that several hundred Serbian tanks, armored vehicles, artillery pieces and aircraft were destroyed, as well as dozens of other military targets and structures. The Serbian army was hurt and the Serbian economy was devastated. Despite the weight of bombs dropped, Serbian civilian casualties were amazingly light, estimated at fewer than 500 dead. More importantly, this was accomplished with near total impunity – only two NATO aircraft were lost and both pilots were quickly recovered. The Serbs were unable to inflict reciprocal punishment on NATO and, as a consequence, their morale declined steadily. Once it became clear that neither world public opinion nor Russian anger would bring a halt to the NATO air campaign, the Serbs realized there was no way to win.

Airmen will no doubt continue to maintain that a rapid and massive application of air power will be more efficient and effective than gradual escalation. They are probably correct. Yet, when the political and tactical constraints imposed on air leaders are extensive and pervasive – and that trend seems more rather than less likely – then gradual escalation will be more appealing. It will be necessary for the UN, NATO and the United States to maintain the moral high ground, to not appear as bullies who use overwhelming force precipitously and flippantly to achieve their ends. A measured and steadily increasing use of air power against an enemy, which gives him ample opportunity to assess his situation and come to terms, combined with a remarkably low casualty rate for both ourselves and the enemy's civilian populace, may be the future of war.

NOTE

A version of this chapter was published under the same title in *Armed Forces Journal International*, October 1999.

12

The Versailles Treaty and Iraq:
On the Road to Munich

Mark Twain allegedly said once that although history may not repeat itself, it does tend to rhyme. While discussing in class one day the aftermath of World War I and the Versailles Treaty, I was struck by the parallels between that era and the one following the Gulf War in 1991. Both wars appeared to end with a decisive military victory; yet, for various reasons, that decision was not pursued to its ultimate conclusion. The reasons for this failure to complete the victory seemed like good ones at the time and, indeed, still do to a great extent. Yet these failures set in train a series of political, economic and cultural events that, over time, tended to reverse the decision of the battlefield. Although the magnitude and importance of these two wars are certainly not comparable, there are nonetheless enough similarities to give us pause.

Over 80 years ago the victorious Allies imposed a peace settlement on Germany to end World War I. The Treaty of Versailles, which Germany had no option but to sign, has gone down in history as a huge mistake. Far from ensuring peace, it was instead, as Marshal Ferdinand Foch phrased it, 'a truce for twenty years'. He was accurate to within a few months. The imposed settlement on Iraq following the Gulf War is now a decade old and is shaping up to be almost as unsuccessful as that of Versailles. The similarities and problems with these two settlements are striking.

The German army was defeated decisively in the fall of 1918 and was flooding backwards in retreat. The Allied high command had to decide whether to pursue the fleeing German army into Germany itself and crush it, or pause at the frontier and let the diplomats arrange an armistice. Both because of divergent political aims – not unusual when alliances approach victory – and also due to the fear of increased casualties they would incur fighting the Germans on their own soil, the Allies elected to hold. The controversy over that decision has continued ever since. German army commanders would later maintain they had never really been defeated; the enemy had never entered German soil; weak-kneed politicians had stabbed them in the back.

At Versailles, diplomats hammered out a settlement, but disagreements among the Allies were continuous and heated. Those countries that had borne the brunt of the fighting against Germany wanted a draconian peace, while the United States was more conciliatory. The result was a compromise treaty often described as both too harsh and too lenient.

Germany was forced to disarm, admit its guilt for starting the war, permanently demilitarize the Rhineland, cede territory to its neighbors and pay reparations. Severe restrictions were placed on the military's size, composition and equipment. It soon became apparent, however, that there were no effective mechanisms established to enforce these restrictions. Only total occupation would have ensured German compliance and no one had the stomach for that. In 1922, Germany signed a secret treaty with another pariah state, the Soviet Union, which allowed them to build weapons and train military forces on Soviet territory in defiance of Versailles. The Allies caught wind of these violations but hadn't the will or domestic support to stop them.

Over time, many of the victors began to regret the harshness of their actions at Versailles. These regrets gained weight as economic realities settled in. Germany had been a major trading partner before the war. By keeping it in a position of economic inferiority, the economies of the Allies suffered as well. Moreover, the reparations were onerous, and the German people, already exhausted from the war and the influenza epidemic that followed, soon defaulted on their payments. In retaliation, France and Belgium occupied the Ruhr in January 1923 in order to force compliance with the Versailles mandates. Surprisingly, it was the French and Belgians who were widely criticized for their use of force and they eventually withdrew.

The dismemberment and demilitarization of Germany, thought essential to ensure it remained de-fanged, similarly came to be seen as excessive. The Rhineland was, after all, German territory. Why should outsiders dictate what it did there? When Germany moved to reassert its rights in this area in 1936, France balked. Unfortunately, of France's three main former allies, Russia had 'gone Bolshevik', the United States had retreated into an isolationist shell, and Britain was exhausted and frightened. Few believed it was worth the price to enforce what increasingly came to be viewed as an ill-conceived policy that attempted to keep Germany out of Germany.

In short, the wartime alliance against Germany cracked apart due to economic imperatives, the cooling of passions a decade after the war, and sheer exhaustion in attempting to enforce what was largely an unenforceable treaty. Germans, of course, were pleased that their strategy of stubborn, passive resistance had paid off. Yet, they still harbored much resentment towards their conquerors and awaited a reckoning.

In March of 1991, the Coalition arrayed against Iraq had thrown the Iraqi army out of Kuwait in a panic-stricken rout that saw both massive desertions and surrenders. At this critical juncture, Coalition leaders called a halt to their pursuit of Saddam Hussein's retreating army. That decision has proven controversial because it allowed the Republican Guard – Saddam's best troops – to escape. The Coalition, however, disagreed over the political wisdom of a US-led army pursuing the Iraqis too far into an Arab country;

they were also concerned over the possibility of increased casualties. Saddam has claimed ever since that his army had not been defeated at all; it was falling back to regroup. The Coalition had stopped because they feared the inevitable battle that would have occurred in the heart of Iraq. He had won and has celebrated his 'great victory' every year since.

Notwithstanding later revisionism, in March 1991 Coalition and Iraqi military commanders met in a desert tent at Safwan airbase and agreed to a truce, much as the Allies and Germans had met in a railroad car in the forest over 70 years earlier. Although there has been no formal peace treaty signed with Iraq, the truce terms of Safwan have remained in force, as have several UN resolutions. These terms and resolutions state that Iraq would make 'compensation' to Kuwait, surrender and/or destroy its weapons of mass destruction and their means of delivery – Scud missiles – and refrain from threatening its neighbors. Unfortunately, there was no mechanism put in place to enforce these requirements other than a group of unarmed UN inspectors who would be permitted to search various locations throughout Iraq and destroy any prohibited weapons or research facilities that they discovered. From the beginning, however, Saddam's stubborn, passive resistance thwarted this inspection team in carrying out its mission and eventually it withdrew from Iraq in December 1998. In response, the United States and Britain launched four nights of air strikes on Iraq to punish Saddam for refusing to cooperate with the UN inspectors, and to destroy a number of suspected military weapons stockpiles and prohibited research facilities. These air strikes were immediately condemned by, among others, the Arab League, Russia, China, France and Italy. The UN inspectors have not been allowed back into Iraq.

The victors have also established large no-fly zones in northern and southern Iraq to prohibit Iraqi aircraft from menacing its neighbors or its own subjects. In the north, Iraqi forces, which had been brutally suppressing a Kurdish uprising, were ordered out and the area was demilitarized. Large portions of northern Iraq have been wrested from Baghdad's control but this has created a thorny problem. There are large Kurd populations in several adjacent countries, including Iran, Syria and Turkey, and these countries are loath to encourage the Kurds in their aspirations for a separate nation or homeland. So, not everyone is supportive of a policy that keeps Iraq out of Iraq, for fear it will foster a rebellion that could spread to other Kurdish areas.

There were also problems in southern Iraq where a large Shiite moslem population is concentrated. (The majority of Iraqi moslems are Sunnis.) Saddam's forces crushed a Shiite uprising in the aftermath of the Gulf War, and in 1994 he massed his forces in the south. This was seen as a provocation directed against Kuwait, so the United States clamped a 'no-drive zone' on that area and the Iraqis were told to pull back. Thus, demilitarized 'Rhinelands' have been created in both northern and southern Iraq. Increasingly over the past few years, Saddam has sent up aircraft, fired antiaircraft artillery and targeted Coalition aircraft patrolling these zones with surface-to-air missiles – there have been over 700 such instances. The coalition responds with force but never enough force to cause him to stop. World opinion would not permit it.

In another parallel with Versailles, in order to enforce its resolutions, the UN has imposed a series of sanctions on Iraq beginning in August 1990. As in Germany, where the Allied blockade remained in place until mid-1921 and caused enormous suffering, so too the UN sanctions against Iraq have generated widespread anguish and sickness throughout that country. Moreover, the UN restrictions on Iraqi oil exports have provided a convenient excuse for Iraq to delay compensation payments and implementing other aspects of the desert settlement and UN resolutions.

Partly as a result of perceived harshness, ten years after the end of the Gulf War, the UN embargo leaks like a sieve. Countries that had once supported it are now asking why it must continue. Clearly, Saddam's position has not weakened among his populace. Worse, those imposing the sanctions are suffering financial losses as a result of it. Markets will always find suppliers. So, despite the strict arms embargo imposed on Iraq, it has still managed to rebuild much of its military, receiving much assistance from China. Indeed, there are disturbing reports that it is inching ever closer to the development of a nuclear weapon.

Saddam insists that Iraq's sovereignty is being violated by the US and British aircraft that patrol his skies and the fleets that blockade his ports. He claims that the sanctions that are willfully and criminally attacking his children are akin to genocide. The UN ruefully admits that hundreds of thousands of Iraqi children have indeed died as a direct result of the sanctions that the UN itself has imposed.

Consensus on Iraq has evaporated, and Russia, France, Turkey, Egypt, Syria, Iran and others are now openly trading with their former adversary, in defiance of the UN. Iraqi oil is a valuable commodity and many nations are willing to pay for it, despite the sanctions. As with Germany after Versailles, Iraqi trade is too lucrative for most of its former trading partners to forego. In short, the wartime Coalition against Iraq has begun to split due to economic imperatives, the cooling of passions a decade after the war, and sheer exhaustion in attempting to enforce what is largely an unenforceable settlement.

The main aspects and results of these two situations are surprisingly similar. Versailles failed in its fundamental purpose of establishing a stable and long-term peace in Europe. The result in Germany was to spawn widespread resentment among the population over what they saw as an overly harsh and unjust peace. These resentments festered and created a climate in which an even worse evil was hatched – Nazism.

So, too, has the aftermath of the Gulf War failed to establish stability, peace and prosperity in the Middle East. Nonetheless, the United States especially has maintained an unrelenting stance throughout. At great cost they have sustained the sanctions while enforcing the no-fly zones. The people of Iraq are frustrated and angry. Their economy, which had been one of the most powerful in the Middle East, is now a shambles; their children are dying at a horrifying rate; their pride is abased. It does no good for the United States to state blandly that it is all Saddam's fault. The people of Iraq don't see it that way, any more than did the people of Germany put the blame on their own leaders. Increasingly, the rest of the world is not seeing it that way either. In fact, Arab countries are beginning to wonder whether the United States is an ally or an enemy. Even Saudi Arabia now questions US policy toward Iraq.

The overall pattern is generating echoes. In the 1930s, France bore the brunt of holding back a resurgent Germany by insisting on its rights as a victor over the defeated – it demanded that the Versailles Treaty be enforced. France's former allies and supporters gradually drifted away from it. For a variety of economic and domestic political reasons, they increasingly declined to sanction actions that attempted to force German compliance with Versailles. Indeed, they even began to side with Germany against France. Over time, even the resolve of the French began to crumble. The victors of 1918 became the appeasers of 1938. By the time of the Munich Conference in September 1938, the only consensus left among the former Allies was that they would no longer stand together to fight. They thought, they hoped, that appeasement would bring peace. When Prime Minister Neville Chamberlain returned from Munich he brandished a piece of paper while stepping off his plane. He said it was 'peace in our time'. He was profoundly mistaken. Instead, Hitler saw French and British appeasement at Munich as a sign of weakness; it whetted his appetite. For six decades since, historians have wondered if war could have been avoided in 1939 by a strong stand against Hitler's Germany – by France alone if necessary.

Today, the United States and Britain stand virtually alone in confronting Iraq. Those who initially comprised the Coalition against Iraq have fallen away. Some condemn the United States and Britain openly for their attempts to enforce decade-old resolutions; others subvert those resolutions quietly or covertly. It seems so much easier to appease Saddam, rationalizing away his threats as being merely the legitimate frustrations of a disgruntled victim. And yet, Saddam now says ever more emphatically that he will destroy Israel; his hatred of Jews is almost as epic as that of Hitler. In the 1930s, few believed Hitler would actually act on that hatred, as now we quickly dismiss Saddam's threats.

US policy regarding Iraq has reached an impasse. The air strikes in February 2001 against radar sites and communications facilities seem like more of the same; indeed, administration spokesmen assured us the attacks were 'routine'. Therein lies the problem. Over the past decade we have conducted scores of 'routine' air strikes against Iraq while also enforcing UN sanctions. We are no closer to attaining our goal of stability than we were ten years ago. What is the plan to resolve this continuing crisis? Saddam is an evil and vicious leader, but our attempts to remove him from power have failed. Our efforts to destroy his military capability, especially his capacity to research and build weapons of mass destruction, have failed. Our support to opposition groups within Iraq has failed – if the Kurds and Shiites could not overthrow Saddam, a handful of dissidents working in secret are unlikely to do so. At the same time, however, our sanctions have caused enormous harm to the segments of Iraqi society we are most eager to protect: the old, the very young and the sick. The effects of these sanctions, combined with the ineffectiveness of our political and military actions, have appalled many of our friends and allies. Like Versailles and its aftermath, our policies seem both too harsh and too lenient.

It is time to re-evaluate our policy towards Iraq. Flexibility and creativity are needed, not stubbornness, emotion or vacillation. Moreover, the events of the 1930s should remind us that if something positive is not done, something negative might. The 'War on Terrorism' may be the justification needed for President Bush finally to end the Saddam Hussein menace. Just as it is difficult to imagine World War II without Adolf Hitler, so too is it probable that the solutions to our problems in the Gulf region must involve the removal of Saddam.

NOTE

This chapter was written in the winter of 2001 during the tenth anniversary of the Gulf War.

13

Aerospace Power and the Post-Kosovo World

Military people, who must by the very nature of their profession be pragmatists, love 'lessons learned'. They want to know what worked and what did not work in a previous case. They hope that such knowledge will allow them to become 'wise before the event' and avoid pitfalls and mistakes when their own crisis occurs. Historians, on the other hand, tend to resist talk of such 'lessons'. Our methodology and the rules of our discipline tell us that we are providers of questions, not answers. Once again, my experience as both a military officer and a historian have forced my two minds to compromise. The US fought in three conflicts during the last decade of the twentieth century – the Gulf War, in Bosnia and in Kosovo. The Gulf War has often been called the last of the 'old' wars, while the events in Yugoslavia have been termed the first of the 'new' wars. Both statements are open to question. Nonetheless, there is little argument that these three conflicts saw something very different happen in warfare. It would be unwise in the extreme to ignore them as 'unique' or 'unimportant'. There are lessons to be learned.

The current geopolitical environment, coupled with domestic issues, shapes US national security policy and the use of military force. These factors are constantly evolving and US military strategy must evolve as well. Long-held assumptions regarding likely adversaries, national goals, the role of allies, the nature of conflict, and the military forces, strategies and tactics used are now being questioned. This is wise, because it is apparent that there is a new set of factors that will shape the new geopolitical environment.

- US vital interests as traditionally defined will not often be at stake. Yet, the nation takes seriously the mantel of world leadership it has acquired. It will, therefore, probably continue to intervene in situations where involvement is believed to be 'the right thing to do' and where this will result in innocent lives being saved. In this sense, what Americans view as their 'key values' often become construed as vital national interests.
- Despite the absence of a major enemy, there are a number of potential difficulties facing the United States around the globe. These threats include the usual bad actors like Saddam Hussein, Muammar Qaddafi and

Osama bin Laden, but also include countries and regions like Colombia, Montenegro, Indonesia/East Timor, Korea, the Middle East and Haiti, where a host of combustible issues could ignite with little notice. All can quite conceivably become serious flashpoints and areas of concern for US interests.

- Crises will generally not be predictable either by location or by scale. Few foresaw that there would be major wars fought in Korea, the Falklands or the Gulf. Similarly, few predicted the duration and expense of military operations short of major war, such as Northern and Southern Watch (the air patrols over Iraq now in their ninth year), or our continued involvement in Bosnia five years after the Dayton Accords were signed. What begins as a limited involvement often is quickly overcome by events.

- Overseas basing will continue to be limited. Our military bases overseas have been reduced by two-thirds over the past decade. As a result, the United States must now be able to project and sustain its military power and influence over great distances when engaging with regional allies. Nonetheless, it is also true that some overseas basing, spread globally, is essential for extended operations and to overcome anti-access strategies of potential adversaries. It is not conceivable, for example, that major military operations could be sustained in the Middle East solely from bases in the United States.

- Civilian casualties and collateral damage avoidance are of increasing importance to US and world public opinion. All operations must continue to be discriminate, measured, restrained and appropriate. The mercifully low casualty rates for US interventions during the past decade have set a dauntingly high level of expectations for US military forces. In this regard, the higher cost of US advanced technology is deemed less important than the lives it will save.

- Just as nuclear weapons drove war down to the conventional level after World War II, so too have the events of the past decade driven it down to the asymmetric level whenever the United States is likely to be involved. The seemingly effortless destruction of the Iraqi and Serbian military forces sent a powerful message to would-be aggressors: the only possibility of success against the United States lies in not fighting it on even terms or in a conventional force-on-force fashion.

- Adversaries will be intelligent, clever and dedicated to their cause. They will devise ways to avoid or limit US technological superiority. Asymmetrical strategies and tactics will include an emphasis on mobility, concealment, hardening, and the commingling of civilian and military targets. Weapons of mass destruction will proliferate as will their means of delivery. Indeed, it will not be necessary for adversaries to develop nuclear weapons in order to be a serious threat. Chemical and biological weapons are also frightening and difficult to defend against. Worse, it cannot be guaranteed that such threats will be directed solely at US forces abroad.

Because of these factors, it is my thesis that in many, if not most, foreseeable situations, aerospace power will be viewed by US policy-makers in the USA as that nation's most versatile and effective military tool, and it will continue to play a key role in US foreign policy.

The United States has committed itself to global engagement. Yet, the past decade has given us some lessons to consider. Lessons can be tricky things, however. There are many examples when military professionals in different countries or services looked dispassionately, logically and rigorously at past events and deduced totally different lessons based on those events. After World War I German officers examined the experience of trench warfare and concluded the only solution was to restore mobility to the battlefield via a combination of armored vehicles and air power. French officers examined that same experience and determined just as conclusively that the answer to the trench stalemate was highly elaborate and defensible static fortifications – the Maginot Line. Learned lessons are not always correct lessons. Proceed with that monition in mind.

Strategists, planners and commanders should remember the axiom that military strategy must match the government's objectives. After civilian leaders have determined the policy objectives, planners must devise a military strategy to fulfill those objectives. It is surprising how often this simple principle has been violated in war. Recent examples are the unhappy US experiences in Somalia and Haiti. Defeating warlords/dictators and restoring democracy and peace were noble goals, but they were simply not achievable given the military resources committed and the strategies employed.

Specifically, regarding the use of aerospace power, planners will begin looking at targets to strike or neutralize. They must ensure those targets do in fact lead them closer to achieving their policy objectives. Targets should not be hit simply because they are hittable, or because they were struck in the last war, or because there are lots of them, or because they are politically 'safe', or because they are less risky to attack than are other targets. Rather, targets should be attacked because doing so will help lead to the policy objectives. If a planner cannot draw a clear connection between the target struck and one of the stated objectives, the targeting strategy needs to be reconsidered.

At this point it would be useful to say a few words about air strategy in more general terms. The object of war is to impose your will on the enemy by destroying his will or capability to resist. An ongoing debate examines whether it is more desirable and feasible to focus on the enemy's will or his capability; consequently, military strategists and thinkers are often put into one of two categories. The first includes those who focus on seeking methods of confusing, deceiving, frightening or influencing the mind of the enemy in the hope of shattering his *will* and thus causing surrender. The other school is more physical and direct; it believes that if one attacks the enemy's military forces or industrial infrastructure, thus removing their *capability* to resist, then surrender must follow. Social scientists have put new terms on these old concepts and now refer to *coercion* and *denial* strategies. Proponents of these two camps have engaged in vigorous debate over the past decade. In truth, it is virtually impossible to separate these two types of strategy in practice. If the point of attacking, say, an enemy's forces is to deny him the ability to fight, then it is highly likely that such an inability will also have a strong coercive effect on the enemy's will. Conversely, if an attack on the enemy's oil refineries is intended to break an enemy's will because it destroys something he values, then, at the same time, the oil supplies lost will decrease their ability to fight. The issue therefore becomes one of emphasis.

To a great extent, the choice of strategy will be driven by objectives and by the nature of the war. In a total war, with surrender and subjugation of the enemy as the goal, it is likely that the destruction of the enemy's will *and* his capability will be necessary. Thus, in World War II the Allies conducted a war directed against both Germany's will and its capability – coercion and denial. Similarly, in the case of Iraq, both strategies were employed, albeit for different reasons: the Coalition wanted to coerce Saddam to leave Kuwait, but it also wanted to deny him the capability of remaining an offensive threat in the region thereafter. Other conflicts, such as that in Kosovo, are more problematic regarding the type of strategy employed. It was NATO's goal to coerce Serbia into stopping its ethnic cleansing in Kosovo. *Coercion* would ordinarily entail the attack of high-value targets in Serbia itself, but planners also employed a *denial* strategy: they hit Serbian military forces and infrastructure in Kosovo. Milosevic surrendered, but was it the coercion or the denial targeting that brought him to that decision? We may never know. Realize, however, that the choice of strategy will have a significant effect on the targets selected for air attack – power lines versus munitions factories versus rail yards versus artillery pieces. Our policy goals and the nature of the war will determine the most effective air strategy to be employed.

Another obvious lesson from the past decade is the importance of air superiority. US military forces, as well as those of its allies, have come to depend on that superiority, knowing that without it, military operations on land, at sea or in the air become incomparably more difficult and dangerous.

Air superiority has two components: it allows us to conduct air operations without serious impedance, and prevents the enemy from doing so. Both of these conditions are important to bear in mind. It is now taken for granted that US forces will be immune from enemy air attack. It is an oft-stated fact that a US soldier has not been killed by an enemy aircraft in nearly 50 years. That is a wonderful record and one we want to sustain. However, too often we forget the other condition of air superiority – that the United States are able to conduct air operations with little or no enemy interference. This is far more problematic.

US air superiority can be tested by enemy aircraft or by ground-based air defenses. Given the quality of US planes, the former has not been a serious problem since the Vietnam War. The F-15 Eagle is approximately 100 to 0 in air-to-air combat over the past two decades, and the F-16 Viper and F-14

Tomcat are hardly less capable. As a consequence, few adversaries are even willing to engage the USA in air combat. In both Desert Storm and over the Balkans, the Iraqi and Serb air forces quickly learned that it was better simply to sit out the war and hope to survive in hiding rather than risk suicide by taking off. Although the F-15, F-16 and F-14 have proven more than a match for anything else in the world, they are aging inexorably. All of these fighters are more than two decades old, non-stealthy and at the end of their technological growth capacity. New air threats are now emerging that are of serious concern. The Eurofighter, French Rafale, Swedish Gripen, and Russian Su-35 are all in some ways superior to the F-15, F-16 or F-14. At this point these new competitors are few in number, expensive and not yet finding their way into the hands of US enemies. However, all of these new aircraft are being marketed worldwide and it is only a question of time before they appear in, what are for the USA, the wrong places. It is useful to recall that friends can sometimes become enemies overnight: the Iranians fly American-made F-14s and the Iraqis fly French Mirages. The lesson is clear: if the USA doesn't keep pace with these new aircraft – if the USA doesn't field a follow-on air superiority fighter – the USA will soon be at a severe disadvantage in air combat.

Having said that, the greatest threat to US aircraft has actually come from ground-based air defenses. This has always been the case – far more aircraft have been lost, from World War II to the present, to surface-to-air missiles (SAM) and antiaircraft artillery fire (AAA) than in aerial dogfights. As US fighters have grown more capable, that situation has intensified. Adversaries see the danger in attempting to meet the USA in the air, so instead have concentrated on ground-based air defenses. SAM and AAA have increased both in numbers and capability. The new Russian-made SA-10 and SA-12 are very dangerous SAM systems; fortunately, neither the Iraqis nor the Serbs have any of these weapons yet. General John P. Jumper, the senior air commander in Europe during Operation Allied Force over Kosovo, admitted, however, that even a single SA-10 battery in Serb hands would have presented serious problems for NATO aircraft. There is no question these systems will proliferate in the years ahead and future adversaries will use them against the USA.

The loss of air superiority could cause the USA serious problems. A few examples should suffice to illustrate how keenly US forces depend on air superiority. The USA conducted a six-week air campaign in Desert Storm prior to the ground offensive. Although estimates vary, virtually all observers have concluded that a large portion – over half – of the Iraqi divisions positioned immediately opposite Coalition ground forces had either been destroyed or driven off by the air campaign prior to the start of the US ground attack. As a result, prewar estimates, which had gone as high as 20,000 US casualties during a ground offensive, were dramatically reduced to fewer than 300. Similarly, in Kosovo, Joint Chiefs Chairman General Hugh Shelton stated that a ground invasion of Serbia would have required 200,000 NATO troops. Although he declined to estimate NATO casualties in the event of an invasion, it goes without saying that they would have been far higher than the zero casualties NATO incurred during the successful air campaign. In smaller conflicts involving unconventional threats, the ability of air power to limit friendly ground casualties is also apparent. On 3 October 1993, US troops found themselves cut off and pinned down in the streets of Mogadishu by Somali 'technicals'. Eighteen American soldiers died and nearly 80 more were wounded that day, but, by all accounts, our losses would have been far greater had US helicopter gunships not been present. Their superior mobility and firepower saved the 100 soldiers who were trapped from being completely overrun and slaughtered.

In sum, air superiority has become a necessary and accepted condition of US military operations. It has dramatically reduced US casualties, while making it far easier to achieve US political objectives. This superiority must not be taken for granted, however. The new warplanes now entering service worldwide are significantly better than anything the USA has had to face previously. If that wasn't bad enough, defensive systems, especially advanced SAMS, are proliferating as well. US options in the face of these new threats are stark: the USA accepts the loss of air superiority that it has enjoyed for three decades and steels itself for higher casualties, or it improves its own technologies in response.

It is also apparent that precision weapons have revolutionized warfare. It is not unlikely that the United States will again face an enemy who, like Iraq, possesses a sizable army complete with heavy artillery, armor and mechanized forces. That does not mean, however, that the USA must confront such an enemy in a head-on land battle. It would be wiser to fight it at arm's length. Although this may not always be possible, there is a difference between preparing to fight a high-tempo and probably bloody land action as a last resort, and assuming that such an action will occur and thus planning for it as the first resort. A number of new air weapons are being developed that offer the hope of severely attritting and halting an enemy before he can get close enough to hurt friendly ground troops. Most of these weapons, many of which have already been used successfully in combat, magnify the ability of aircraft to neutralize enemy facilities, vehicles and ground forces.

Precision Guided Munitions (PGMs) have arrived in force. In the Gulf War, only 9 per cent of the bombs dropped by Coalition aircraft were precision-guided. In the Balkans, the percentage jumped to 69 per cent in Bosnia and 35 per cent in Kosovo (virtually all targets in populated areas were hit with PGMs). They have become the weapon of choice in US military operations. There are several reasons for this. First, PGMs are essential when one's goal is to limit enemy civilian casualties and collateral damage. Because US vital interests are not usually at stake, the USA must maintain the moral high ground whenever it chooses to intervene in a foreign crisis. The USA cannot be seen as a bully who uses excessive force. Precision weapons are therefore essential. Moreover, the USA must be able to deliver these weapons so as to minimize its own casualties. Whether or not the American public is 'casualty-averse' is open to question. But what seems irrefutable is that political and military leaders *assume* the public feels that way, and US military policies and strategies are based on that assumption. Second, PGMs are cost-effective: a 2,000lb laser-guided bomb costs approximately $25,000 and the new Joint Direct Attack Munition (JDAM) costs about $15,000, whereas the tanks they destroy cost over $1 million each. Third, increased accuracy allows a target to be neutralized with far fewer weapons. This has implications for the number of aircraft required to deliver such munitions, the trained personnel to maintain and fly those aircraft, the logistics to deliver and support the planes, weapons and personnel and, perhaps most importantly, the number of lives put at risk in delivering those weapons.

For example, a common measure of combat efficiency is the 'tooth-to-tail' ratio: the number of fighters versus the number of support personnel. A military force with a low tooth-to-tail ratio – few fighters relative to the number of supporters – is seen as inefficient and wasteful. In the age of PGMs, this is an outmoded concept because it assumes that a large number of attack assets is both necessary and desirable. It is not. If the same amount of damage can be performed by a far smaller number of personnel, then the size of the support structure backing them up – out of harm's way – is of minor import.

Precision capability requires an intelligence-gathering and analysis effort far greater than anything we have had previously. This requirement includes air and space systems that collect intelligence, analyze it and disseminate it to users worldwide in near-real time. It also includes surveillance, reconnaissance, navigation and communication systems. The purpose of this network is to give a joint commander a complete and accurate picture of the battlespace, while also providing timely and accurate intelligence and targeting support to aerospace forces.

Supplying near-real-time intelligence to the cockpit is becoming a reality. During Allied Force, for example, space sensors were able to update intelligence data, have it analyzed, and then have the information passed to airborne B-2 aircraft, allowing re-targeting en route. This in-flight 'flex' targeting enhanced efficiency and effectiveness, while also reducing risk. In another instance, a Predator unmanned aerospace vehicle (UAV) flying over Kosovo took video of events on the ground, relayed that video via satellite back to the USA, where it was fused with three-dimensional satellite imagery taken earlier to generate precise coordinates. These coordinates were then relayed to orbiting AWACS aircraft and thence to airborne F-15E strike aircraft, which used satellite-guided precision munitions to strike the target. All of this happened in a period of minutes and demonstrates the rapid growth in what is termed 'sensor-to-shooter' capabilities.

It is imperative to point out, however, that nothing argued up to this point is to imply that aerospace power should be employed by itself. On the contrary, aerospace power would always be more effective when employed as part of a joint force. In fact, it is precisely the redundancy of US military force that makes it so daunting to a potential adversary. If the United States had 'simply' the world's best army, or air force, or navy or marine corps, it is possible that an enemy could focus on that single threat and determine a way to thwart it – or at least render the US cost of engagement too high to continue. But the USA have the best army *and* air force *and* navy *and* marine corps, so it becomes almost impossible for an adversary to counter all of the many weapons the USA could throw at him. This redundancy has become the US Way of War – a quiver-full of very capable arrows.

Nonetheless, there are still a number of challenges facing US aerospace forces which must be addressed. The first of these is that of assessment: how does the USA know if it is achieving its objectives? This problem has haunted airmen for decades. Bomb damage assessment has certainly improved, but this is largely a tactical concept that can give little insight into the overall progress of the air campaign. In other words, although one may have the ability to determine whether or not a bomb or missile struck its target, that does not necessarily tell one what effect, if any, that destruction will have on the overall war effort. Common sense tells one, for example, that if a capital city loses its electrical power, telephones and public transportation systems, then the ability to coordinate and direct a war effort will be greatly impaired. But how impaired? Assigning a number to such a degradation of performance is extremely difficult. This problem ties directly to the objectives–strategy issue noted above. One must devise a method for measuring aerospace power's effectiveness so as to determine whether one is moving closer to one's overall objectives.

Another difficult task facing airmen today is the ability to detect, track and destroy mobile targets, especially in bad weather or when they are camouflaged or hidden. This problem was seen in the Gulf War, when finding and destroying Iraqi Scud launchers proved enormously difficult. It was noted again in Allied Force when, despite a far more capable reconnaissance effort that included JSTARS aircraft, UAVs and space assets, airmen still had trouble in locating and destroying Serb tanks, artillery pieces and other vehicles. There are new systems soon coming on-line that will move us closer to this vision, but it will remain a daunting challenge.

An issue that is causing concern among all the services is that of 'access'. This term reflects the fear that potential adversaries will be able to hinder or even prevent one's access to a crisis area, thus denying one the ability to intervene effectively. An enemy can do this by attacking US forces as they attempt to disembark in port, attacking US supply depots or airbases, or simply using diplomatic pressure to prevent US use of such facilities near the crisis area. Adversaries are smart enough to see what happens when the United States is given time to deploy its forces unimpeded. Yet, it is precisely this ability to deploy massive forces worldwide that the United States currently relies upon to exert its influence in a crisis. Given its drawdown of overseas bases, concern over its ability to use remaining facilities is a significant problem.

Specific US concerns center on cruise and ballistic missiles that are proliferating worldwide, sophisticated air defenses, advanced sea mines, increased availability of space-based intelligence satellites that would give an adversary a clear picture of US deployments, and the spread of weapons of mass destruction. All of these threats would make it difficult for US forces to deploy rapidly and smoothly.

The solution to the access problem would appear to be a joint team, based on aerospace power, that would seize a lodgment area, defend it against air, land and sea attack, and would also begin conducting meaningful offensive strikes against the enemy. The composition of such a notional joint team would include long-range, land-based stealth aircraft, air-superiority fighters, sea-based aircraft and cruise missiles, space-based intelligence and communications assets, defensive missile batteries and a soldier/marine contingent. In addition, airlift and air refueling assets would be immediately available to support and expand the lodgment. At that point, heavier forces and the logistics to sustain them could begin flowing into the area. To be sure, this is still merely a concept of how the United States would overcome an access problem, but it is certainly wise to begin serious planning on how to counter such a threat.

Aerospace power has increasingly come to dominate modern war. Paradoxically, what is often seen as one of its greatest weaknesses – the inability to take and hold ground – is in some circumstances precisely what makes it such a useful tool of diplomacy. It is less provocative and less risky than ground forces, while, at the same time, it lessens the danger of mission creep. It was thus more politically acceptable for NATO to bomb Serbia than it would have been to invade it, as the Russians warned us repeatedly. Similarly, it has been more advisable for aircraft to patrol the skies over Iraq than to deploy tens of thousands of ground troops there.

We are in an era where US interventions may be seen as important but are not always seen as vital. In such instances, US leaders, supported by public opinion and allied governments, may be willing to use military force to save lives, make the peace or enforce it. But when doing so, this force must be used providently: it should not harm noncombatants; it must limit friendly casualties; it must not irritate one's friends, and, thus, it should probably not involve a large or permanent presence in the region.

US political leaders, military commanders and the American public must realize that every problem is not amenable to the use of military force. For those that are, however, aerospace power has a substantial contribution to make – whether it be in direct combat with enemy forces or in vital support of a joint command or our allies. Will it always work? No. Given the trends of the past decade in technology and US political activism around the globe, however, aerospace power will be viewed increasingly as the force of first resort.

NOTE

This chapter is the outcome of a number of lectures given at war colleges, both in the United States and abroad. The written version was completed in the fall of 2000.

14

Strategic Implications for the Aerospace Nation

Virtually all air theorists have noted that a definition of air power or aerospace power must include far more than simply machines. It includes also a robust aerospace industry – airframe, engine, avionics, and equipment manufacturers. In addition, air power must also encompass the myriad workers in the commercial and private aviation sectors. For example, military airlift capability is absolutely dependent on civilian airline companies and their willingness to contribute air fleets in the event of a crisis. This occurred on a massive scale in the Gulf War. Incidentally, a large percentage of civilian airline pilots were once military pilots, and in many cases still fly as Reserve or National Guard pilots. Added to these industrial elements is the airway structure itself, to include runways and airport terminals, weather stations, navigation aids and space-based positioning satellites. Finally, air power includes a codified doctrine on how all of these air and space assets should be employed. Using such a broad interpretation, the United States is an aerospace nation. Its dominance in most areas, both militarily and commercially, is obvious and significant. On the other hand, there are competitors who are chipping away at that superiority, so US dominance is by no means assured.

The United States is the world's first and only aerospace nation. That fact is evidenced in its dominance of aerospace technology and infrastructure, as well as in the future visions shared by its political, economic, military and cultural leaders. This domination has important implications for US national security. Unfortunately, many Americans have come to view aerospace dominance as their birthright. It is not. The events of 11 September 2001 have dealt a body blow to the US aerospace industry. It must take steps now to ensure that the setback is temporary.

A number of factors have combined to make the United States an aerospace nation. The vast size of the country generated the development of transportation systems to link its markets and resource areas. As a consequence, the United States led the world in railroad development in the nineteenth century. Similarly, air travel exploded in that country during the twentieth century – leading the world into the commercial air age.

In addition, the United States' rich and varied natural resources not only provided national wealth, but also helped it to become an industrial giant. It excelled not only in the production of steel, for example, but also in many of the products made from that steel – automobiles, trucks, locomotives, ships and airplanes. However, other regions and countries have also been blessed with an abundance of minerals and fertile soil, yet they were unable to capitalize as well on those riches.

Americans have always looked to technology to ease their problems. This technological determinism was coupled with a progressive belief that all processes, systems and products could be perfected through a rational, analytic and scientific approach. Americans took naturally and quickly to aerospace power, the epitome of advanced technology and progressivism. The United States was the birthplace of aviation, and modern airline designs trace their roots to the sleek, all-metal models introduced by Boeing, Lockheed, Douglas and Northrop in the 1930s.

In addition, there has always been wanderlust in the American spirit which has led to great feats of exploration and discovery – Lewis and Clark, John Frémont and Zebulon Pike. Four decades ago, John Kennedy called space the final frontier and urged the United States to explore it. They did, putting a man on the moon and pioneering in other such celestial voyages of discovery.

Air and space now dominate much of what we do on a daily basis. It is difficult to imagine life without our television satellites, cell phones, internet and air travel. The shutdown of all air traffic after the 11 September terrorist attack stranded thousands, disrupted business and had a major effect on the mundane – canceling hundreds of sporting events across the USA and elsewhere. Nonetheless, as Figures 14.1 and 14.2 illustrate, when Americans travel commercially, they travel by air.

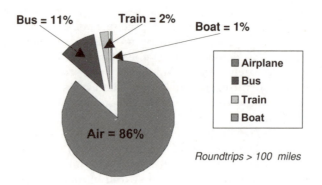

Figure 14.1: How People in the USA Traveled Using Commercial Transportation in 1995 (*Source:* US Dept of Transportation, 2000)

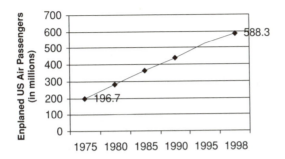

Figure 14.2: US Air Passenger Growth (*Source:* US Dept of Transportation, 2000)

Speed is the engine of commerce and economic growth. Rapid means of transportation have been essential for nations seeking economic dominance. The rise of Britain in the eighteenth century was based on global trade carried by its large merchant fleet, which, in turn, was protected by the Royal Navy, the world's largest and most powerful navy.

In the twentieth century, speed meant aircraft, and expanding US aviation generated economic power. Over the past 40 years, the growth of the US airline industry has been dramatic, in contrast to the decline of its shipping industry. As Figure 14.3 shows, since 1960 the number of airliners has quadrupled (and aircraft have more than doubled in size), while the size of the US merchant fleet has dropped 84 per cent.

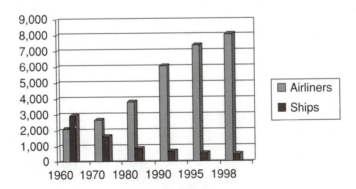

Figure 14.3: Airlines vs. Merchant Ships (*Source:* US Dept of Transportation, 2000)

The size of the US merchant fleet relative to that of the world fleet has declined even more dramatically. Today, the 463 ocean-going merchant ships of the USA comprise barely 2 per cent of the world's total, down from 17 per cent in 1960. In the year 2000, of the 1,192 major vessels ordered worldwide, only 16 will be built by US shipyards. Also, at a time when old rail terminals are being converted into shopping malls, airport expansion is taking place all over the country. For good reason. Airline passenger travel is expected to double over the next decade. Moreover, fully 95 per cent of the world's air cargo capacity flies in Boeing aircraft. The value of goods shipped is also telling. In 1997, the average pound of cargo traveling by boat was worth 7 cents; by rail it was 10 cents but by air it was a whopping $25.59. When Americans have something important and valuable to ship and it needs to get there quickly, they send it by air.

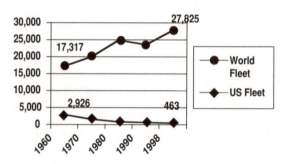

Figure 14.4: Size of World Fleet vs. US Fleet (*Source:* US Dept of Transportation, 2000)

In addition, aerospace trade has significantly increased over the past few decades. As Figure 14.5 shows, the black ink in the aerospace balance of trade rose to over $32 billion in 2000, making it the largest net exporter in the US economy. At the same time, the *overall* US trade balance has been negative for 27 of the past 30 years and the deficit now exceeds $250 billion annually. Given all these statistics, it is apparent that the United States is now far more an aerospace nation than it is a maritime one.

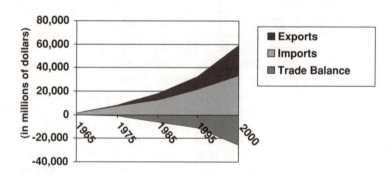

Figure 14.5: Aerospace Imports/Exports and Balance of Trade (*Source:* AIAA, 2000)

The USA once led the world in transportation technologies, but over the past two centuries it has relinquished this dominance in many areas such as shipbuilding and auto manufacturing. (The US share of the world auto market has fallen from 48 per cent to 15 per cent over the past 40 years.) The USA cannot allow its lead in aerospace to similarly evaporate.

NATIONAL SECURITY

Military strategy has evolved dramatically over the past decade. The basic factors that shaped our geopolitical environment during the Cold War era are now different. The Soviet threat is gone, but other threats and other commitments remain. In fact, US military deployments have increased fourfold, while the size of our military forces has declined by 40 per cent. Even so, the character of these engagements has altered. It is ever more essential that the United States maintains strong public support for its actions. This, in turn, means it must be extremely careful about both inflicting and sustaining casualties. In this sense, the air campaign over Kosovo in 1999 could haunt the United States in the future – it suffered no casualties while, at the same time, causing remarkably little collateral damage or injury to noncombatants. It is too much to ask that all US future military involvements will be as similarly successful and bloodless, but the bar has been set and the United States will, by necessity, be forced to aim for it from now on.

It is obvious, however, that if such sterilized warfare is one's goal, then certain types of strategies, tactics and weapons are more desirable than others. Precision or non-lethal weapons delivered by air platforms, ideally either unmanned, unseen or located out of range of enemy fire, are the instruments of choice. To be sure, identifying, tracking and destroying mobile targets – tanks, trucks and terrorists – remains one of the most difficult challenges, but this problem is being addressed using a combination of space- and air-based sensors tied to strike aircraft by communication satellites. A solution may be in sight.

Only hubris would tempt a nation's leaders to think that aerospace power could be effective in any crisis, but it has now become a weapon of first resort. The American people intuitively realize this: recent Gallup Polls reveal that 42 per cent of those surveyed believe the air force is the most crucial arm of national defense, twice as many as voted for any other service; a like number believe it should be built up to a greater extent than the other services.

Just as the US commercial air fleet is the world's largest and most modern, so too is its military air power. Figure 14.6 compares the number of US military aircraft to the totals of other leading countries. US dominance is obvious, but that superiority is even greater than indicated. Although China has many airplanes, most are obsolescent, including over 6,000 Vietnam-era MiG-17s, 19s and 21s. Certainly, quantity has a quality, but most of the

Chinese air force would stand little chance against a front-line adversary. Similarly, Russia's air force has atrophied catastrophically over the past decade. Once the pride of the Soviet state, much of this vaunted air force now sits rusting and out of commission.

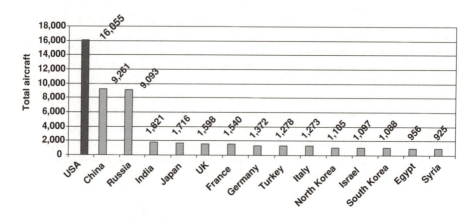

Figure 14.6: Leading Nations in Total Air Power (*Source: Aviation Week & Space Technology*, Jan 2001)

Examining the *types* of military aircraft comprising the world's air forces is also revealing. The majority of combat aircraft worldwide are short-range fighter-bombers like the F-16, Mirage 2000 and MiG-21. The United States, which has nearly 4,000 such aircraft, has far more capability than that. It is the airlift and aerial tanker fleets that allow it to project power anywhere in the world on short notice. The United States possesses the vast majority of the world's large military cargo aircraft like the C-17 and C-5, while also having four times more tankers than the rest of the world combined. Tankers turn US tactical fighters into strategic bombers. No other nation has such an impressive capability to project power and influence. China, for example, has fewer than 50 modern cargo aircraft and virtually no aerial refueling capability.

US dominance in space is equally compelling. At the present time, there are approximately 550 operational satellites in orbit around the earth. Nearly half of these were launched by the United States, and approximately 100 of these are military satellites. In addition, the large Global Positioning System constellation of 28 satellites provides precise geographical data to users all over the world. In contrast, Russia now has only 90 operational spacecraft and much of its space infrastructure – its missile launch detection system for example – is moribund. Although China can be expected to become a serious space competitor – it is currently working on an anti-satellite system – it has launched an average of fewer than four satellites per year over the past decade.

What is even more compelling is the realization that within the US military services there is an increasing reliance and emphasis on aerospace power. There is an old saying that if you want to know what's important, follow the money. In the US military, that trail is pretty clear. The backbone of the navy is its aircraft carriers, which cost over $5 billion each (without their aircraft and support ships), and the navy spends nearly as much on aircraft procurement each year as does the air force. The marines' top funding priority is the tilt-rotor V-22 cargo planes which will cost in excess of $80 million apiece. The army has major production and modernization programs for Black Hawk, Apache and Comanche helicopters which will total around $70 billion. Indeed, over the past decade the army has spent more on aircraft and missiles each year than it has on tracked combat vehicles. In sum, over 60 per cent of the US defense budget is devoted to aerospace forces. In fact, in Figure 14.7 a comparison of the size of the USA's four air arms with the rest of the world shows that each *individually* is greater than the total military air assets of most major countries. The qualitative superiority of the aircraft makes US aerospace dominance even more profound.

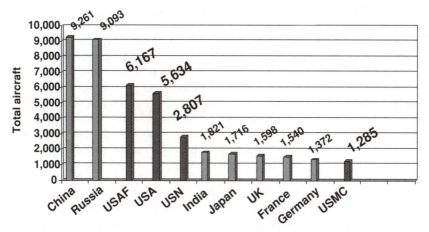

Figure 14.7: US Air Power vs. the World (*Source: Aviation Week & Space Technology*, Jan 2001)

The reason for this emphasis on aerospace power among the services is the realization that military operations no longer have a likelihood of success without it. It has become the US Way of War. Indeed, the major disagreements that occur between the services today generally concern the control and purpose of aerospace assets. All covet those assets, but their differing views on the nature of war and how it should be conducted shape their ideas on how aerospace power should be employed. Thus, there are heated debates regarding the authority and scope of the Joint Force Air Component Commander, the desirability of a Joint Targeting Board, the role of the corps commander in the deep battle, who should pay for additional airlift assets, which service should control and maintain US satellites, and whether attack helicopters should be controlled by the air commander or the ground commander. All the services trumpet the importance of joint operations, but all also understand the dominance of aerospace power within that joint construct. Aerospace strategy increasingly has become US primary joint strategy.

IMPLICATIONS

There are many implications that follow from the USA's status as the aerospace nation. Its political and military leaders, as well as the public in general, should reflect on this unique capability and consider its meaning, how it can be maintained and how it can shape the future.

Over the past decade, nearly two-thirds of US overseas bases have been closed and the troops stationed there have been pulled back to the United States or disbanded. The bulk of the forces and bases overseas had supported a strategy of Soviet containment in Europe. Large and stable bases, depots and family communities grew up to support this unitary threat. Today, the Soviets are gone and so are most of the bases.

Problems still remain. Although US military forces may not deploy to the same bases or even the same countries as they did previously, they deploy nonetheless. In many cases, as in the 1991 Gulf War and again in the airwar over Serbia in 1999, US forces had to conduct operations in new and unfamiliar locations. Aerospace power allowed this to happen. US airlift and tanker fleets ferried aircraft, crews, maintenance and supply personnel, combat forces and logistical support into airbases throughout the Middle East and then southeastern Europe. In the Gulf War, 99 per cent of the US personnel deployed to the Middle East went by air. In support of the Kosovo operation, the USAF deployed to 21 different locations. Long-range, rapid power projection has become an essential element of US foreign policy.

Some have argued that future US security strategy will place an increased emphasis on the Pacific theater. As in Europe, the number of US bases in that area has declined over the past decade. In one sense, however, a discussion of primary versus secondary theaters is of little relevance for a global aerospace nation. Nonetheless, if it became necessary to move military forces quickly into the Pacific, it would not be difficult. There are over 650 airfields in the western Pacific region that could accommodate US aerospace forces. All of these airfields, located in the territory of its friends and allies, are only a plane ride away from the United States. The air expeditionary forces of the USAF are designed to deploy to such locations and begin combat operations in less than 72 hours. As importantly, such deployments will be far less demanding in terms of logistics, which further increases how rapidly the USA can deploy. At the same time, it has a dozen carrier battle groups that can project air power ashore from international waters.

The American public has always been ambivalent about being the 'world's policeman', but if such a role is chosen by its leaders, aerospace power will allow its implementation. It has become increasingly apparent that military intervention can be wielded through the air with less cost, risk and political turmoil than via the introduction of ground forces.

It has long been said that aerospace power's greatest weakness is its inability to occupy and hold ground. Although that may be true, such a vision of military force and its importance is fading. There are many instances when occupying ground is politically impracticable and also unwise. There are dozens of terrorist camps in Afghanistan, but it would be folly to contemplate an occupation of that country in order to eradicate those camps. The unhappy Soviet experience there should teach that much. Throughout the Vietnam War, the US Army's leaders recommended an invasion of North Vietnam. In their view, only the occupation of North Vietnamese territory would stop the flow of troops and supplies moving south to the Viet Cong. President Johnson rejected such suggestions because he feared such an invasion would bring Chinese or Soviet intervention. For those who waved off such fears, Johnson merely noted that the generals had not taken Chinese intervention seriously in 1950 either.

Instead, Johnson chose an air interdiction campaign against North Vietnam for the specific reason that it could *not* hold ground. Air power was less provocative and less politically risky than the use of a ground invasion force. The fact that no amount of military forces on land, at sea or in the air was able to break the desire of the North Vietnam leadership to carry on the war for control of the south should not obscure the rationale behind President Johnson's decision.

It was the same logic that caused President Bush and Coalition leaders to halt short of Basra in the 1991 Gulf War, and why President Clinton rejected the idea of invading Serbia in 1999 to stop ethnic cleansing in Kosovo. A march on Baghdad may have toppled Saddam Hussein in 1991, but it was a politically impossible option for our Arab allies. Similarly, a ground invasion in 1999 might have driven the Serbs out of Kosovo, but it would have taken longer and incurred far more casualties – on both sides – than did the air campaign. This price was why several NATO countries, including the United States, rejected the ground option. Moreover, echoing LBJ's fears, NATO was concerned about Russian threats to intervene in the event an invasion of Serbia was attempted. Once again, aerospace power was chosen because of its inability to hold ground. Aerospace power's greatest weakness is becoming one of its greatest strengths.

Aerospace dominance also provides US civilian leadership with flexibility. Although intelligence is never complete or perfect, US leaders now have unprecedented information regarding what military actions can or cannot accomplish and how much risk is involved in a given course of action. Over Serbia, for example, NATO understood how many aircraft and weapons would be needed to produce a given military effect, the accuracy of those weapons, the collateral damage that might occur and the risk to aircrews involved. This allowed leaders to fine-tune the air campaign. Although some have labeled this 'interference', it is in keeping with the US military tradition. Political leaders control and direct the US military. The capabilities of aerospace power allow those leaders to exercise that control and direction more rapidly and effectively than was ever previously possible.

There are other factors affecting the way we will fight in the future. There is much talk today of a 'revolution in military affairs' and 'transforming the military' to meet new threats. Warfare has changed dramatically over the past decade. The Gulf War, Bosnia and Kosovo – and for that matter Somalia and Haiti – indicate that traditional methods, weapons, forces, tactics and strategy will often no longer be successful.

Stealth, precision weapons and space-based communication and intelligence-gathering systems are examples of this new form of war. Certainly, the human element in war can never be ignored. At base, it is people who make war, and all their strengths and weaknesses must be considered. Yet, it would be foolish not to exploit new technologies that remove part of the risk and human burden in war. It is not always necessary for people to suffer. It may not even be necessary for them to expend the prodigious efforts characterized by traditional forms of war. Aerospace power permits new types of strategies that make war on things rather than on people and which employ things rather than people. It capitalizes on the explosion in computer, electronic and materials technologies that so characterize the modern era. This is the USA's strength and one that must be ensured.

DANGERS AHEAD

Perhaps the greatest challenge facing the aerospace nation today is conceptual. Although Americans have become dependent on aerospace in many aspects of their daily lives, and although their military has come to realize the dominance of aerospace power in operations, they have yet to think through sufficiently all its implications or how to maintain its momentum.

Aerospace power is not merely a collection of airplanes or spacecraft, although these assets are essential. It is not even the combination of machines with an effective command and control network and intelligence-gathering capabilities. Rather, aerospace power is the totality of US military air and space assets from all the services, plus the US commercial airline industry and the pilots and mechanics who comprise it, plus the US commercial aerospace industry with its thousands of engineers and designers, plus the massive airport and airways structure stretching across the nation and, indeed, the world, plus US codified doctrine on how all this power should be employed. All of these facets are essential for the United States to remain the world's aerospace nation.

One problem is a tendency to focus on individual services and weapons, or specific airport and air traffic control problems, thus failing to see aerospace power in the broadest sense. There is no agency in the United States chartered to examine its military aerospace force structure in its totality. There are attempts to look at parts of the problem – 'tactical' aircraft, airlift requirements or air traffic control sequencing issues – but such attempts are limited by their myopia. In the tactical air debate, for example, there is never a discussion of attack helicopters – their cost, vulnerability or role in conjunction with fixed-wing air assets. Similarly, airlift requirements are tied to army deployments that may or may not be relevant in the future. Other issues that need to be addressed include: How does one measure the relative value of land-based versus sea-based air power, or rotary versus fixed-wing? What are the trade-offs between the use of aerospace power versus ground troops or maritime forces? In an even broader sense, how do we articulate a vision for all of our aerospace assets, military and civilian? How does the US ensure the viability and superiority of its industrial base and the competitiveness of its commercial airline companies?

Aviation Week & Space Technology, one of the world's leading publications on aerospace matters, has, over the past few years, often referred to the 'crisis' in the US aerospace industry. Despite the USA's dominant position in many areas, there are problems brewing. Our scientific and engineering force is graying – the average age of the US aerospace worker is 47. Airline profitability is down – they face huge losses for 2001 due largely to the shutdown after the 11 September terrorist attacks and subsequent new and expensive security procedures. Tens of thousands of airline employees were laid off and several companies have talked bankruptcy. Legislation and government credit were necessary to get through this crisis. Also, international competitors like the aircraft manufacturer Airbus are garnering a greater market share of a field traditionally dominated by US legends like Boeing, Lockheed and McDonnell-Douglas. Now, many of our venerable companies have disappeared: Curtiss, North American, Convair, General Dynamics, Fairchild. Even those attempting to move forward face a rocky path: some worry that Boeing is betting too heavily on its futuristic sonic cruiser as the airliner of the future; if it flops, so will the company. Industry analysts continue to maintain that the long-term future of aerospace is bright, but for the short term there are major problems that need to be addressed.

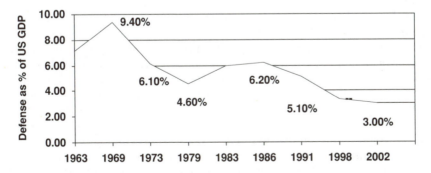

Figure 14.8: Defense Outlays as per cent of US GDP (*Source:* US Dept of Defense)

Overall, spending on aerospace research and development is down nearly 20 per cent in the past decade; shareholder return among the major aerospace companies is down; company stocks are down; defense spending as a percentage of GDP is down to 3 per cent, a post-World War II low; the US share of the world aerospace market is down 20 per cent over the past 15 years; the number of technology graduates who seek a career in aerospace is down by 57 per cent since 1990; and the aerospace industry's net debt is up. What can the nation do to reverse these trends?

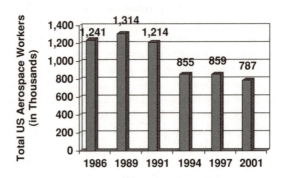

Figure 14.9: Employment in the US Aerospace Industry (*Source:* AIA, 2001)

First and foremost, there must be a broad-based examination of all aspects of the aerospace nation. The problems of the airline industry must be addressed. Difficulties concerning aerospace industry profitability, as well as international competitiveness, are in need of someone with both vision and strength. Overcrowded airports and late departures are becoming endemic. Herb Kelleher, the retired head of Southwest Airlines, argues that a mere '50 miles of paved highway' – essentially 30 new runways nationwide – will solve the airport overcrowding problem. Although Kelleher's claim too easily ignores the task of building the ramps, terminals, parking garages, etc. that must accompany the new runways, as well as environmental concerns, such a vision would require someone with both power and persistence to implement it.

As for military aerospace power, the problems, if anything, seem even more intractable. Since taking office, Defense Secretary Donald Rumsfeld has labored to reform and transform his department. It will be difficult. The F-22, the new US air superiority fighter that will incorporate advanced stealth, supercruise ability (it can fly supersonic without a gas-guzzling afterburner) and fused avionics, has only recently received Congressional approval for low-rate production. The F-22 was designed 20 years ago. The weapons acquisitions process is broken. Over the past decade there have been numerous studies on US Department of Defense organization and virtually all of them cite the need for acquisition reform. It has not yet happened and help is not imminent. Relatedly, it is a common practice for Congress to delay, stretch out and reduce the number of weapons to be purchased. This creates havoc with the manufacturer, while also driving costs through the roof. Originally, Congress authorized the purchase of 750 F-22s. Over the past few years, it has cut the planned buy to 295. Testimony before Congress reveals that these cuts have raised the unit price of the F-22 by over $20 million. That's real money. We cannot afford to have the aerospace star hitched to a Model T acquisition system.

The other danger lies in the realm of grand strategy. It became clear during the Gulf War and operations against Serbia that US aerospace strength not only exceeded that of US adversaries, it exceeded that of US allies. The vast majority of some key air and space assets – stealth, precision munitions, electronic jammers, intelligence satellites, tankers and strategic airlifters – were provided by the United States. This made it very difficult to devise an effective and balanced air plan. Interoperability has been a goal of NATO for decades but it is now of even greater concern. If strategy will call for increased reliance on aerospace power and the continual quest for technological advances, this interoperability problem can only get worse.

At the same time, it is also apparent that US foreign policy will require closer relations with our allies. If it is to maintain the moral high ground when intervening globally, it cannot be seen as the lone ranger. This was never more apparent than in the aftermath of the September terrorist strikes. The United States must have the political top cover provided by either a formal alliance like NATO, or an ad hoc coalition of major and minor powers as in the Gulf War. Clearly, the imperative to operate in an alliance/coalition will clash with US technical disparity relative to those allies. We must find a way to bridge this gap.

In one sense, the infusion of funds into the military after 11 September will alleviate many of the problems facing the US military and hence its aerospace forces. It is not yet clear, however, if sound planning and a coherent vision are behind this unexpected financial bounty. Throwing money at a problem is seldom sufficient to solve it.

CONCLUSION

The United States is the world's first and only aerospace nation. There are many reasons why this is the case but the most basic reason is that it wished to be. It developed the technology, infrastructure and mentality – at great cost and effort – to achieve its dominant status. The fact of this pre-eminent US position is reflected in political, economic, military and cultural lives. The United States must not take this dominance for granted. If the United States intends to maintain its position and make full use of the benefits that aerospace power provides, then there are certain things it must do.

The United States must have a comprehensive plan to develop, improve and coordinate the commercial and military aspects of its policy. It must stem the decline in its R&D efforts, while also rebuilding and expanding its aerospace infrastructure and educational base. It must change the way it develops and buys its air and space technologies to take advantage of new ideas and advances, ensuring its equipment is not out of date before it is even fielded. At the same time, the United States must remember that it is part of a world community that looks to it for leadership. That means it needs to cooperate not dictate and become true partners with its allies.

The United States must look closely at the fundamental principles and assumptions underpinning its military strategy and force structure. Much of what it does today militarily is based on tradition. Old ideas and old ways may not work in the twenty-first century. Aerospace power offers a cost-effective, rapid and discriminate weapon for political leaders. Let's sharpen that weapon.

NOTE

This chapter was written in the summer and fall of 2001. When I had almost completed it, the terrorist attacks of 11 September occurred. The subsequent huge drop in airline passenger revenues pushed several companies, worldwide, near bankruptcy. The US government, recognizing the importance of the aerospace industry, began immediate resuscitation efforts. The United States remains an aerospace nation, but is now more aware of the challenges that involve possessing such a status.

Index